SCREENING SPACE

The American Science Fiction Film

SECOND, ENLARGED EDITION

VIVIAN SOBCHACK

Rutgers University Press
New Brunswick, New Jersey, and London

Fourth printing, 2001

Library of Congress Cataloging-in-Publication Data

Sobchack, Vivian Carol.
    Screening space : the American science fiction film /
Vivian Sobchack. — 2nd, enl. ed.
        p.   cm.
    Rev. ed. of : The limits of infinity. c1980.
    Originally published: New York : Ungar, 1987.
    Includes bibliographical references and index.
    ISBN 0-8135-2492-X (paper : alk. paper)
    1. Science fiction films—United States—History and
criticism.   I. Sobchack, Vivian Carol. Limits of infinity.
II. Title.
PN1995.9.S26S57   1997
791.43′615—dc21   97-16074
                                          CIP

Manufactured in the United States of America

Contents

Preface to the Enlarged Edition

This volume was first published in 1980 under the title *The Limits of Infinity: The American Science Fiction Film.* It is being reprinted as it originally appeared (including its original introduction), but with the addition of a new chapter and an up-dated selected bibliography. The new chapter, "Postfuturism," continues the original work's discussion of the aesthetic character of the genre as it relates to many of the American SF films released since the appearance of *Star Wars* and *Close Encounters of the Third Kind* in 1977. The chapter's primary aim is not the entire recuperation of nearly a decade's worth of American SF films. Rather, its intent is to explore the cultural implications of the genre's contemporary aesthetics as they are informed by and constitute the socially symbolic narratives of what Fredric Jameson has termed a culture's "political unconscious." Although our culture is more heterogeneous and fragmented than such a unitary concept admits, the assertion of the existence of a "political unconscious" is significantly based on the understanding that "there is nothing that is not social and historical —indeed, that everything is 'in the last analysis' political," and that all cultural artifacts are constituted as "socially symbolic acts."[1]

Written almost ten years ago, the first three chapters of this book primarily concentrate on describing the formal structures that make up the specific nature and function of the American science fiction film. Their aim was to "redeem" and illuminate a genre that, at the time, had been completely neglected by film scholars and merely valorized by film buffs. Times, however, have changed. The SF film now enjoys wide-ranging critical and scholarly attention, and has been acknowledged in the last few years not only for its aesthetic and technical sophistication, but also for its ideological complexity.

This increased interest in the genre has emerged coincidentally with two phenomena. The first is the major "renaissance" of the SF film, which, as previously mentioned, dates from 1977. Since then, the genre's production and popularity have increased so greatly that the films and their cultural significance can no longer be easily ignored or dismissed. The second phenomenon is a major shift in the critical theories, methods, and vocabulary informing the practice of film scholarship in general, and genre criticism in particular. Over the last ten years, film scholars have enriched their understanding and description of the cinema as art and cultural artifact by drawing upon the knowledge and vocabularies of other disciplines. For example, it is now a relative commonplace to discuss the horror film within the context of neo-Freudian psychoanalytic theory. Similarly, the least dogmatic and most dynamic of Marxist descriptions of cultural production have been extremely useful in looking at genre films as part of an ideologically charged symbolic economy. Thus, formal descriptions or the "poetics" of genre have recently begun to contextualize their attention to the structures of the film text with a correspondent "politics" of genre that enriches and dynamizes structural considerations with social and historical significance.

Both the popular "renaissance" of the American SF film and the changed terms of genre scholarship have made their mark on the shape and style of the present book. That there is a "new and enlarged" edition of this work signals the new popularity and interest in the genre. That the new chapter "enlarges" the discussion of the aesthetics of the contemporary American SF film to entail history and ideology signals the recent changes in the approaches and methods of film study. In sum, the substance and style of the new chapter are quite different from those of previous chapters, but this difference is not casual. Rather, it quite seriously marks the scholarly recognition that the poetics of the SF film need to be interpreted as socially symbolic and historically situated. Today, one need not "be a Marxist" to realize that aesthetics, politics, economics, technology, and social relations are interdependent cultural phenomena.

I hope, therefore, that the new last chapter (the current "last analysis") will, in part, enrich the formal analysis of the previous chapters. In an ambitious, but limited way, it aims to close the "structural, experiential, and conceptual gap" between the poetic and the political articulations of the contemporary SF film, and to reveal some of the cultural meanings of the genre's changed and newly charged aesthetic activity.[2] To this end and to encourage further debate, I have drawn heavily on a recent (but already seminal) essay by Fredric Jameson that considers changes in contemporary American aesthetic "styles" as symptomatic of the historical emergence of a new form of cultural understanding. Entitled "Postmodernism, or The Cultural Logic of Late Capitalism"[3], it seems particularly useful not only to an explication of the new aesthetics of SF, but also to an understanding of the genre's periodization into a first and second "Golden Age." Thus, the first three chapters of this book transparently, if rigorously, explore what will only later be revealed — through the benefit of time and hindsight — as the American genre's first historical grouping. This later revelation is the charge of the last and newest chapter — which is not yet and never will be the last "last analysis" of a genre that most specifically responds to and represents our cultural imagination of the possibilities for social being in a technological world.

Notes

1. Fredric Jameson, *The Political Unconscious: Narrative as a Socially Symbolic Act* (Ithaca, NY: Cornell University Press, 1981), p. 20.

2. Ibid.

3. *New Left Review*, No. 146 (July–August 1984): 53–92.

Acknowledgments

This book was first conceived at U.C.L.A. (Division of Motion Pictures/Television) where, long ago, I had the happy occasion to spend a year completing graduate work in their Critical Studies program. The constructive criticism, support, and faith offered by Professors Steven Mamber, Howard Suber, and Lou Stoumen were of inestimable value — for they followed me from Los Angeles to my home in Utah and sustained me during a period of intellectual isolation. The University Film Association financially supported my efforts with their annual Critical Writing Fellowship awarded to a portion of this book; I thank them with gratitude. I also cannot ignore the pervasive helpfulness of the Department of Communications at the University of Vermont where I was teaching during the major editorial work on the manuscript; particular thanks go to Frank Manchel and Woodrow W. Leake, Jr., for making life easier than it would have been without them. And, finally, throughout the writing and production of the first version of this book, Thomas Sobchack offered invaluable criticism and support.

This expanded edition was written almost ten years after the first — and under quite different circumstances. I should most like to acknowledge the nurturant attitude of my colleagues and the institution where I now happily teach. Work on the new chapter of this book was supported by Faculty Research Funds granted by the University of California, Santa Cruz. My gratitude also to dear friends and movie buffs Lisa Jensen and Jim Schwenterley for their cheerful assistance. Last, but not least, I want to offer heartfelt thanks to Lester Glassner for the use of his private collection of stills. For both editions of the book, his creative research and sensitivity to my aesthetic demands were quite extraordinary.

A portion of this book, in modified form, previously appeared as "The Alien Landscapes of the Planet Earth" in *The Film Journal* 2, no. 3 (1974): 16-21.

Santa Cruz, 1986   V.S.

Introduction
to the First Edition

There have been few book-length critical studies of the science fiction (SF) film—and there are currently only two in English which are more than picture books: John Baxter's *Science Fiction in the Cinema,* and *Focus on the Science Fiction Film* edited by William Johnson. Baxter's study is ambitious but ultimately self-defeating because it is so broad; he deals with SF film from its beginnings in the films of Méliès through Stanley Kubrick's *2001: A Space Odyssey,* and attempts to cover the genre on an international scale and from a number of critical approaches. The book ends up an informative survey of factual data, critical insights, personal preferences, and plot summaries, but it remains no more than a survey—skimming the top of a film genre which deserves more intensive discussion. *Focus on the Science Fiction Film* also offers a broad view of the genre; it is a collection of reviews, essays, interviews, and data which provides the reader with an overview of the genre, again from its beginnings to the approximate present. Both books are extremely intelligent and together might well be used in an undergraduate university class studying the SF film. However, as works which closely inspect the films and those aesthetic and thematic elements which bind them together to form an identifiable genre, both books are inadequate when placed alongside the serious critical work devoted to genres like the Western and the gangster film. Given the current resurgence of popular interest in the genre, it now seems appropriate that the SF film receive more intensive analysis than it has received in the past. It is the purpose of the following work to fill in only a small part of that vast black hole in space which metaphorically represents the lack of aesthetic criticism available to serious film scholars (and fans) of the genre.

To deal in depth with the particular idiosyncrasies of the SF film, it is necessary to limit the scope of any study. In the following pages, therefore, I have chosen to confine my attention exclusively to the American SF film; this decision, however, has not been dictated solely by arbitrary considerations of length. Film genres, as we critically recognize and speak of them, first arose out of the American system of film production, distribution, and exhibition. It also seems remiss that no American has written a lengthy study of American SF films—although several Europeans have concentrated on them (viewed, of course, from a foreign perspective and with an eye toward their political undertones). Then, more personally, the American SF film is most familiar to me (and my readers) and the most accessible for intensive study; I grew up in the fifties and can rank my weekly visits to the neighborhood theater to see the latest SF film equal in importance to other adolescent *rites de passage*. I come to this study, therefore, with what I hope will be considered the enthusiasm and love of a buff and the discipline and impartiality of a scholar.

It has also seemed productive to narrow the time span the following study will cover. Although somewhat influenced by my intimacy with those films made from 1950 on and by limitations of space, my exclusion of SF films made before 1950 is really principally based on the fact that what we might call the "prehistory" of the genre has been covered quite adequately in a number of books and articles, including the two works cited earlier. In addition, 1950 marked the year that *Destination Moon* was released, initiating the spate of SF films which filled American movie theaters in the subsequent decade; prior to the early fifties there was hardly a spate—in fact, barely a trickle. It was only after 1950 that SF film emerged as a critically recognized genre; that is, reviewers and critics (sometimes one and the same) began to talk about the films by grouping them together.

Finally, limiting the scope of this study even further, after attempting to generally explore and define the parameters of the SF film as a genre, I have chosen to deal intensively only with those visual and aural elements which seem to define the genre formally. The reasons for approaching the SF film on a primarily formal basis may be various, but the main impetus behind my method of study is that the SF film has seemed to defy the kind of current genre analysis which is dependent upon iconographic, thematic, or even structural considerations. As a result, and despite the resurgence of the genre's popularity with the commercial success of and critical awareness given to *2001: A Space Odyssey* in 1968, and more recently *Star Wars* and *Close Encounters of the Third Kind* in 1977, the SF film continues to be one of the least critically observed genres in American cinema. What seems to be called for, then, is a new approach to the SF film—and, perhaps, to genre study—one which is able to deal with structural relationships between images and sounds as well as those between thematic elements. It is my hope, therefore, that the following pages will not only illuminate the aesthetic structure of the American SF film from 1950 to the present, but will also cast some light on hitherto unconsidered paths genre study might care to follow.

Finally, some mention should be made of certain stylistic decisions. In as many instances as possible, I have chosen to use the pronoun "one" to avoid the problems provoked by preference for one gender over another. However, in those cases where clarity and/or brevity demanded a "he" or "she," I generally chose the former because it is—currently—less distracting. The choice was conscious and always considered, the final responsibility my own. Less controversial, perhaps, has been my choice to include the director's name as well as the release date after a film's initial mention in each chapter. Although this is not current practice in most genre studies and may be construed as "auteurist," it seemed both informative and appropriately respectful of the films in a genre not usually treated with respect.

Screening Space

1

The Limits of the Genre:
Definitions and Themes

What is Science Fiction?

One of the difficulties inherent in discussing the science fiction (SF) film is that the critic has to deal with the nagging conviction that he or she ought to define it before describing it, that the very act of definition is, indeed, an academic requirement as well as a personal cathartic. The tyrannical phrase *define your terms* can, however, if followed too slavishly, imprison the critic in an ontological construct which has little to do with cinematic reality. Definitions strive, after all, for exclusivity, for the setting of strict and precise limits which, when they become too narrow, seem glaringly and disappointingly arbitrary. As Lawrence Alloway says: "One of the dangers of genre theory is that the categories may be taken rigidly. When that happens they lose their descriptive usefulness and assume a normative function."[1] On the other hand, there is also something suspect about a critic who plunges into his subject with the optimistic assumption that his readers know—a priori—precisely what he is talking about. Obviously, there must be some sensible and productive middle ground, a way of defining the limits of a genre while remaining as inclusive as possible so that the definition will seem neither too arbitrary and personally manufac-

17

tured nor so general that it becomes useless as a critical tool. Above all, if it is to remain relevant, a definition must accommodate the flux and change which is present in any living and popular art form.

One potentially useful tool in arriving at a serviceable definition of the term "science fiction film" is the body of critical material written about SF literature. From Utopian literature to pulp literature to mainstream literature, written science fiction has existed as a recognized genre long before there was a body of film which lay claim to the name "science fiction." We might assume, therefore, that certain previously established definitions would be handy for cinematic application, that by now there would be a consensus of critical opinion as to precisely what science fiction is. This, however, is not the case. The problem of satisfactorily defining science fiction has also plagued critics and writers of SF literature; although there is some small agreement here and there, contradictions and simplifications predominate, and the variety of definitions remains as problematic as it is useful.

For example, Judith Merril (SF writer, editor, and critic) admits:

> I never did know just what "science fiction" meant: in all the nights I stayed awake till dawn debating definitions, I do not recall one that stood up unflinchingly to the light of day. They all relied, in any case, on certain axiomatic assumptions about the meanings of "science" and "fiction." [2]

Although Ms. Merril prefers description to definition in breaking down recognizable types of SF stories, she does end up making a general statement as to what constitutes the "essence" of science fiction. She identifies three basic SF stories: the Teaching Story, whose function seems to be the popularization of science and technology; the Preaching Story, which essentially warns and prophesies; and a type of story which she labels Speculative Fiction, "whose objective is to . . . *learn* . . . something about the nature of the universe, of man, of 'reality.' " [3] It is in this last type of story that she finds the heart of science fiction and, in fact, ends up with a definition after all:

> I use the term "speculative fiction" here specifically to describe the mode which makes use of the traditional "scientific method" (observation, hypothesis, experimentation) to examine some postulated approximation of reality, by introducing a given set of changes—imaginary or inventive—into the common background of "known facts," creating an environment in which the responses and perceptions of the characters will reveal something about the inventions, the characters, or both. [4]

Sam Moskowitz (SF editor and writer) comes up with the following definition, which is of interest because of its catholic conception of science, a conception which was not always as broad nor as acceptable to practitioners and readers of science fiction as it is today: [5]

> Science fiction is a branch of fantasy identifiable by the fact that it eases the "willing suspension of disbelief" on the part of its readers by utilizing an atmosphere of scientific credibility for its imaginative speculations in physical science, space, time, socal science, and philosophy. [6]

More succinct and even more general is the aesthetic definition of the genre given by SF writer Theodore Sturgeon as quoted by his colleague James Blish: "A good science fiction story is a story with a human problem, and a human solution, which would not have happened at all without its science content." [7]

British author and critic Kingsley Amis, however, sees science fiction a bit more narrowly than do Merril, Moskowitz, or Sturgeon:

> Science fiction is that class of prose narrative treating of a situation that *could not arise in the world we know,* but which is hypothesized on the basis of some innovations in science or technology, or pseudo-science or pseudo-technology, whether human or extraterrestrial in origin. [Italics mine.][8]

Amis seems to emphasize the futuristic nature of science fiction and clearly does not consider the application of existent scientific theory or technology the stuff of which science fiction is made. Critic Richard Hodgens, on the other hand, seems to recognize that the present and the past are both very much a part of science fiction:

> Science fiction involves extrapolated or fictitious science, or fictitious use of scientific possibilities, or it may be simply fiction that takes place in the future or introduces some radical assumption about the present or the past. [9]

Lastly, there are implied definitions which rest uneasily upon what amounts to an act of faith by critics and scholars who are generally more specific. Michael Butor believes:

> It is enough to say: "You know, those stories that are always mentioning interplanetary rockets," for the least prepared interlocutor to understand immediately what you mean. This does not imply that any such apparatus occurs in every SF story; it may be replaced by other accessories which will perform a comparable role. But it is the most usual, the typical example, like the magic wand in fairy tales. [10]

And Carlos Clarens is feeble when he deals with the question of what science fiction is: "Hard to define abstractly, science fiction is instantly recognizable on the printed page." [11]

Literature and Film

It is ironic, then, that a great many SF writers and critics—unable to agree even among themselves what sort of beast SF literature is—have chosen to find only the most specious connection between written and filmed science fiction. This negative criticism of SF movies has caused the film critic to become extremely defensive, and forced him at times—perhaps out of strong feelings of self-preservation—to play the devil's advocate, either denouncing the films or ashamedly admitting he loves them even if they're not really very good. Certainly, if we are to make evaluative statements, few SF films are great; most are not even good. But the same is true of SF literature. Unfortunately, since the written literature was there first and is both more plentiful and accessible than film, the common tendency is to remember all the good—and therefore, frequently anthologized—SF literature and compare it to the worst SF films. The films, of course, suffer in comparison. As a result, there has been much discussion about whether the SF film even has the right to bear its name and thereby claim an alliance with the literature. Indeed, it has been blithely pointed out by many critics like John Baxter and Richard Hodgens that the very nature and emphasis of the literature and the films are opposite.

John Baxter believes SF literature and SF film have little common ground: "Contact is tangential, a genuine coincidence of outlook rare in the extreme." [12] He sees the basis of the SF film as superstition, horror, and a fear of science, whereas the literature rests on an optimistic and positive base "sustained by the mystique of technology and a belief in the desirability of mathematical order in human affairs." [13] Seizing upon a line of dialogue now considered "classic" ("There are some things Man is not meant to know"), he builds what seems a pretty strong case for the existence of a wide philosophical gap between SF literature and film. That line of dialogue becomes, for Baxter, paradigmatic and "expresses the universal fear all men have of the unknown and inexplicable, a fear science fiction rejects but which has firmly entrenched itself in the sf cinema." [14] Following this line of argument, it is not at all surprising that Baxter unequivocally states: "Science fiction supports logic and order, sf film illogic and chaos." [15]

The problem with Baxter's reasoning, however, is that he makes the very questionable assumption that the major bulk of SF literature is, in fact, optimistic and unafraid, that almost all written science fiction has its roots in what we know as "the visionary literature of the Nineteenth Century."[16] He also assumes that the majority of SF films are non-visionary, not concerned with movements and ideas, and not idealistic. These generalizations are simply not true. They refuse to recognize that neither literature nor film are static arts created in one moment of historical and philosophical time. After Hiroshima, SF writers were neither as optimistic about nor as unafraid of science as they had previously been, and their stories and novels reflected their age and anxiety. Utopia became anti-Utopia. Logic itself became suspect as witness all those stories which deal with computers, robotics, and cybernetics, in a not particularly positive way. The literature, like the film, may always have a base in science and the application of science, but its attitudes toward this base are never constant. The visionary science fiction of the nineteenth century bears little attitudinal resemblence to written science fiction of the twentieth. After Hiroshima, literature recognized, according to Thomas Clareson, that:

> Man might not conquer the stars ... mushrooming technology might reduce him to a robot existence, if it did not annihilate him. By its concern for the anti-utopia, the genre ended a largely self-imposed exile by moving toward the essentially anti-scientific mood and themes of the main body of twentieth century literature.[17]

In this context, it must also be remembered that although the SF film existed in isolated instances before World War II, it only emerged as a *critically* recognized genre *after* Hiroshima. Therefore, even if one mistakenly accepts Baxter's all-inclusive statement that the SF film is antiscience and antiorder, it is not in a historical sense surprising. The film genre, emerging when it did, had no roots in the philosophical attitudes of the nineteenth century. Baxter's separation of the impulses in SF literature and film, his insistence that they are at odds with one another, does not take into account the constantly changing attitudes and themes in both media. Not all SF literature is proscience and not all SF film is antiscience. Indeed, the two seminal films (both adapted from literary sources) which together, at the beginning of the 1950s, seemed to describe the limits of the genre and caught the critics' attention, reveal the duality of attitudes present in both media.

Destination Moon (Irving Pichel, 1950), despite its possible interpretation as a film about a military rather than a scientific expedition,[18] was meticulously concerned with authenticity, with logic, with the wonders of scientific achievement, and, as Denis Gifford has pointed out, was prophetic of the manned Apollo Moon flights.[19] Taken from a Robert Heinlein novel (*Rocketship Galileo*, 1947), it purposefully omitted the novel's treatment of the discovery of Neo-Nazis on the Moon and retained only the space voyage to and from the Moon. Rejecting the "scare" appeal of the novel and its even then illogical premise of life on the moon, the film became what Baxter pejoratively—and self-contradictorily in light of his comments on the differences between SF film and literature—calls "a routine voyage to the moon yarn." [20] They very "routine" quality of the trip, however, revealed the extremely optimistic belief that man and science and the machinery dependent on both could, indeed, conquer the stars. Respect for science was evident not only in the competence and confidence of the astronauts (a word not yet coined), but also in the extreme care given to set design and special effects, and in the fact that producer George Pal hired a real astronomical artist (Chesley Bonestell) and a real rocketeer (Hermann Oberth) to work in creating the high level of authenticity the film attains. *Destination Moon* was certainly not a movie which concentrated on fear or despised science and scientists.

The second seminal film (and the one which has been used most often to support the thesis that SF films are really not SF but horror films because they are antiscientific) was *The Thing* (Christian Nyby/Howard Hawks, 1951). Again the source for the film was a short SF novel (John W. Camp-

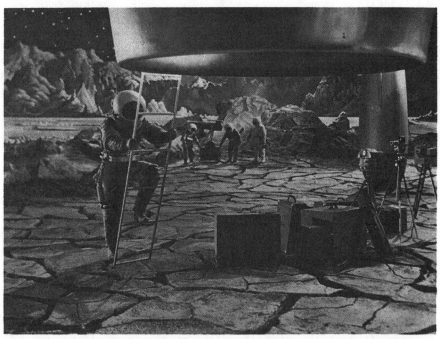

Destination Moon (Irving Pichel, 1950) was meticulously concerned with authenticity, logic, and the wonders of scientific achievement. (United Artists/Eagle-Lion)

The Thing (Christian Nyby/Howard Hawks, 1951) is "pro-fear" and "anti-science." Its heroes are the "regular guys" in the U.S. Air Force and its villain a professor/scientist whose desire for knowledge approaches madness. (R.K.O./Winchester)

bell's *Who Goes There?*, 1938), and again certain changes were made in the adaptation; the most conspicuous alteration was that Campbell's alien was not an exotic vegetable, but a creature which could assume the human shape of the people it attacked. In the film, however, instead of the ambiguity of watching an alien walking around in human form, we have an extremely recognizable "other," something definitely detached from Man, something concretely different to be afraid of.[21] The film is, indeed, profear ("Keep watching the skies" is its last warning message). It is also antiscience and antiscientists. The latter are shown to be foolishly curious, their abnormal desire for knowledge dangerous to the whole human race and, more immediately and specifically, to the United States Air Force—the latter a bunch of "regular" guys whose biological curiosity extends only to the opposite sex and not pervertedly to intelligent vegetables. What is ironic about *The Thing*, however, is that although it is considered a horror film by a critic like Richard Hodgens, he refers to the story upon which it is based as "one of the most original and effective science fiction stories, *subspecies* 'horror' "[22], as if horror were a normal part of SF literature but

23

insupportable in SF film. Also provocative is the fact that many SF writers such as Arthur C. Clarke and Michael Crichton consider *The Thing* one of the best SF movies ever made.[23]

The SF films which followed *Destination Moon* and *The Thing* have continued to display dual and opposing attitudes toward science, logic, and order. Anyone who has examined the themes in these films can no longer accept Baxter's notion that the attitudes expressed towards science, order, logic, and the application of technology in the literature and the film are significantly and consistently different.

Another myth which should be laid to rest is that the SF film cannot possibly be as thoughtful, as profound, or as intellectually stimulating as SF literature, that because of the nature of the medium itself film is incapable of dealing with ideas as effectively as does literature. To quote Baxter again (although this view is upheld by an extraordinary number of literary critics and writers in areas far removed from science fiction):

> Science fiction's concern is not with individuals but with movements and ideas. . . .
> Contrast with this utilitarian field the fantasy and illusion of film. Even the greatest of cinema artists cannot do more than approximate in symbols the intellectual development of an abstract premise on which science fiction depends so much for its effects. . . .
> Science fiction film, then, is an intellectual impossibility.[24]

Presented here is the rather naive assumption that because a writer always uses words (which, after all, are abstractions themselves) he is in a better position to deal with the abstract than an artist working in another medium. Baxter suggests that because a filmmaker expresses himself primarily through images, he is hampered because he can't take a picture of an abstraction, he can't photograph an idea; at best, he can create a symbol.

What is ignored in this line of reasoning is that we are discussing *fiction*: fictional literature and fictional film. Certainly, abstractions and ideas are best communicated through written language and mathematical formulae. There is no way a film could approximate or adapt the verbal "development of an abstract premise" in a philosophical tract, a scientific essay, an economic theory. But—and this must be emphasized—SF literature is also in no way able to duplicate this kind of abstract thought and still remain fiction or, for that matter, literature. Good fiction may provoke ideas but it does not present them in the raw. They are not offered to the reader as in a scientific paper, the object of the latter being to communicate them as comprehensively and clearly as possible. Narrative is located in characters, things, places, and events; these are not abstractions. If, in their action and interaction, an idea is expressed it is expressed through them and thus indirectly. Fiction cannot be written without these concrete and particularized carriers of meaning, and once they are particularized and concrete they are not abstract. Abstract information in a fairly pure form may—at worst—be given to the reader through the intervention in the story of the voice of the author. It can also be presented through the characters themselves. But good science fiction does not have its author or its scientist-hero present in detail a paper on nuclear physics in the middle of the work. Facts may be overtly presented from time to time but never at the expense of the narrative.

The SF writer or filmmaker may want to present intellectual thought, ideas, and concepts to his reader, but his primary goal is not to inform, nor to philosophize, but to create a narrative which dramatically—through its style and structure, its characterizations, its events and objects and places—provokes the reader to think, to observe, to draw his own abstract conclusions. The good SF writer realizes that if it is pure abstract theory or factual information a reader wants, he will not turn to stories or novels, but to scientific journals or *Popular Mechanics;* similarly, the good SF filmmaker is not interested in creating a science film, a documentary whose primary reason for being is to show step by step process and detail. Viewed in this manner both the SF writer and filmmaker must deal with the "intellectual development of an abstract premise" dramatically and, therefore, indirectly. Both may create works which can be—and are—as banal, boring, and talky or as significant, compelling, and profound as the artist's ability to control his medium. That medium may be words or it may be moving images, but both are equally capable of leading the reader or viewer to abstract considerations. In other words, the medium is only as good as the talent which uses it, as profound as the vision which informs it.

One of the reasons, of course, for the evolution of this myth that SF literature is inherently more profound than SF film is that there have been many banal SF films. Because any film, however poor, comes to the attention of an extraordinary number of people, the bad SF film is likely to attract more notice than the bad SF story or novel which simply goes unread and doesn't get reviewed or anthologized. It is also true that many SF films were made by people who had neither particular interest in nor understanding of science fiction, productions which were bent on making a quick buck, capitalizing on a previous offering but diluting it beyond recognition and meaning, exploiting the American habit of sending the kids to a Saturday matinee. Most SF literature has been written for adults, while most, although certainly not all, SF films have been made for children and teenagers. This may say something about movie production or publishing habits, but it really indicates nothing about the capabilities of the media themselves. It is clearly evident since 1968 and the huge success of Stanley Kubrick's *2001: A Space Odyssey* (certainly an intellectually provocative film on a number of levels) that the film medium can accommodate "adult" science fiction. And it is also interesting to note that since 1968 and Kubrick's film, SF movies have been made primarily for adult audiences.

It would not be fair, however, to leave the reader with the impression that all—or even most—SF writers despise the SF film or deem it incapable of achieving profundity. Richard Matheson, for example, interviewed in a poll of writers in William Johnson's *Focus on the Science Fiction Film*, assesses the situation quite reasonably, even though two film adaptations of his own novels greatly disappointed him. After choosing *The Andromeda Strain* (Robert Wise, 1971), and *Colossus—The Forbin Project* (Joseph Sargent, 1969) as examples of intelligent, literate, and exciting SF film, indicative of what the film medium could achieve, he agreed with the majority of writers polled that most SF film was puerile compared to SF literature. This, however, was the reason:

> Hollywood, as in all areas of imaginative thinking, is years behind the pace. Only in recent months—perhaps years—has the attitude begun to alter so that films can be made which are fully adult, totally acceptable as grown-up fare, and yet are science fiction. If one were to conceive the Solar System as full possibility in the realm of science fiction films, with the basic concepts starting out from the sun, Hollywood is not quite to Earth yet in the radiating expansion of its thought. The two films I mentioned plus *2001* and a few others, indicate some effort to get away from the old Monster from Outer Space concept—although, amusingly enough, *The Andromeda Strain* is nothing else *but* that concept—done so maturely that one never notices.[25]

And lest the reader think too harshly of the SF writer who presumes to be a film critic (and, after all, why shouldn't he be?), let him fully appreciate the implication of Sturgeon's Law: "But 90% of *everything* is crud!"[26]

Transylvania on Mars: Horror and Science Fiction

Before we can arrive at a useful definition of the SF film, its relationship to the horror film needs exploration. Their uneasy connection has bothered many critics. Carlos Clarens' *An Illustrated History of The Horror Film* devotes two chapters to the SF film.[27] John Baxter's *Science Fiction in The Cinema* discusses many films—particularly those influenced by German expressionist cinema—more often considered horror films than they are SF films.[28] In numerous books and articles, the same films are claimed by both genres while others are rejected by both, each claiming they belong to the

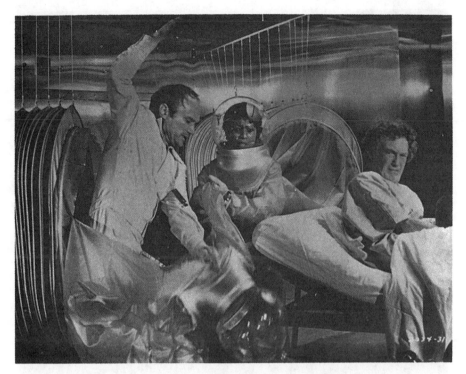

The Andromeda Strain (Robert Wise, 1971). A modern treatment of the fifties' "Monster from Outer Space" plot. (Universal)

other. Critics of both genres have been anxious to differentiate science fiction from horror, to separate the two irrevocably. Those hybrid films which combine equal elements of both—and there are quite a large number of them, as we shall see—are generally found to be "aesthetically" dissatisfying, one of the reasons being, perhaps, that they present problems of classification and create a gray area—a no-man's-land—linking the two genres more than purists in either camp would like.

Richard Hodgens, for instance, deplores the misuse of the term science fiction for those films whose "tone and implications . . . suggest a strange throwback of taste to something moldier and more 'Gothic' than the Gothic novel," [29] and he flatly asserts that to "the film audience, 'science fiction' means 'horror', distinguished from ordinary horror only by a relative lack of plausibility." [30] Neil Isaacs laments:

> The fantasy visions of alien monstrosities or evolutionary missteps have refused to acknowledge their kinship with traditional horror films and persist in explaining themselves out of all their dramatic potential. [31]

To explain some of the similarities between the two genres, it has

The Mummy (Karl Freund, 1932). Publicity still of Boris Karloff in the title role: the horror film's version of the SF robot. (Universal)

often been suggested that SF cinema arose directly out of the "traditional" horror film. Michel Laclos sees the relationship in this way:

> Science fiction cinema . . . assimilated all the themes of traditional fantasy. Martians, Venusians or mutants evolved from vampires, while robots imitated the trance-like states of zombies and the Golem. The confined setting of the haunted house expanded to the dimensions of a satellite populated by invisible extraterrestrial presences.[32]

One can recognize in these comments—whether receptive or hostile to the fact—acknowledgement that the horror film and the SF film have, at times, a tendency to cover the same dramatic territory.

On the surface a case can certainly be made that the SF film developed out of the traditional horror film, that it *is* the horror film sufficiently "technologized" to suit the demands for "modern" horror from an increasingly pragmatic and materialistic audience. One can equate Dracula's embrace with alien mind control, mummies and zombies with robots, Frankenstein's monster with the machine that's run amok. Both genres contain their laboratories, their experiments, their creatures, their empirical litanies. Are the stake and cross used "correctly" in the horror film so different from the application of the proper antidote to the alien invasion in the SF film? As Dr. Van Helsing himself remarked in *Dracula* (Tod Browning, 1931), "The superstition of yesterday can become the scientific reality of today."[33] One has to ask, however, if it is simply technology which separates the two genres; is the SF film merely the horror film brought up to date?

One major difference between the genres lies in their sphere of exploration, their emphasis. The horror film is primarily concerned with

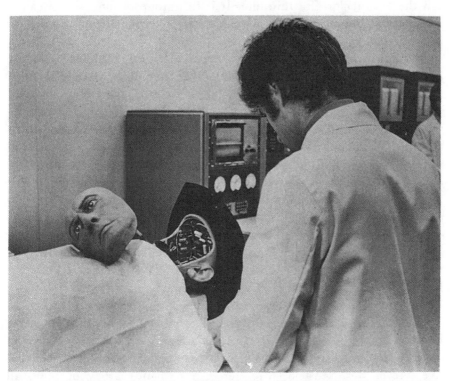

Westworld (Michael Crichton, 1973). The horror film "technologized" for an increasingly pragmatic audience becomes science fiction. The machine running amok replaces Frankenstein's monster. (Metro-Goldwyn-Mayer)

29

the individual in conflict with society or with some extension of himself, the SF film with society and its institutions in conflict with each other or with some alien other. Therefore, the arena for conflict in the horror film is usually as small as a minute town tucked in the Carpathians, an old castle, or an English village, while the arena for the SF film is most often the large city, the planet Earth itself. If one genre is as large as the human soul, the other is as large as the cosmos. Both genres deal with chaos, with the disruption of order, but the horror film deals with moral chaos, the disruption of natural order (assumed to be God's order), and the threat to the harmony of hearth and home; the SF film, on the other hand, is concerned with social chaos, the disruption of social order (man-made), and the threat to the harmony of civilized society going about its business.

There are, however, frequent cases of congruence between the SF and the horror film; there are films in which it is not so easy to distinguish whether the chaos is moral or civil, whether the order threatened is God-given or man-made. The films which most typify what is considered by some to be the "miscegenation" of the two genres are what we commonly call the Monster or Creature film. It is this group of films which causes purist critics the most trouble when they try to make abrupt distinctions between the two genres.

The Creatures and Monsters of certain SF films seem to roam the Earth almost as if by accident. They may fall from outer space to threaten the planet, invade it, destroy it, or they are accidental byproducts of "the Bomb." In the horror film, however, the Monster seems less accidental; he seems to arise inevitably out of a personal Faustian obsession or the inherent animal nature of Man. There has been no SF film made in which an individual Edmond Teller does battle with himself or his creation on a personal and moral level. Because of this somehow organic link between man and Monster in the horror film, it seems absolutely dramatically necessary for the Monster to have an anthropomorphic form —something which is not dramatically essential to the SF film. There are no blobs or creeping fungi or exotic vegetables or tentacled Martians in the traditional horror film. Lawrence Talbot may turn into a wolf, but he walks upright and looks distinctly human within his animal form; he is morally and mortally torn between his instinctive animal nature and his human, civilized nature. Dracula is terrifying in his lust for blood because he appears so sophisticated, so urbane, so much in control of his instincts, so much aware as well of the corrupt desire in all of us to live forever. Frankenstein's Monster is a pathetic parody of Man, all bits and pieces of human flesh crudely and grotesquely sewn together, but still reaching for natural and celestial light.

Dracula (Tod Browning, 1931). The horror film deals with moral chaos, the disruption of natural order, and the omnipresent threat to the harmony of hearth and home. (Universal)

Since the horror film emphasizes individual moral conflict, the Monster—again of dramatic necessity—must be a significant and personalized antagonist. To make the moral struggle truly protean, both Man and Monster must be given equal weight and equal time. Thus, in the horror film, we are involved in personalized conflict and combat: Dracula vs. Dr. Van Helsing, Frankenstein vs. his Monster, Lawrence Talbot vs. his animal

31

The Wolf Man (George Waggner, 1941). Since the horror film emphasizes individual moral conflict, the Monster must be equal in stature to the forces for good, and both must finally meet in personalized conflict and combat. (Universal)

alter ego. Once we have seen the Monster in a horror film and marvelled at his physical deformity, we become no less interested in him as the film progresses; he may initially fascinate or frighten us with his form, but we continue to be fascinated by what he represents long after his form has ceased to amaze us.

In the SF film, the Creature is less personalized, has less of an interior presence than does the Monster in the horror film. Usually we are given only form, physical attributes; the Creatures of science fiction distinctly lack a psyche. After the initial shock at the Creature's appearance, our interest lies not in why the Creature will do what it does, not in what it thinks or feels, but solely in what it will do and how it will do it—in other words, its external activity. Our sympathy is never evoked by an SF Creature; it remains, always, a thing.

Conversely, in the horror film there is always something sympathetic about the Monster, something which gives us—however briefly—a sense of seeing the world through his eyes, from his point of view. He is not other than Man; he is the darker side of Man and therefore comprehensible.

Frankenstein (James Whale, 1931). There is always something sympathetic about the horror film Monster. He is not other than Man; he is the darker side of Man and humanly comprehensible. (Universal)

Frankenstein's Monster moves us as a child would for he is totally innocent at the beginning of the first film (Henry Frankenstein says of him, "He's only a few days old." [34]), and we cannot help but feel as the film progresses that Frankenstein, in refusing responsibility for his creation, has acted like an irresponsible parent or—worse—an indifferent God. We long for Dracula's death not only to reestablish the harmony of the status quo, but to give rest and peace to a tormented if suave soul who can say with such quiet and caressive intensity: "To die . . . to be *really* dead . . . that must be glorious."[35] Certainly Lawrence Talbot commands our sympathy in his struggle with the known but uncontrollable animal within him because he is—in human form—eminently likable, eminently earnest, and decent. We identify with him, and we are told constantly by the verse which is repeated throughout *The Wolf Man* (George Waggner, 1941), that we, too, are possibly in similar danger:

> Even a man who is pure in heart,
> And says his prayers by night,
> May become a wolf when the wolfbane blooms
> And the Autumn moon is bright.[36]

We are all potential victims of ourselves, our passions, our animal lust, our unholy and earthly desires. We all live as the offspring of Original Sin and we are all Monsters but for the grace of God which is not logically comprehensible. This is what the horror film in its traditional guise suggests to the viewer. Hence all the physically deformed human characters who lurk peripherally in its corners, the cripples and the hunchbacks. Maimed bodies indicate maimed souls.

If the traditional horror film is about anything, it is about Man's fall

Frankenstein (James Whale, 1931). **The cripples and hunchbacks who appear in the horror film exteriorize moral deformity. Maimed bodies indicate maimed souls. (Universal)**

Dr. Jekyll and Mr. Hyde (**Rouben Mamoulian, 1932**). **The world of the horror film is constant in its values and predestined to find Man struggling with evil, menaced by protean outcasts who have been denied Eden. (Paramount)**

from grace, his expulsion from Eden, his dependence on the potentially redemptive power of love. Thus the horror film presents us with a world which remains ever constant in its values, a world which is predestined to find Man struggling with evil, a world which accepts the inevitability of evil and Man's susceptibility to it, a world graced by lovers who are not lustful, and menaced by protean outcasts who have been denied Eden and the hope of heavenly forgiveness because they lust. The recognition of this inevitable struggle for redemption through suffering and love runs through all the traditional horror films—echoes, for example, in the litany chanted by Maleva the gypsy over the bodies of her son and Lawrence Talbot in *The Wolf Man:*

> The way you walk is thorny through no fault of your own. For as the rain enters the soul, and evil enters the sea, so tears run to their pre-destined end. Your suffering is over. Now find peace for eternity, my son.[37]

There is no such sense of predestination in the SF film. Danger does not arise from what men inevitably are, but rather from what they do or from what is done to them. And, most definitely, the danger is seen as separate and distinct from the animal within. The animal—or vegetable—when he appears in the SF film is no hunchbacked eruption of internal evil. In those films in which Creatures stomp cities, wreck Coney Island, etc., the human characters feel little sense of responsibility for the appearance of the Creature; they have divorced themselves from any but the most minimal connection with it. Many critics have seen these Creatures as personifications of the Bomb (and there is certainly a good deal of evidence to support this theory), but despite occasional dialogue about the misuse of atomic energy or some aspect of applied science, the Creature is a threat which exists apart from personal or collective guilt. The "He" (or on occasion "She") of the horror film thus becomes the "It" or "Them" of the SF film. Its relationship to Man is virtually nonexistent; It is an accident, something disconnected from human experience and human intention.

In Jack Arnold's *Tarantula* (1955), for example, the scientist, who would be held morally responsible for the very fact of the giant spider in a horror film, is instead seen as a victim of a horrible accident, as essentially noble in his desire to create a nutrient which will feed the world's hungry. There

Tarantula **(Jack Arnold, 1955). The scientist is not held morally responsible for the giant spiders, but is seen instead as the victim of a horrible scientific accident. (Universal)**

is almost always the feeling in the SF film that however misguided men's actions may be, however many accidents there may be, men are essentially able to control their own destinies in either an affirmative or negative manner. Even in films which present us with a world already destroyed by the biggest accident of all—nuclear war—there is often the promise of a new Eden.

Because the Creature in the SF film is so unparticularized (we generally know it only by its external appearance and by the destruction it causes) and because it threatens men rather than Man, it is never so horrible as the Monster in the horror film. Even doing Its worst—killing the populace and laying waste to cities—we do not see it seeking personal revenge; it does not possess a tortured soul. Since we view it primarily as an externally realized object with no "insides" to speak of, it is not terrifying beyond the first shock of seeing it. Since it does not menace one lone individual, it threatens us all and as a result, the individual viewer does not feel singled out as victim. Thus, as Susan Sontag notes, there is not much horror in SF films:

Suspense, shocks, surprises are mostly abjured in favor of a steady in-

An unidentified "ape woman" from one in a series of films dealing with female "animals." The fear in the horror film is the eruption of the animal, which dehumanizes, bestializes, men and women.

exorable plot. Science fiction films invite a dispassionate, aesthetic view of destruction and violence—a *technological* view. Things, objects, machinery play a major role in these films.[38]

Because the emphasis in the SF film is so often on the external, because it does not usually concentrate on internally realized characters, our interest in these types of films is objective and often based on scale. Not threatened into a recognition of personal guilt, and never feeling much identification with summarily developed human characters, we view the SF Creature film dispassionately; the aesthetics of destruction please us as a well-mounted slide might please a scientist. The passion and human hunger of the horror film is replaced by the satisfactions of objectivity. Terror is replaced by wonder.

If the SF film expresses or elicits any fear, it is a fear which is far removed from the fear and terror of the horror film—and it is milder by comparison. The SF film is not concerned with the animal which is there, now and for always, within us. It produces not the strong terror evoked by something already present and known in each of us, but the more

The Stepford Wives (Bryan Forbes, 1975). Publicity still. The fear in SF films springs from the possibility that we may turn into machines, dehumanized by the rational rather than bestial side of our nature. (Columbia)

diluted and less immediate fear of what we may yet become. The terrifying aspect of traditional horror films arises from a recognition that we are forever linked to the crudeness of our earthbound bodies; the fear in SF films springs from the future possibility that we may—in a sense—lose contact with our bodies. Susan Sontag observes:

> The dark secret behind human nature used to be the upsurge of the animal.... The threat to man, his availability to dehumanization, lay in his own animality. Now the danger is understood as residing in man's ability to be turned into a machine.[39]

What we fear now is the rational side of our nature, but that fear is never quite pitched to the intensity of horror. It is diluted by the alternative attraction of pure rationality. Thus in *Invasion of the Body Snatchers* (Don Siegel, 1956), we can see dual feelings expressed: the desire to rid ourselves of the disruptive, unreasonable animal within and the simultaneous need for the good aspects of that animal which includes the ability to love. (One of the "taken over" characters, quite pleased with his transformation into a nonfeeling being, tries to persuade the hero to accept the invasion and its results: "Love, desire, ambition, faith—without them life is so simple."[40]) In the SF film, then, our fears are more confused and more complex than they are in the horror film, and—more often than not—we experience anxiety rather than terror.

It must be recognized that this general discussion of some of the differences between the traditional horror film and the SF film neither encompasses all the areas of divergence between the two genres, nor does it deal with the similarities between them (something which will be discussed in part in the next section). It does point, however, to the major differences of approach to the genres' respective material, their different thematic emphases which influence their visual and verbal content, their characterizations and conventions. In discussing the SF film in this section, particular attention has been paid to the kind of films which seem to be most confused with horror films because of the presence of a distinctly visible Creature or Monster in them. With regard to those films which seem to contradict the general thrust of this argument, suffice it to say that this critic recognizes that *Forbidden Planet* (Fred Wilcox, 1956), for example, has a Monster from the Id; yet although this particular Monster comes from within the individual—in the film's present, Dr. Morbius—and has destroyed a civilization of the highest intelligence, the film's emphasis is less on Dr. Morbius' moral crisis than it is on Robby the Robot and the landscape and machinery and decor of Altair IV. *Forbidden Planet* is certainly science fiction. It tends to explain the animal within us in the scientific terminology of Freudian psychology, to view it—if not tame it—

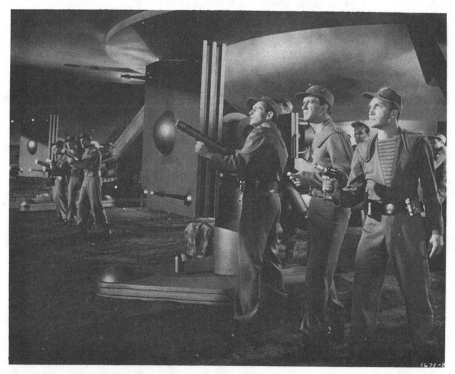

Forbidden Planet (Fred Wilcox, 1956). This SF film's Monster is "from the Id," yet the emphasis is less on the eruption of moral evil than on the alien landscape and wondrous machinery. (Metro-Goldwyn-Mayer)

dispassionately and analytically. The Monster from the Id is not seen from the same vantage point we watch the Wolf Man.

Conversely, although *Frogs* (George McCowan, 1972), overtly voices considerable concern about ecology, pollution, insecticide spraying, etc., it little resembles science fiction in its evident attitudes toward its material content. Despite the realistic nature cinematography, the faddish concern with the "environment," structurally and thematically it is a horror film. A normally corrupt family, isolated on an island with their house guests, becomes the personal victim of frogs, snakes, and lizards who systematically wipe most of the family out. The creatures are, in a sense, anthropomorphized, given an implicit human intelligence, and their destructive actions are calculated and personally directed. *Frogs* is more about morality and revenge than it is about ecology.

Science fiction films, then, differ from traditional horror films in their focus of attention, their thematic emphases, their visual way of looking at their subjects, and particularly in their total intensity. T. J. Ross notes in *Focus on the Horror Film:*

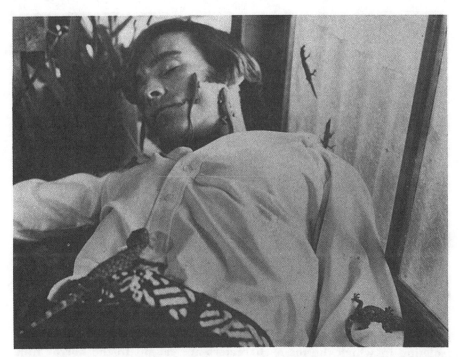

Frogs (George McCowan, 1972). A horror film despite its ecological concern, the movie anthropomorphizes its creatures and makes them selectively vengeful. (American International)

Films of Gothic horror are expressionist in their style and atmosphere and humanist in the drive of their meaning and concern. They are most akin to expressionist art in their overriding emphasis on distorted emotional capacities and quests, on energies wildly miscast. Thus, their ominously stark landscapes are peopled by wailing giants, brutal hunchbacks, compulsive scientists, raging mobs, fierce dark ladies, and swooning blond heroines. Nor does the fevered pitch of the scene—and its shocks of horror—depend simply on the appearance or antics of a freakish-looking creature, but rather on a situation which determines the whole action of the film. We are more moved and scared by the freakishly profound isolation in which every one of the main characters is caught up than by a gimmickry of things that go bump in the night . . . the moral is inseparable from the terror.[41]

Such a description of the SF film would tend to use "cooler" adjectives than Ross does; the type of passion and compulsion and heat that exists in the horror film does not exist in SF. Neither does the sense of personal isolation. And although there are SF films like *Robinson Crusoe on Mars* (Byron Haskin, 1964), and *Silent Running* (Douglas Trumbull, 1972), in which the main characters spend much of their time away from other men, their

House of Wax (Andre de Toth, 1953). We are moved and frightened by the isolation in which the main characters are caught in the horror film. (Warner Brothers)

Silent Running (Douglas Trumbull, 1972). Personal isolation in the SF film is tempered by the presence of civilization and society in the very artifacts that surround the lone protagonist. (Universal)

isolation is always tempered by the presence of civilization and society in the artifacts which surround them. It is also true that there are SF films which evoke shudders and occasional screams from the characters (stereotypically female), but we do not usually associate those shudders and screams with the audience. Ultimately, the horror film evokes fear, the SF film interest.[42]

The Trouble with Creatures and Monsters

In the last section, the Creatures of the SF film were considered together, not only for the purpose of making certain observations about the different emphases of horror and science fiction, but also because they are most usually considered together by critics. It is necessary, however, in order to understand why a limbo of films exists between horror and science fiction, to make certain distinctions between those types of SF Monsters which seem to have an affinity with the Monsters of the horror film and those SF Creatures which, scaled and tentacled, claim major alliance with the SF film. (For the purpose of clarity, the former will henceforth be called Monsters and the latter Creatures.)

Two particular types of antagonists have continually caused the SF critic (literary and film) no small amount of discomfort. In SF literature, one was pejoratively referred to as the BEM—an acronym for bug-eyed monster—and it appeared most often in the "space opera," a type of story which had more to do with physical and broad comic strip art than it had to do with literature; the BEM was the monstrous antagonist—a symbol of unparticularized evil—which the silver-suited space jockey had to slay before he could win the scantily clad girl. In the film, the BEM has found its equivalent in the Creature who stomps cities, dissolves people, and inexorably worms or flies or walks its way from the Arctic, the sea, the desert, to a highly populated area where it mindlessly destroys anything it happens upon. The second type of antagonist seems to follow in the tradition of Dr. Jekyll and Mr. Hyde: a human being is transformed—through contact most usually with radiation—into a Monster, but his destructive or murderous exploits are followed in more detail than are his moral agonies. The respective films in which these two types of antagonists appear are most often disavowed by both the SF critics who claim that science only activates the antagonist and has little to do with the film's emphasis, and the horror film critics who claim that the antagonist is not morally worthy company for the Wolf Man, Dracula, or Frankenstein's Monster.

It must be emphasized that the Creature who is equivalent to the BEM of literature is not the *intelligent* alien invader, but the conceptually un-particularized living organism that provides the pivotal focus of a narrative having less to do with science and technology than it does with what Susan Sontag calls "the aesthetics of destruction, with the peculiar beauties to be found in wreaking havoc, making a mess."[43] The destructive actions of the Creature may be viewed dispassionately, appreciated aesthetically, but the manner in which the filmmaker usually introduces the Creature is calculated to shock or arouse the audience to terror or fear, an element (a rather small one, at that) which superficially connects it to the horror film. The overt reasons for the Creature's existence, however, ostensibly connect it to the SF film; it is the Bomb which creates or liberates the evil, or—less frequently—it is brought to Earth by scientifically explainable transportation (the meteorite, or the spaceship which unwittingly plays cabbie). The major fact is, however, that neither genre wants much to do with the Creature; it possesses neither the "soul" so crucial to the horror film's antagonist nor the "mind" so necessary to the SF film's antagonist. Thus, the films are rarely discussed intelligently. And it is only recently that they are beginning to be considered as something other than either SF or horror

Them! **(Gordon Douglas, 1954). The Creature films of the fifties are about the preservation of social order. What is called for is teamwork, coopera-tion, and organization. (Warner Brothers)**

films—and as having a fascination and aesthetic value of their own. (Whether they are actually something "other" from SF and horror is questionable if "other" means isolated or apart from; the films combine elements of both genres and are therefore not really isolated from either.) Fortunately, this new critical stance allows for a less defensive and more positive look at these hybrid films.

Brian Murphy in an essay entitled "Monster Movies: They Came From Beneath the Fifties," says: "What makes the Fifties' monster movies a species unto themselves is the combination of the two forms—the horror and sci-fi—and the ideological purpose to which they were put in that age." [44] He indicates that these films "are like nineteenth century operas ... in their degree of structural stylization," [45] and he sees the essential elements of that stylization embodied in the Creature film's plot: "A team of U. S. military-scientific types discover, precisely, a 'thing' and must use all of their military and scientific knowledge corporately to destroy the monster." [46] In the bulk of these Creature films, the giant insect or reptillian mutant, the awakened Rhedosaurus, etc., is, in a sense, "spontaneously generated" by the Bomb, but the antiscientific implications of this must be counter-balanced by the proscientific implications of the fact that science is called upon to destroy the Creature as well. As Murphy notes:

> Those beasts and things—Them generally—are awfully real, and, it seemed, we could deal with them only by going back to the very people who spawned them: the scientists working "in full cooperation" (such an important word, that "cooperation") with the military. [47]

The Creature films of the fifties (and the early sixties as well) are less about horror and science than they are about the preservation of social order. There is no salvation for the disorganized mob, running amok under the Creature's feet. What is called for is teamwork, cooperation, and, above all, organization. In this type of film, Murphy accurately notes that "the monster . . . is not the principle character," [48] a truism which removes it further from the ranks of the horror film. The mutants and beasts which threaten the architecture as much as they do the populace in films such as *The Beast from 20,000 Fathoms* (Eugene Lourié, 1953), *Them!* (Gordon Douglas, 1954), *It Came from Beneath the Sea* (Robert Gordon, 1955), *The Deadly Mantis* (Nathan Juran, 1957), and *The Monster that Challenged the World* (Arnold Laven, 1957), have no *personae*; they are intentless. They act only as foils to the collective hero (the organized institutions of the society: scientific, military, political).

John Denne, in an essay about various types of Monsters and Creatures, notes that in what we are calling the Creature film, the Creature's "motivations are for the most part inconsequential, as we view the monster as a

It Came From Beneath the Sea (**Robert Gordon, 1955**). **The mutants and beasts that threaten the architecture as much as they do the populace have no personae; they are intentless. (Columbia)**

problem which society faces in different ways." [49] Denne designates the Creature film the *bipartite* (or *bipolar*) monster film and suggests that it is closer to SF films than to horror films because it is "relatively asocial in its approach, leaving the audience freer to observe more of a tactical battle . . . a struggle between strong opposites." [50] (By asocial, Denne is not suggesting that the films are not concerned with society, but that the *presentation* of the conflict is more objective than in other sorts of films which contain monsters.)

Joe Kane, in an article "Nuclear Films," presents a related thematic classification of Creature films: the Bestial Invocation theme; in these films the Creatures are seen as "instruments of punishment for nuclear misuse." [51] The elements of both the SF and the horror film can be found in the linking of "punishment" and "instrument" in that one phrase, much as the films themselves combine elements from both genres. We usually connect punishment with themes primarily found in the horror film, associated with crime and guilt; it is a word charged with moral connotations. The Creature who brings punishment, however, is seen as an instrument, a tool or device which causes social disaster and affects social organization. Thus, the Creature film sits (awkwardly, for some) between horror and SF, because the films can be viewed as either retributive fantasies or as a call for social order and organization. Interpreted from the latter perspective, the films are primarily objective, dispassionate, and allow the viewer to respond on a removed aesthetic level to destruction and disaster. If one sees the films as retributive fantasies, however, destruction and disaster become part of a nightmare construct.

Many critics have, of course, pointed out that the Creature films are a dream-like representation of—if not collective guilt—collective nuclear fear, definitely related to group anxiety about the uses of atomic energy. Susan Sontag sees them as indicative of

> ...the trauma suffered by everyone in the middle of the 20th century when it became clear that from now on to the end of human history, every person would spend his individual life not only under the threat of individual death, which is certain, but of something almost insupportable psychologically—collective incineration and extinction which could come at any time, virtually without warning.[52]

And Brian Murphy sees the Creature as "the symbol of what we have to fear: it is not fear itself; it is the horror of what we have done, scientifically and militarily to bring the world to the brink of destruction." [53] John Baxter, as well, talks about the Creature cycle in words which evoke the moral tone of the horror film, the idea of retribution and the possibility of atonement:

> To American audiences the havoc wreaked on their homes by various dinosaurs is as welcome as the lash to a flagellant while ritual phrases like "There Are Some Things Man Is Not Meant to Know" assume the importance of a litany; affirm, abase, adore—the prescribed reactions of audiences and congregations are too similar to be accidental.[54]

Margaret Tarratt, too, sees the dream-like quality of the Creature film but relates it to Freudian psychoanalytic theory rather than to nuclear anxiety or guilt. Approaching films like *The Thing* and *20 Million Miles to Earth* (Nathan Juran, 1957), from a psychoanalytic point of view, she refers most definitely to the Creatures in these films and others as the embodiment of the sexual and unreasoning animal within which threatens domestic harmony, and its attendant sedated and institutionalized sexuality. The themes she sees in the Creature films are the themes of the horror films. She finds in the Creature films structures which relate to Freud's work on dreams. The hero (and she sees him as an individual rather than part of a collective whole) and his battle against the Creature is "a dramatisation of the individual's anxiety about his own repressed sexual desires,

Them! (Gordon Douglas, 1954). Freudian interpretation sees the "Insect" films as concerned with impotence and frigidity. There is a great narrative preoccupation with stopping the Queen from mating and breeding. (Warner Brothers)

which are incompatible with the morals of civilised liife." [55] She particularly notes the thematic concerns of the Insect films as impotence and frigidity and sees the insect phobia as a "fear of castration and dread of the phallic mother." [56] To some, this may seem to be making a mountain out of an anthill, but it must be noted that in many Insect films there is a great narrative preoccupation with stopping the Queen of the species from mating and breeding. Ms. Tarratt's Freudian analysis also holds up quite well in those Creature films which predominantly feature adolescents as victims and heroes (i.e., *Horror of Party Beach,* [Del Tenney 1964]); their battle seems, quite reasonably, one against eruptive sexual impulses and may explain why such films, shoddy as most of them are, continued to be made long after the Creature cycle with adult heroes wore itself out.

It is Richard Hodgens, however, who deals the *coup de grâce* to those who insist the Creature film is pure science fiction because of its "scientific" philosophizing about the Bomb, and its presentation of the Creature as a symbol of the Bomb:

It may be argued that all the atomic monsters of SF films are symbols, and I suppose that they are, but they are inapt, inept, or both.

If the creators of monster films had intended any comment on the problems raised by the atomic bomb, or even feelings about it, as some kindly critics have assumed, they would not have made their monster films at all. The most obvious advantage of science fiction, and the three films mentioned above [Hodgens praises as SF *Five,* Arch Obler (1951); *The World, the Flesh, and the Devil,* Ranald MacDougall (1959); and *On the Beach,* Stanley Kramer (1959)], is that one can deal with such problems and feelings by extending the situation into the future and showing a possible effect or resolution. There is no need for indirect discussion or for a plot with a "symbol" as its mainspring. A twelve-ton, woman-eating cockroach does not say anything about the bomb simply because it, too, is radioactive, or crawls out of a test site, and the filmmakers have simply attempted to make their monster more frightening by associating it with something serious.[57]

Hodgens is echoed by Frank Hauser who, although he admits their disquieting effect, sees the "Beast from 20,000 fathoms, the Godzillas and other sports" as little but "bugaboos dressed up in atomic hats."[58]

The Creature cycle tends, then, to be disowned by both horror and SF purists. Yet it is obvious that there are elements of both genres in it. Susan

The Beast from 20,000 Fathoms **(Eugene Lourié, 1953). The Creature films place their primary emphasis on disaster and destruction, but also display the fifties' anxiety about nuclear annihilation. (Warner Brothers)**

Sontag sees the films' primary emphasis on disaster and destruction but does regard them also in relation to nuclear anxiety. Murphy sees them as rendering the particular social fears of the 1950s when "it seemed that all America was tunneling through its bowels to build bomb shelters, and theologians argued about the morality of shooting a radium-contaminated neighbor at the door of your family's private shelter." [59] He evaluates the Creature films' major function as reassuring us that "the soldier was good enough and the scientist wise enough to take care of us." [60] If the Creature films are not primarily about abstract or applied science (and there are often considerations of both in them to some degree), they are most definitely about science as a *social force,* as an institutional aspect of contemporary civilization. While they may not be about scientific theory or about the Bomb, they are extremely cognizant of science as an arm of institutional power and it is in this latter sense that they can be approached as science fiction.

Let us turn now to the second type of antagonist who sits in limbo between horror and science fiction, the Monster. In the SF–Monster film, it is a *human being* who—most often as a result of scientific accident—becomes the Monster and who, although he may go mad by the end of the movie, is through a great portion of the film at least semirational. Unlike

The 4-D Man **(Irving Yeaworth, 1959). The SF Monster is almost always a misfit and does not conform to accepted modes of social behavior. Isolating himself, he alone becomes contaminated. (Universal/Fairview)**

his Creature counterpart, his actions have purpose and intent. The Monster can be a scientist, a gangster, a "hero," but he is almost always a misfit in the sense that he does not conform with accepted modes of social behavior, or does not obey orders, and thus places himself in isolation, away from society, so that he alone is contaminated. *The 4-D Man* (Irving Yeaworth, 1959), for example, is a member of a scientific institute whose researchers work in teams; he, however, chooses to work secretly on a project which—in conjunction with other factors, the most interesting being his penchant for privacy—ultimately results in his transformation from man to Monster. *The Most Dangerous Man Alive* (Allan Dwan, 1961), is a gangster who has escaped apprehension to revenge himself against his associates; wandering in a desolate area he is exposed to radiation from an atomic blast and turned into a combination of flesh and steel. *The Amazing Colossal Man* (Bert I. Gordon, 1957), is affected by a plutonium bomb explosion when he disobeys his commander's orders and rushes onto the test site to save another human being.

Despite the constantly radioactive cause of the transformation or mutation, what results is very much akin to the physical eruption of spiritual deformity found in the horror film—the evil within finding its way to the surface to take external form. In so many of these SF Monster films, the punishment seems to fit the crime; the Monster is a physical manifestation of some characteristic flaw—usually of an antisocial nature—in the pre-monstrous human and what we see is visual poetic justice. Jealousy and passion force the scientist in *The 4-D Man* to clandestine experiments and antisocial behavior; as a Monster he becomes dependent upon other people's "life forces" to sustain him and with his kiss he turns a young woman into a desiccated and incredibly aged hag. The *Most Dangerous Man Alive* was figuratively "as hard as nails" before his accidental exposure to radiation; after the blast, the figurative becomes literal and his body which is turned into a molecular combination of tissue and steel can absorb bullets. The heroic but insidiously individual action of the Colonel who disobeys orders in *The Amazing Colossal Man* can—despite its supposedly social aim of saving another human being—be seen as evidence of *hubris,* pride, separation from society; his "heroism" is literally translated into "bigness" and he grows to a size which actually separates him from the social world and the rest of humanity.

John Denne, previously cited, categorizes films with this kind of Monster as *atmospheric* Monster films which "can be viewed as the struggle between good and evil." [61] He sees the Monster "as protagonist, malevolent, antisocial, and strong in the sense of moral consistency of behavior." [62] Joe Kane notes this Contamination-Mutation theme as well and suggests that one of its necessary factors is the *isolation* of the individual.[63] He also adds that the

... message following the usually ironic and ambiguous ... destruction of the civilization-stripped mutant is invariably a variation of the "when will we (or Man or Russia) learn not to mess with the ways of nature (or God or the United States)." [64]

Theoretically, then, the Monster film bears a great resemblance to the horror film; we are concerned with an isolated individual who—science or no—is in conflict with his animal nature, who defies law, and who suffers and dies for his personal sins. The messages of the films—sometimes overtly stated—seem, however, to be more anti-Faustian in content than antiscience. On the whole one is reminded of Dr. Jekyll and Mr. Hyde or the Wolf Man.

In practice, however, these films are not as closely connected with the horror film as they might theoretically appear to be. True, all the proper ingredients are there, but the emphasis placed on them—other than the structural similarities of plot—is fairly negligible. Even though, for example, *The Amazing Colossal Man* may ask himself "What sin could a man commit in a single lifetime to bring this upon himself?," he spends little time— if any—answering the question. The film itself is not at all concerned about the answer to the question. It is not really concerned with the breaking of moral laws. Instead, it emphasizes in great detail the physical effects of the transformation—the process and progress of the Monster—and pays little attention to internal moral struggle. In the case of all but the gangster-mutant, the films ignore the Monster's initial crime (*hubris* or antisocial behavior). The Monster is really seen as the victim not of himself—despite the physical form his monstrousness takes—but of an accident. In all these films, then, it is always required that the Monster murder a number of people before it seems morally right to destroy him. He is evil because of what he does, not because of what he is. Sin and personal guilt are never a real issue in these films as they seem to be in their horror film counterparts; there are only social crimes in this type of Monster film and they are usually evaluated quantitatively rather than qualitatively. Murder in large numbers is worse than a single murder; destruction on a grand scale is more immoral than small scale destruction. Sin and guilt as it is conceived of in the horror film is never practically considered in the SF Monster film.

As a result of this lack of preoccupation with sin and guilt, the narrative presentation of the SF Monster is nearly always objective. He becomes an object to look at, not one to feel for. Despite the supposed emphasis on the individual, closeups of the Monster are fairly infrequent and we never find ourselves identifying to any great degree with him, either in his human or mutated form. Even in such films which present us with apparently "sympathetic" characters (*The Amazing Colossal Man,* or *The Fly* [Kurt Neumann, 1958]) we become engaged with the external qualities of their

X, The Man With X-Ray Eyes (Roger Corman, 1963). The messages of SF Monster films seem to be more anti-Faustian than antiscience. The protagonist/antagonist defies society and suffers and dies for his sins. (American International)

mishaps and not with their individual psyches. The camera keeps its distance. We are not hypnotized by them as Dracula can hypnotize us; we feel none of their pain and suffering as we do the Frankenstein Monster's or the Wolf Man's.

The Creature cycle of the fifties and the Monster films discussed in this section are often considered embarrassments. For one thing, a great many

53

The Fly (Kurt Neumann, 1958). Even when the SF Monster is apparently "sympathetic," we are engaged with the external qualities of his mishap and not with his individual psyche. (20th Century Fox)

Creature from the Black Lagoon (Jack Arnold, 1954). Publicity still. The Creature cycle and Monster cycle are hybrid forms, neither horror nor SF films. (Universal)

of them are shabbily made. And, for another, they get in the way of the purist in either genre who might be able to come up with a fairly neat generic definition if only they were not around to be seen. It is quite natural, therefore, that these films come under the most critical fire and are—in fact—often hated, usually for the least objective of reasons. There are, however, some exceptionally well-done films which fall into these hybrid forms, and they cannot be ignored; SF critics extract them, with various strained arguments, from this intermediate area between science fiction and horror and bring them into the mainstream of SF films. But films like *The Thing, Them!, Creature from the Black Lagoon* (Jack Arnold, 1954), *Most Dangerous Man Alive, X, The Man with the X-Ray Eyes* (Roger Corman, 1963), and *Night of the Living Dead* (George Romero, 1968), are neither horror nor SF films. There is no way of either ignoring or purifying them. Hopefully, in the next section, we can arrive at a more moderate evaluation of these hybrid films by coming up with a definition of SF film which can, instead of being threatened by such films, accommodate them.

Magic, Science, and Religion: Towards Synthesis and Definition

There have been two major camps in SF film criticism which, each in its own way, have perhaps obscured the path to a meaningful definition of the genre. The first sees the "ideal" SF film as being opposite to and totally separate from the horror film; it eschews those so-called SF films which overtly or surreptitiously present elements that are not empirically based, elements of superstition, mysticism, or religion (the magical and the miraculous) most often associated with the horror film. The SF purist sees science fiction as a kind of "prophetic 'neo-realism', which reality corroborates after the fact." [65] The second critical camp sees the SF film as a modern replacement or substitute for the horror film, growing out of it and superseding it; the magical and miraculous become—simply—the empirically explainable. Thus, Robert Brustein can echo Michel Laclos' suggestion that robots are merely comprehensible zombies:

> The alchemist and devil-conjuring Dr. Faustus, gives way to Dr. Frankenstein, the research physician, while the magic circle, the tetragrammaton, and the full moon are replaced by test tubes, complicated electrical apparatus, and Bunsen burners. [66]

Unfortunately, however, both views are too simple to be satisfying and do not explore the relationships which have always existed in society and in its art among magic, religion, and science, relationships which have existed in the most primitive of societies and which still exist in the most complex. Both critical camps tend to concern themselves primarily with the paraphernalia of the films as if they held the key to the genres' respective differences, their attitudes, themes, and visual emphasis. And both camps have trouble dealing with the paradoxical nature of the actual films.

Certainly, for example, *2001: A Space Odyssey* can be regarded in terms of its technical extrapolation, its paraphernalia, as a purist's dream; it is, indeed, in one sense prophetic neo-realism. Yet the purist could not find it in himself to interpret the ambiguously presented Monolith as anything other than an empirically based device, a technological *tour de force* pulled off by a "superior" civilization, despite all the transcendental and religious connotations with which the film surrounds it (heavenly choirs, etc.). The purist critic finds himself in the uncomfortable position of having to deny the ultimately mystical implications of Arthur C. Clarke's Third Law which says, "any sufficiently advanced technology is indistinguishable from magic." [67] He also cannot comfortably consider the possible alternate or multiple meanings behind what he sees and hears. How would he deal with the following provocative critical interpretation of SF films about space and astronauts offered by Mandell and Fingesten:

> We see that the new mythology is a subtle point-for-point exchange of traditional religious doctrines for "modern" concepts ... the spaceship ... displaces the church as a vessel of salvation ... the pilot or astrogator leads his community of saints like a savior ... the dashboard paraphernalia and control dials become as potent and dominant as icons and sacraments—faith is placed in technical efficiency ... the breakthrough into space, the bursting through gravitational pulls, constitutes a baptism or a climactic initiation into the heavenly mysteries. [68]

The second group of critics also have their problems. Suggesting that the SF film is the modern equivalent of the horror film makes a certain amount of good sense until we realize that the horror film—with all its mythic, magical, and religious emphases—is still around and thriving, apparently filling certain needs which still exist in even a highly technologized and pragmatic society. Ivan Butler points out:

> The apparently indestructible interest in the supernatural and fantastic Horror Film is an extra-ordinary phenomenon in an age which increasingly rejects religious beliefs and upholds the materialistic values of science and technology. To say that nobody takes such stories seriously is begging the question. It is not wholly correct, and if it were it would only increase the difficulty of explaining their fascination. Nor is their continuing profusion solely due to the fact that vampires, ghosts

and monsters are often extremely photogenic, and can also provide an easy excuse for staging scenes of sadistic or erotic sensationalism. It is, rather, as if, despite our protestations of the triumph of common sense over superstition, something very deep inside us is loth to bid farewell to the ancient beliefs, the "old religion" of our less enlightened but perhaps more imaginative ancestors.[69]

In support of Butler's statement, one need only look at the current crop of television series and movies which deal with possession by the devil, occult practices, witchcraft. And, as a poetically just rebuttal to those critics who think that SF films have replaced horror films because the former are more "realistic" and therefore more credible to contemporary audiences, Stanley Kubrick makes the following observation:

People in the twentieth century are increasingly occupied with magic, mystical experience, transcendental urges, hallucinogenic drugs, the belief in extraterrestrial intelligence, et cetera, so that, in this sense, fantasy, the supernatural, the magical documentary, call it what you will, is closer to the sense of the times than naturalism.[70]

The Dunwich Horror (Daniel Haller, 1969). It seems not enough to say that the horror film is about magic and religion and that the SF film is about science. Both genres involve interaction among all three elements. (American International)

57

If one considers the actual complexity of the films themselves, then, it seems not enough to say that the horror film is about magic and religion and that the SF film is about science. What is important is to recognize that both genres involve *interaction* between magic, science, and religion—and the only thing which really separates the genres is the dominant emphasis given to either the sacred or the profane. We cannot legitimately say, viewing the films themselves, that there is no science in the horror film, no empirically credible material, nor can we say that there is no magic and religion in the SF film. Rather than futilely attempting to isolate the genres from each other, it is far more critically useful to see them as the two ends of a spectrum. If the horror film is infrared (with its moral passions, its magical and religious motifs), then the SF film is ultraviolet (cool and intellectual, empirically oriented). In between, however, is a whole range of films which represent those colors perceptible to the human eye, blending into each other from one end of the spectrum to the other, containing both passion and dispassion, magic, religion, and science in varying degrees of intensity.

Since almost all the films in the range from horror to science fiction contain some elements of magic, religion, and science, it is not particularly enlightening—in the service of definition and analysis—to simply note their appearance and mathematically calculate the percentage of each in a specific film. Far more important in arriving at any meaningful distinctions is an attempt to evaluate and analyze the function—not merely the presence and amount—of each. As social phenomena and the bases of social institutions, magic, science, and religion may be related and coexistent, but they have different social functions, serve to fulfill different social needs. And, in doing such, they are not mere abstractions. Each represents a mode of action as well as a system of belief.

Anthropologist Bronislaw Malinowski, in a fascinating essay "Magic, Science and Religion," examines the cultural functions of these three systems of belief, pointing out the visible similarities between the three as well as their inherent differences. A look at these similarities and differences helps to explain why critics feel compelled to separate the two film genres on the basis of their differences; on the bases of their similarities, however, it also explains why the genres ultimately refuse amputation. Magic, science, and religion *interact* in the SF film as they do in society, fulfilling our need for comprehensible answers to cosmic questions. All three—in some way—attempt to reconcile man to the unknown.

To begin, magic is seen by Malinowski as similar to science in many ways:

Magic is akin to science in that it always has a definite aim intimately

58

associated with human instincts, needs, and pursuits. The magic art is directed towards the attainment of practical aims ... it is also governed by a theory, by a system of principles which dictate the manner in which the act has to be performed in order to be effective.[71]

What, then, is the cultural (and perhaps cinematic) function of magic? Magic is, like science, essentially optimistic—a system of belief which is based on the assumption that man is capable of affecting his environment and his own destiny. And magic, like science, depends on process and product. Thus, on one hand, it is quite possible to see the alchemist-like Dr. Praetorius observing his live miniaturized human beings in *Bride of Frankenstein* (a horror film) as equivalent to *The 4-D Man* in his laboratory attempting to penetrate steel with a pencil. On the other hand, what distinguishes magic from science, the horror film from the SF film, amounts finally to how much we know about the process and the product, how much we are told about the cause and effect. Dr. Praetorius is essentially a magician, a witch-doctor, not because he can miniaturize human beings and put them in bell jars, but because we don't understand or see how he did it; the film emphasizes only the result of an unseen process we must

The Bride of Frankenstein (James Whale, 1935). Dr. Praetorius is essentially a magician, an alchemist, not because he can miniaturize human beings, but because we don't understand or see how he did it. (Universal)

The Fly (Kurt Neumann, 1958). The protagonist is a scientist and the film SF because it attempts to explain and show a process the viewer is supposed to understand. (20th Century Fox)

take on faith and so that result is magical. Unlike Dr. Praetorius, the 4-D man is a scientist because the film attempts to explain "how he does it" and sets up and shows a process which we, the audience, may understand—or pretend to understand. (The fact that the scientific premises may be bogus is subordinate to their empirical elaboration in any given film.) Magic, then, is the term born from our collective lack of knowledge about something which works anyway.

Obviously the unexplained—although ritualized—process we call magic functions in and serves society (and both the horror and SF films which are concerned in various ways with society) in areas which cannot be served by the demonstrated process of science. Magic answers a need when logic and desire are incompatible, when practical effort and desired result seem to have little in common. The function of magic is—as Malinowski concludes—"to ritualize man's optimism, to enhance his faith in the victory of hope over fear." [72] What distinguishes the superstition or magic of yesterday from the scientific reality of today or tomorrow, what distinguishes the horror or fantasy film from the SF film, is how much of a burden of faith we, the audience, are asked to assume.

This emphasis on faith is, of course, what primarily links magic to religion in both society and cinema. But what separates magic and religion is the function of ritual; religious ritual—unlike magical ritual which aims at practical, concrete results—does not seek to affect man and nature in a pragmatic manner. It celebrates what is, the *fait accompli*. In this sense, religion is pessimistic in its system of belief; man, himself, is not seen as able to control his destiny or much of his environment, and must place his faith not in the efficacy of action through process, but in the benevolence of a superior power, a Godhead who grants gifts or takes them away without logic or reason and not as the result of process or ritual. The rituals of magic indicate a faith in process itself; religious ritual, however, denies the importance of process and affirms only faith. Despite these differences, both magic and religion:

> ... arise and function in situations of emotional stress. ... Both ... open up escapes from such situations and such impasses as offer no empirical way out except by ritual and belief into the domain of the supernatural. ... Both magic and religion are based strictly on mythological tradition, and they also both exist in the atmosphere of the miraculous, in a constant revelation of their wonder-working power.[73]

Zardoz (John Boorman, 1974). Religion is pessimistic in its system of belief. Man is seen as not able to control his destiny and must place faith not in his own actions but in a Godhead who grants gifts or punishes. (20th Century Fox)

61

Similarities not withstanding, the cultural function of religion is opposite to the cultural function of magic. Based on negative and pessimistic assumptions of man's ability to control or affect his destiny, religion's function is to socially affirm and make supportable man's inadequacies. This function results in group activity which gathers man into a congregation to control his fear and terror of the inevitable, the uncontrollable, and the unknown. Thus, it is perfectly appropriate (and highly mimetic) that the SF film apply religious and/or magical balm to its narrative lesions, that it provide nonempirical answers to those empirical questions its scientist-characters and its social order cannot adequately answer. When an SF film's postulated society is forced to face its own inadequacies, its own inability to deal with and control the unknown and insupportable, then (as in "real" life) that society will simultaneously hide and celebrate its lack of effect by congregating and by making of its failure something holy. No one and no effected empirical solution is able to stop the Martian onslaught in *War of the Worlds* (Byron Haskin, 1953); it is fitting, therefore, that the film end with the survivors congregating in churches, praying and singing in an acceptance of their inadequacies and impending doom— while outside the Martians are halted and destroyed by bacteria, germs, what the narrator tells us are "the littlest things God in His wisdom put on the earth." Similar is the mutant society's religious worship of a nuclear bomb in *Beneath the Planet of the Apes* (Ted Post, 1970). Total annihilation is finally unknowable, unimaginable—and an artifact like the bomb which reminds men of their lack of control over their destiny (and their history) is, itself, logically destined to become a religious icon, a symbol of a Godhead as well as a warhead. Visually and ironically, the worshipped bomb physically resembles an inverted cross; and science is thus alchemically transformed to religion (with a precipitate of associations to the magic of Satanism).

Science, too, needs some definition here—if not equal time. (It is, after all, supposedly less murky than either magic or religion.) Science— derived from observation, experimentation, logical critique and modification—attacks the problem of man's fear of the uncontrollable by practically controlling what it can through technology. Science is a system of belief, technology a mode of action whose purpose is to overcome man's physical inadequacies. The cultural function of science, then, "by acquainting man with his surroundings and by allowing him to use the forces of nature" [74] is to give empirical evidence to man's optimistic belief in his biological supremacy, his ability to control and affect himself and his environment as no other life form on Earth is able to do. In brief, the cultural function of science is to empiricize man's optimism.

These three systems of belief and modes of action exist, as Malinowski has pointed out, in every society, serving different specific functions yet overlapping in both subtle and visible ways. What magic, religion, and science have most in common, however, and what creates a profound and irrevocable bond between them in spite of their differences is that they all attempt to describe and confront the unknown in a manner which will satisfy man's hunger for security and control. Since all three modes of action affect man in society, they are always in constant interaction in every society, cooperating or battling with each other for social dominance. And, since they all deal with the unknown, where one fails to satisfy, another will step into the breach. It is, therefore, not surprising that in today's highly complex and technologized world, magic and religion still flourish.

The pertinence of Malinowski's observations to science fiction should be clear. If science fiction is about science at all, it is not about abstract science, science in a vacuum. In the SF film, science is always related to society, and its positive and negative aspects are seen in light of their social effect. Dealt with in this way, science is bound to interact in some way with other social constructs, institutions, modes of action, and most particularly, with magic and religion. Thus, despite the urge to separate magic and religion from science, SF (film or literature) critics tend to use a "mixed" vocabulary which clearly indicates this interaction; in a sense, they can't help themselves. To discuss control dials as "icons" and their manipulation as "sacraments," or to combine seemingly opposing impulses to come up with the apt phraseology of Kubrick's "magical documentary", is as natural as is the combination and interaction of magic, religion, and science in society itself. The magical and religious elements of the horror film are as present in the SF film as science is present in the horror film. They exist as shadings on a spectrum of need, moving from one end to the other and back, shifting emphasis from magic and religion to science or resting in the middle in a type of stasis between the two poles.

The definitions of science fiction cited at the beginning of this chapter are not incorrect; they are, however, inadequate. Their emphasis on science, empiricism, and technology and their relation to man are fine as far as they go, but they don't go far enough. They ignore one extremely important factor which must be added to any definition of science fiction to make that definition meaningfully inclusive of all those films usually rejected by SF writers and critics who want to purify the genre of its horrific elements. We need a definition of science fiction which gladly recognizes these hybrid forms as part of a spectrum which moves—on a sliding scale—from the sacred to the profane. Such a definition might read: The SF film is a film genre which emphasizes actual, extrapolative, or speculative science and the empirical method, interacting in a social context with the lesser emphasized, but still present, transcendentalism of magic and religion, in an attempt to reconcile man with the unknown.

2

Images of Wonder:
The Look of Science Fiction

Although a great deal has been written about the images in science fiction (SF) films, most often that writing has been more descriptive than analytic. There has been only minor consideration of the nature of SF images and their function in the creation of a film genre which—in photographic content—is unlike any other. Instead, discussions of the visual surface of the films have usually seemed to degenerate into a delightful but critically unproductive game film enthusiasts play: "Swap that Shot" or "The Robot You Love to Remember." Although there is absolutely no reason to feel guilty about swapping nostalgically remembered images like baseball trading cards, it does seem time to go beyond both gamesmanship and nostalgia toward a discovery of how SF images—in content and presentation—function to make SF film uniquely itself. What, if anything, do all the films have in common in their visual surface?

Iconography

One approach to the images in genre films (most often the Western and Gangster film) has been iconographic. Jim Kitses, one of the first critics to discuss the relationship of iconography to the genre film in his *Horizons West,* explains the basis of the approach: "As a result of mass production, the accretions of time, and the dialectics of history and archetype, characters, situations and actions can have an emblematic power."[1] And Colin McArthur, in *Underworld U.S.A.,* emphasizes the "continuity over several decades of patterns of visual imagery, of recurrent objects and figures in dynamic relationship" which "might be called the iconography of the genre."[2] McArthur goes on to say: "The recurrent patterns of imagery can be usefully divided into three categories: those surrounding the physical presence, attributes and dress of the actors and the characters they play; those emanating from the milieux within which the characters operate; and those connected with the technology at the characters' disposal."[3]

In certain groupings of films, then, the visual units which manifest—and often dictate—character, situation, and action have been examined as those elements which not only link the films together, but which also carry meaning and emotional nuance beyond their physical particularity in any one film. Because these elements of visual content appear again and again in film after film, they have become visual conventions or icons, pictorial codes which are a graphic shorthand understood by both filmmaker and audience.[4] The Western topography (whether photographed in the United States or Spain) is not just any place; beyond the specificity of badlands, mountains, rangeland, desert, its appearance evokes associations in the viewer which are, perhaps, more metaphysically than historically based. The same could be said of the city of the Gangster film; buildings and alleys, rooftops and fire escapes surround themselves with clusters of meaning and yet-unplayed actions, with emotional reverberations which have little connection with the same physical objects represented, for example, in an urban comedy like Preston Sturges' *Christmas in July* (1940), or an urban musical like Robert Wise's *West Side Story* (1961). Costumes and tools also become objects of totemic significance in certain film genres; the gun of the Western is different in significance as well as in kind from the gun of the Gangster film.

This recognition of iconography is, perhaps, what Michael Butor was trying to indicate when, attempting to define science fiction, he felt it was sufficient to say: "You know, those stories that are always mentioning interplanetary rockets."[5] His statement, however, brings us to a crucial issue regarding any iconographic consideration of the SF film. Butor, himself, acknowledges that rocketships are not—in themselves—necessary to science fiction.[6] And one could create a list of such SF "objects" as the spaceship which do indeed *evoke* the genre, but which are—specifically and physically—not *essential* to it: the New Planet, the Robot, the Laboratory,

Star Wars (George Lucas, 1977). SF iconography: those stories that are always mentioning interplanetary rockets. While such objects evoke the genre, they are not essential to it. (20th Century Fox)

Radioactive Isotopes, and Atomic Devices. On the other hand, it is extremely difficult to think of a Western which does not take place in a visually represented "West" with guns and horses, or to recall a Gangster film which does not show a nightclub or which has no guns and no automobiles. These settings and objects seem physically essential to these genres and their iconographic significance seems readily approachable and comprehensible because they appear and send the same messages to us in almost every film.

It is also highly significant that both these genres are visually circumscribed by an awareness of history, the Western even more so than the Gangster film. This linkage of situation and character, objects, settings, and costumes to a specific *past* creates visual boundaries to what can be photographed and in what context. This historical awareness, which leads at least to an imaginative if not actual authenticity, demands repetition and creates consistency throughout these genres. This is not true, however, of the SF film, a genre which is unfixed in its dependence on actual time and/or place. There is, then, a very obvious reason for the fact that most iconographic analysis has focused on the Western and the Gangster film. Simply, these genres play out their narrative in a specific, visually identifiable and *consistent* context, and the objects of these films accrue their meaning not only from repetitious use, but also because they function in a much more

Silent Running (Douglas Trumbull, 1971). There is no consistent cluster of meanings provoked by the image of a spaceship. (Universal)

circumscribed and limited way than do objects in other genres. This limitation of meaning should in no way be considered a cinematic, aesthetic, or thematic liability—but it should point to why iconographic analysis serves a less potent critical function when it is used as a method to seek meaning in settings and objects in other film genres less affixed to history.

Consider, for example, the railroad—a frequent, although not mandatory, icon in the Western. The meanings which are suggested by its appearance on the screen are both complex and richly paradoxical, yet they are also circumscribed in scope from movie to movie. The railroad is not merely its physical manifestation; it *is* progress and civilization. It threatens the openness and freedom of the West and individual enterprise, but it also promises the advantages of civilized life and brings the gentling influence of the Eastern heroine who plays the piano and uses an English saddle if she rides horses at all. The ambiguity and paradox contained in the Western's images of the Iron Horse are as rich as our mixed feelings about civilization and progress, but they are also limited to those feelings and those feelings only. The railroad is not interchangeable with other means of transportation in the Western; its meanings are not those which surround the images of a stagecoach, horse, or covered wagon. From its first silent chugging to its clangorous present, the railroad in the history of the Western film has not altered in its physical particularity or its specific significance; it is, indeed, an icon.

Now let us examine one of the most potential icons of SF cinema: the spaceship. Any inspection of the genre leads one inevitably to the conclusion that there is no *consistent* cluster of meanings provoked by the image of a spaceship. The visual treatments of the ship vary from film to film—and sometimes even vary within a single film. Beyond the fact that seeing a spaceship on the screen signals the viewer that he is watching a film which does not take place in the present (and even that signal is weakening since space flight is now a reality), there is no constant meaning generated by that image; because there is no consistent meaning, there is little accumulation of "emblematic power" carried by the object from movie to movie.

There are those films, for example, which treat the spaceship lovingly, positively, optimistically. There is no doubt as to the "goodness" of a technology which can produce such a magnificent toy (although this goodness does not necessarily extend to the men who created the technology nor to the men who employ it). The ship itself is "good." It is aesthetically beautiful. It is fun to play with. It promises positive adventure, an ecstatic release

When Worlds Collide (Rudolph Maté, 1951). **The film presents us with a positive image of the spaceship, an "interplanetary Noah's Ark." (Paramount)**

from the gravitational demands of Earth, and it can remove us from ourselves and the complexity of life on our planet, taking us to new Edens and regeneration. In *Destination Moon* (Irving Pichel, 1950), the silvery sleekness of Ernest Fegté's single-stage spaceship almost palpably glows against the velvet black and star-bejewelled beauty of a mysterious but nonhostile space; it is breathtakingly beautiful, awe inspiring, and yet warmly comforting like the night light in a child's bedroom. In the interior of the ship the crew delights in its weightlessness, playing games with gravity like children released in a schoolyard for recess. *When Worlds Collide* (Rudolph Maté, 1951), although its plot and themes evoke what John Baxter sees as "a Thirties vision of Armageddon," [7] presents us with the positive image of a spaceship as an "interplanetary Noah's Ark," [8] destined to carry a group of potential colonists from a doomed Earth to a new world. The spaceship— plumper and looking more fecund than its predecessor in *Destination Moon* —is visually divorced from the chaos and squabbling on Earth. Completed, it sits horizontally on its launching pad on a mountainside high above the confusion and it "glows like gold, while the sky is in perpetual sunset." [9] It visually promises, in contrast to the orange and dying hues of Earth, a golden dawn. Among other films which visually celebrate the spaceship and

Forbidden Planet (Fred Wilcox, 1956). Another celebratory image of the spaceship is this flying saucer operated by "quanto-gravitetic hyperdrive and postonic transfiguration." (Metro-Goldwyn-Mayer)

dwell on its surfaces with a caressive photographic wonder which precludes any ambiguous interpretation of its essential worth are *Conquest of Space* (Byron Haskin, 1955), with its lavish treatment of takeoffs, manueverings, and landings, and *Forbidden Planet* (Fred Wilcox, 1956), whose "palatial flying saucer" [10] operates "via quanto-gravitetic hyperdrive and postonic transfiguration." [11]

There is, however, a demonic side to the spaceship. In many films it is a trap from which there is little hope of escape. Its sleekness is visually cold and menacing, its surfaces hostile to human warmth. It functions mechanically and perfectly, ignorant of its creators and operators—or it malfunctions with malice, almost as if it could choose to do otherwise but prefers to rid itself of its unsleek and emotionally tainted human occupants. Instead of glowing like a night light, it coldly glitters like the blade of a stiletto. Instead of humming, it ticks. It evokes associations not of release, but of confinement. The womb-like and protective warmth of a positive visual treatment is nowhere apparent; rather, the ship is seen negatively, viewed with antitechnological suspicion, the images of it suggesting a tomb-like iciness, a coffin-like confinement. Its corridors and holds echo the sounds of human isolation or provide a haven for alien and lethal dusts and slimes; in unseen corners the subversion of human life begins.

In *20 Million Miles to Earth* (Nathan Juran, 1957), a spaceship returning to Earth from Venus crashes into the sea, carrying aboard the gelatinous embryo of an alien monster who subsequently hatches and proceeds, after growing, to terrorize Rome. The ship of *Mutiny in Outer Space* (Hugo Grimaldi, 1964), harbors a deadly fungus and transports it to a space station from whence it threatens to infect the Earth. These rockets and countless others harbor, support, and transport alien "things" which ultimately threaten not only Earth, but life itself as we know it. Even more menacing is the ship "Discovery" which is to take astronauts Bowman and Poole to Jupiter in *2001: A Space Odyssey* (Stanley Kubrick, 1968). Although the film does not in any way deny the aesthetics of technology, it gives us in "Discovery" a mechanism which barely tolerates and finally rejects human existence. Despite the vastness of the ship, the visual treatment impresses upon us a sense of claustrophobic and stifling confinement, cold, and death. Most of the crew are temporarily frozen in cryogenic beds which resemble the sarcophagi of "Egyptian mummies." [12] Their movement from life to death because of a computer malfunction is discernable only through the impersonal and yet somehow malevolent red lights and computer print which let us know that their life support systems are no longer operative, and by the needles on the screens above their glass coffins which "run amok on the graphs and then record the straight lines of extinction." [13] Vast as it is, the ship allows no room for privacy; Bowman and Poole at-

2001: A Space Odyssey (Stanley Kubrick, 1968). The hostile spaceship: Discovery I. Astronauts Bowman and Poole attempt to hide from main computer HAL's omnipresent surveillance. The ship and its computer finally reject biological life. (Metro-Goldwyn-Mayer)

tempt to hide from the main computer HAL's omnipresent eyes and ears and unctious voice so they can discuss a possible solution to their predicament, but HAL can read lips and we are given a subjective camera shot to prove it. The astronauts are forced into their bulky and oppressive spacesuits by the ship and its computer's increasing rejection of biological existence; HAL's paranoia is the ship's madness as well. This sense of entrapment and confinement is echoed in a more "realistically" plotted film, *Marooned* (John Sturges, 1969), which "was released during the week the world waited for Apollo 13." [14] Three astronauts are confined in a malfunctioning space capsule; almost all the visuals are in close-up, showing the men cramped in their potential coffin orbiting the moon. The capsule is dubbed "Ironman One," a name perhaps suggestive of the medieval torture chamber, called the "Iron Maiden," in which the victim was most securely confined. And, in *Silent Running* (Douglas Trumbull, 1972), the space freighter "Valley Forge" literally becomes a coffin for its crew, murdered by Freeman Lowell (the ecologically minded protagonist) to protect his specimens of plant life from destruction. In this film, the visuals emphasize the vastness of solitary confinement, the deadness of a hermetically sealed existence which is silent and unyielding in its evocation of eternal loneliness.

The spaceship need not, however, be treated either positively or negatively. In numerous SF films, it is seen and used neutrally; its wonders are deemphasized visually, made to seem commonplace, accepted not only by the characters but by the camera as well—matter-of-factly. The ship is merely a means to get from here to there—and has about as little visual impact and iconic power as a Greyhound bus. The dials and lights and

Marooned (John Sturges, 1969). The hostile spaceship: Ironman One. Three astronauts are confined in a malfunctioning space capsule. (Columbia)

Silent Running (Douglas Trumbull, 1972). The hostile spaceship: Valley Forge. The visuals emphasize the vastness of solitary confinement; the ship literally becomes a coffin for its crew. (Universal)

Star Wars (George Lucas, 1977). The spaceship need not be treated either positively or negatively. In much SF film, it is seen and used neutrally. (20th Century Fox)

switches are neither warmly supportive nor coldly sinister. They exist—like an automobile dashboard—as something familiar, conquered, and forgotten. The complex workings of the ship pose no problems to the garage-mechanic confidence aboard. In *Marooned,* when the capsule malfunctions, one astronaut helplessly and impotently refers to the good old days in contrast to a present whose technology no longer admits salvation through tinkering. "We used to fix the planes we flew with paperclips," he says, frustration apparent on his face. In those films which treat the spaceship like a Ford, repairs on malfunctions can be affected with the equivalents of paperclips and hairpins—or the problem is so "understood" by the crew in their mechanic-like overalls that there is no mystery whatsoever connected to the malfunction. Films like *Rocketship X-M* (Kurt Neumann, 1950), *The Angry Red Planet* (Ib Melchior, 1959), and *Queen of Blood* (Curtis Harrington, 1965), treat the spaceship as a mechanical convenience which, devoid of wonder, will carry the crew to visually exciting adventures having little to do with a technology already accepted and dismissed. To be nostalgic for a moment, but also to the point, I fondly remember a scene aboard the spaceship in *The Angry Red Planet* in which the attitude toward

73

Star Wars (George Lucas, 1977). The ship is merely a means to get from here to there. The controls exist like an automobile dashboard—something familiar, conquered, and forgotten. (20th Century Fox)

The Angry Red Planet (Ib Melchior, 1959). The spaceship is treated as a mechanical convenience to carry the crew to exciting adventures having little to do with a technology already accepted and ignored. (American International)

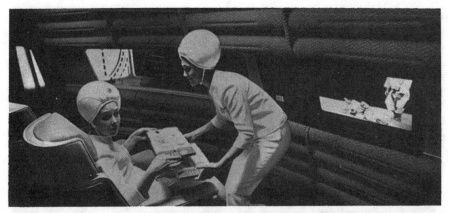

2001: A Space Odyssey (Stanley Kubrick, 1968). Space conquered and domesticated, the spaceship commercialized. (Metro-Goldwyn-Mayer)

the voyage to Mars is visually encapsulated: one sees the hero shaving with an electric razor and the heroine putting perfume behind her ears while a tape bank records a mundane log entry. This domestication of the spaceship leads one to recall the recent terminology used by actual astronauts on the various moon flights and aboard Sky Lab, their references to "housekeeping." Perhaps no film to date, however, has visually evoked the reduction of space flight to "the ultimate in humdrum" [15] as has *2001: A Space Odyssey* in the section in which space scientist Floyd flies Pan American to an orbiting spaceport and from there to the moon. As Joseph Morgenstern aptly comments: "We see that space has been conquered. We also see it has been commercialized and . . . domesticated. Weightless stewardesses wear weightless smiles, passengers diddle with glorified Automat meals, watch karate on in-flight TV and never once glance out into the void to catch a beam of virgin light from Betelgeuse or Aldebaran." [16]

The spaceship of the SF film, then, is in no way comparable to the railroad of the Western in the latter's ability to communicate by its standard physical presence a constant and specific cluster of meanings throughout an entire genre. Unlike the railroad, in so far as the spaceship is a means of getting from here to there, it is, at times, functionally interchangeable with other modes of transportation like the time machine. In films such as *The Time Machine* (George Pal, 1960), and *The Time Travelers* (Ib Melchior, 1964), there are definite mechanisms which are at least physically differentiated from the spaceship, but in *World Without End* (Edward Bernds, 1956), and *Planet of the Apes* (Franklin Schaffner, 1968), the spaceship *is* the time machine. Unlike the railroad, not only can the spaceship's meanings and functions change from film to film and from decade to decade, but its very shape and color are plastic and inconstant—ergo, the sleek and

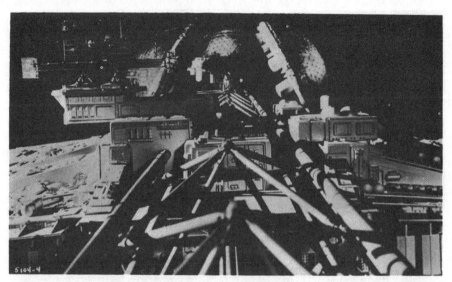

Silent Running (Douglas Trumbull, 1972). The spaceship as plastic and malleable: the "Valley Forge," a combination of dark awkward bulk and delicate latticework. (Universal)

The Day the Earth Stood Still (Robert Wise, 1951). A thing of beauty, the alien flying saucer's ascetic design evokes the Platonic virtues of clarity, sanity, and reason. (20th Century Fox)

silver body of the ship in *Destination Moon,* the circular perfection of the flying saucer in *Forbidden Planet,* the bright yellow of the minaturized submarine in *Fantastic Voyage* (Richard Fleischer, 1966), and the combination of dark awkward bulk with the latticed delicacy of the plant domes on the "Valley Forge" of *Silent Running.*[17] In addition, one can draw no conclusions from the films as to a tendency to visualize positively those ships which belong to us (Earthlings) and to visualize negatively those ships which belong to "them" (aliens). Treated as a thing of beauty, the alien Klaatu's 350-foot flying saucer in *The Day the Earth Stood Still* (Robert Wise, 1951), is so pure in line, so ascetically designed by Lyle Wheeler and Addison Hehr, that it concretizes the Platonic virtues of clarity, sanity, reason—virtues sadly lacking in the Washington, D.C., *mise en scene* in which the saucer comes to rest.[18] On the other hand, the Martians' individual war ships in *War of the Worlds* (Byron Haskin, 1953), could hardly be more sinister (and eerily beautiful) in their realization; their shape suggests a cobra or the ocean's deadly manta ray, their silent movement over city and countryside metaphorically turns Earth's atmosphere turgid, their inexorable progress is punctuated only by the hissing of their incinerating rays.[19] The morally ambiguous and finally reprehensible Metalunans of

War of the Worlds **(Byron Haskin, 1953). The Martians' individual war ships are both sinister and beautiful. (Paramount)**

77

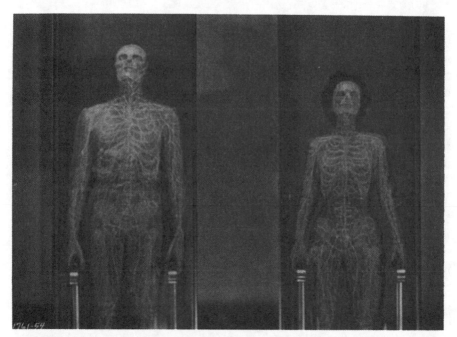

This Island Earth (Joseph Newman, 1955). The alien spaceship as visual marvel: a series of translucent tubes that transform their occupants' molecular structure to accommodate space travel. (Universal)

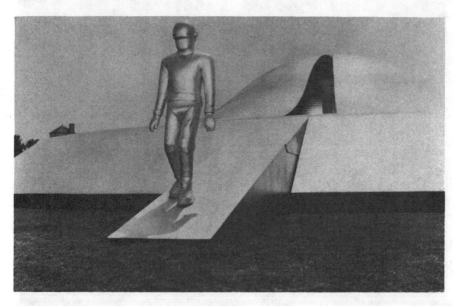

The Day the Earth Stood Still (Robert Wise, 1951). Gort, the huge intergalactic policeman, is a perverse visualization of the medieval knight in shining armor. (20th Century Fox)

This Island Earth (Joseph Newman, 1955), kidnap two Earth scientists and transport them to another world aboard a spaceship which is pointedly emphasized as a marvel of design, containing as it does such visual delights as a main control center composed of a brightly lit and revolving replica of the atom, and a series of translucent tubes which transform their occupants' molecular structure before our eyes.

Even more obvious in their capacity to change shape and color and evocative power than spaceships are SF robots, all too frequently considered *en masse,* lumped together superficially and erroneously for critical convenience as emblematic of that vague term "SF technology." Yet, again, after seeing robots in a wide range of films, the viewer must be drawn inevitably to a recognition of their essentially expressive singularity. Gort, the huge intergalactic "policeman" of *The Day the Earth Stood Still,* is definitely mysterious and menacing. Shot much of the time from a low angle, he is faceless; the otherwise smooth and metallic impenetrability of his blank visage is broken only by a visor which slowly opens to reveal a pulsing light or to emit incinerating rays after which it silently closes. His metallic surface, that visor, is a perverse visualization of the medieval knight in shining armor, and the images of Gort are far removed from those of the lumbering

Tobor the Great (Lee Sholem, 1954). Tobor, the "answer to the problem of human space flight," is treated with the reverence one usually reserves for a can opener. (Republic)

Forbidden Planet (Fred Wilcox, 1956). Robby, the Robot, the most famous of the fifties' SF film robots. (Metro-Goldwyn-Mayer)

but pleasant clumsiness of *Tobor the Great* (Lee Sholem, 1954), devised as the "answer to the problem of human space flight." [20] Tobor is treated with the reverence one usually reserves for a can opener, and in one highly comic scene, the robot—operated by a scientist's young grandson—walks stiff-leggedly about the house crashing into furniture and through doors in what amounts to a parody of Frankenstein's Monster. Tobor becomes a mindless hero because of his inexplicable emotional attachment to the little boy, explained away in the film as "a new synthetic instinct, race-preservational concern for the young."

Perhaps the most celebrated robot of all SF film, Robby of *Forbidden Planet,* bears no resemblance whatsoever to either Gort or Tobor. He was "one of the most elaborate robots ever built for a film production. More than two months of trial and error labour were needed to install the 2,600 feet of electrical wiring that operated all his flashing lights, spinning antennae and the complicated gadgets that can be seen moving inside his transparent dome-shaped head." [21] Visually, Robby looks like the offspring of some mad mating between the Michelin tire man and a juke box. He is "a phenomenal mechanical man who can do more things in his small body than a roomful of business machines. He can make dresses, brew bourbon whiskey, perform feats of Herculean strength and speak 187 languages . . . through a neon-lighted grille. What's more, he has the cultivated manners of a gentleman's gentleman." [22] Although essentially a servant and programmed according to Isaac Asimov's famous Robotic Laws of SF literature (whose prime directive is that robots shall not harm human beings), Robby has a distinct personality. He is comically humorless and proud. ("This is my morning's batch of Isotope 217. The whole thing hardly comes to ten tons," he says, carrying the "whole thing" around.) He is alternately petulant and helpful; "when Francis [Anne Francis, who plays the role of Alta in the film] asks him for star sapphires, he croaks, 'Star sapphires take a week to crystallize. Will diamonds or emeralds do?' 'So long as they're big ones,' Francis says. 'Five, ten, fifteen carats are on hand,' Robby replies smugly." [23] Robby's personality—although treated positively—prefigures to a degree the more sinister HAL of *2001: A Space Odyssey,* the computer (an immobile robot) who pushes Robby's comic *hubris* over the edge of reason. "It is when HAL cannot admit he has made a mistake that he begins to suffer a paranoid breakdown, exhibiting overanxiety about his own infallible reputation and then trying to cover up his error by a murderous attack on the human witnesses." [24] Ultimately, despite their similarity of manner, Robby and HAL are decades apart in both visualization and meaning. Even if HAL were physically realized as more than "a bug-eyed lens, a few slabs of glass," [25] it is hard to imagine him becoming the darling of the toy industry as Robby was to become after the release of *Forbidden Planet.* Robby's cute rotundity and comic primness, however, did not influence the subsequent screen images of robots. He was revived the following year in *The Invisible Boy* (Nicholas Nayfack, 1957), as "the playmate of his inventor's ten-year-old son" [26] and then he disappeared.

Through the fifties and sixties, mobile robots continued their singular ways, sometimes visualized negatively, sometimes positively. And they also occasionally functioned interchangeably with other SF manifestations. In

The Invisible Boy (Nicholas Nayfack, 1957). Robby's second and last movie appearance. (Metro-Goldwyn-Mayer)

Kronos (Kurt Neumann, 1957), the robot is not an instrument of an alien race as was Gort in *The Day the Earth Stood Still;* brought to Earth by a fireball, Kronos *is* the alien, a "strange machine, half creature, half construction." [27] The huge electronic robot of *The Colossus of New York* (Eugene Lourié, 1958), is a monster also, but his technologically devised exterior is motivated by impulses found in the most traditional horror films. The robot's brain is not a complex gadget or an incomprehensible alien mind; it is the transplanted human brain of a scientist's son and it turns against its father, its creator, as Frankenstein's monster had done years before.

Perhaps the most innovative and intellectually complex treatment of robots was in the low budget *Creation of the Humanoids* (Wesley Barry, 1962), a film which considers the robot both positively and negatively. Here is posited and visualized a "history" of robotics which leads to the creation of humanoids. The rationale for making the machines look and act human is that "Humans found it psychologically unbearable to work side by side with machines." Finally, the dividing line between robot and human is totally extinguished. Interpreting Asimov's Robotic Laws literally, the robots have been transferring and duplicating sick humans and accident victims into perfect mechanical bodies; as one robot says, "Humanity doesn't always

The Colossus of New York (Eugene Lourié, 1958). Publicity still. This electronic robot was motivated by impulses found in traditional horror films. (Paramount)

know what is in its best interest." The film's protagonist, antirobot and member of the Order of Flesh and Blood, turns out to be a humanoid himself and —along with the heroine—is finally raised to the humanoid level R100 by undergoing an operation which will enable him to "humanly" contribute to the reproductive process, a function which the robots see as crude but which "fulfills a psychological need." The film ends with a close-up of a pleasant-looking "man"—our narrator—who smiles directly at the viewer and says,

"Of course the operation was a success or *you* wouldn't be here."

The mixed treatment of robots is still apparent in the seventies, in the new group of SF films which followed the commercial success of *2001*. The mechanical "drones" of *Silent Running* are affectionately named Huey, Louey, and Dewey, but although they waddle, their visual realization reminds one less of Disney than of Tolkien. (Paul Zimmerman has aptly called them "iron hobbits." [28]) They are unaesthetic squat boxes on stumpy short legs, neither marvelous nor sinister in their physical realization. It is their very ordinariness which makes them endearing. The drones are not super-human like Gort or Robby, nor are they capable of insubordination like HAL; they don't even talk and their literal interpretation of the English language results occasionally in functional *faux pas*. And yet, as the film progresses and they are programmed to play poker, to perform a surgical operation, to be "companions" to the isolated Lowell, the camera's treatment of them becomes progressively sympathetic and subjective, suggesting the merest hint of an animate life of some kind tucked away in their circuitry. As William Johnson points out in an excellent review of the film: "They are machines with at least as much claim to animate being as a responsive and well-trained pet." [29] The subjective camera lets us see out of

Silent Running **(Douglas Trumbull, 1972). The mechanical "drones" are programmed as companions to crewman Lowell. (Universal)**

Silent Running (Douglas Trumbull, 1972). The drones seem nearly sentient, and man is linked to his own creation "in a single circuit of consciousness." (Universal)

their monitor-screen "eyes" in a way which does not deny their machineness (the images are obviously poor TV quality and in black and white), but promotes as well a feeling of sentient watchfulness. "When two drones, standing side by side, bury a dead crewman, Lowell sees part of the body through one drone's eye and part through the other's. Later, this odd subjectivity is taken a stage further: when Lowell is talking to the two drones, we (the audience) are shown their monitor screens, through which we look at Lowell and Lowell looks at us. . . . Here, through the drones' eyes, "man is linked with his creation in a single circuit of consciousness." [30]

Such is not the case in *Westworld* (Michael Crichton, 1973). The subjective camera may let us in one instance look through the scanner-eyes of the robot gunfighter (coldly played to mechanical perfection by Yul Brynner), but what we see is so remote from human vision that we are emphatically made aware not of a "single circuit of consciousness," but of the vast separation between man and his creations. The little colored cubes which move geometrically over a graph paper-like grid may be aesthetically pleasing in their pastel visualization, but they deny any but the most tenuous connection between the robot's vision and our (the audience) vision of a warm-blooded and ungeometric human being trying to escape from mechanical retribution. The robots which run amok in this night-marish extension of Disneyland do so for no known reason. The initial competence of the scientific staff who run the resort, the calm and often boring visual emphasis on computers and monitor screens under expert control, the close-ups of mechanical "operations" and repairs which in their detail suggest a technology thoroughly understood, routinized and con-quered—all are quickly subverted by images which emphasize chaos and claustrophobia in the control center, and a world outside which has been stolen from its anthropomorphic gods in white lab coats. The robots' malevolence which goes beyond mere malfunction is inexplicable in scien-tific terms. And Asimov's Robotic Laws seem purposefully mocked by the mechanical creations turned perfect and skilled killers.

The fluctuating meanings of what superficially seem to be iconic objects in SF films can be demonstrated many times over. Time and place are not con-stants either. The temporal setting of science fiction has no obligation to his-

Star Wars (George Lucas, 1977). Robots C3P0 and R2D2 are iconic in their visual function as wondrous pieces of machinery. It is the very plasticity of objects and settings that defines SF film. (20th Century Fox)

tory; it may be a speculative past (*Creation of the Humanoids*), the present (*Seconds*, [John Frankenheimer, 1966]), the immediate future (*The Andromeda Strain*, [Robert Wise, 1971]), the distant future (*Forbidden Planet*), or a combination of times as in the *Planet of the Apes* series. As well, the settings of science fiction know no geographical boundaries and may be found literally anywhere—from small town USA, to distant and undiscovered galaxies, to the interior of a human body. Inevitably, then, we must be led away from a preoccupation with a search for consistent visual emblems into more ambiguous territory. It is the very plasticity of objects and settings in SF films which help define them as science fiction, and not their consistency. And it is this same plasticity of objects and settings that deny the kind of iconographic interpretation which critically illuminates the essentially static worlds of genres such as the Western and Gangster film.

Visual Functions

Although it lacks an informative iconography, encompasses the widest possible range of time and place, and constantly fluctuates in its visual representation of objects, the SF film still has a science fiction "look" and "feel" to its visual surfaces. This unique look and feel embraces all the films of the genre, is quickly recognized by the viewer, and begs for some kind of critical identification. Yet, if the visual connections between the films cannot be located in the repetitious and therefore emblematic use of specific visual representations, where do we find them? The visual connection between all SF films lies in the consistent and repetitious use not of *specific* images, but of *types* of images which function in the same way from film to film to create an imaginatively realized world which is always removed from the world we know or know of. The visual surface of all SF film presents us with a confrontation between and mixture of those images to which we respond as "alien" and those we know to be familiar. This observation, however, is more complex than it may first appear. Certainly, if we think in terms of alien images in SF, what first comes to mind are the imaginative "impossibilities" of the special effects men and designers: creatures, flying saucers, the terrain of Mars, etc. Yet whether an image evokes a sense of strangeness—a sense of wonder—or whether it seems familiar is not always dependent upon the inherent strangeness or familiarity of its actual content. In *Invaders From Mars* (William Cameron Menzies, 1953), a small town police station becomes a setting as visually jolting and alien as any other-worldly planet, and in *Soylent Green* (Richard Fleischer, 1973), a tomato and a wilted stalk of celery are as strange and wondrous as any alien plant life designed in the studio.

The major visual impulse of all SF films is to pictorialize the unfamiliar, the nonexistent, the strange and the totally alien—and to do so with a verisimilitude which is, at times, documentary in flavor and style. While we are invited to wonder at what we see, the films strive primarily for our belief, not our suspension of disbelief—and this is what distinguishes them from fantasy films like *The Seventh Voyage of Sinbad* (Nathan Juran, 1958), or *Jason and the Argonauts* (Don Chaffey, 1963). This is not so rhetorical a distinction as it may seem, for it determines the unique visual construct of every SF film. For in order to be believed, to achieve credibility, the SF film must also deny its alien images at the same time it promotes them. To make us believe in the possibility, if not probability, of the alien things we see, the visual surfaces of the films are inextricably linked to and dependent upon the familiar; from the wondrous and strange and imagined, the cameras fall back on images either so familiar they are often downright dull, or neutralize the alien by treating it so reductively that it becomes ordinary and comprehensible. Thus in every SF film there is a visual tension which exists in such earnestness in no other genre—a tension between those images which strive to totally remove us from a comprehensible and known world

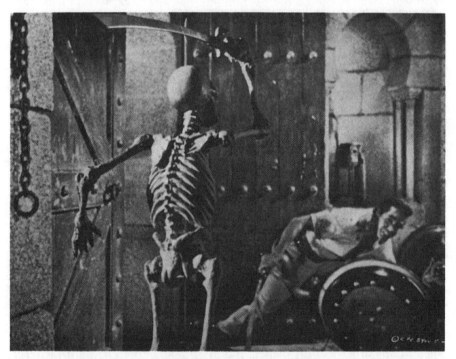

The Seventh Voyage of Sinbad (Nathan Juran, 1958). What distinguishes fantasy from SF films is that the latter strive for the viewer's belief, the former his suspension of disbelief. (Columbia/Morningside)

Jason and the Argonauts (Don Chaffey, 1963). The fantasy film feels no obligation to make itself credible in relation to the world outside the film. (Columbia/Morningside/BLC/World Wide)

into romantic poetry and those images which strive to bring us back into a familiar and prosaic context. For a better understanding of this visual tension unique to science fiction, it becomes useful to isolate the two basic kinds of images (the alien and the familiar), examine their components, and then deal with their interaction.[31] But we should not, in the following process, forget that this isolation of types of images is arbitrary, useful only in so far as it allows us to see how *all* the images of science fiction interact and function in the films themselves, in films seen as whole and complex entities.

The Alien

The Speculative

Science fiction writer and critic Damon Knight has asked the question: "If your alien planet is just like Broadway, or even just like Uganda, what the devil is the use of leaving Earth at all?"[32] Implied here is the expectation we all have of SF film—that it show us things we've never seen before, that it move us beyond the confines of the known (Broadway)

Star Wars (George Lucas, 1977). "If your alien planet is just like Broadway, or even just like Uganda, what the devil is the use of leaving Earth at all?" (20th Century Fox)

Star Wars (George Lucas, 1977). The expectation we have of SF film is that it shows us things we've never seen before. (20th Century Fox)

Invaders From Mars (William Cameron Menzies, 1953). The Martian "mastermind" is never reductively defined by human activity. (20th Century Fox)

or even the known of (Uganda). On the most obvious level, the SF film attempts to meet our expectations by using the magic of design and special effects cinematography to show us things which do not exist, things which are highly speculative, which astonish us by the very fact of their visual realization on the screen since they have no counterparts in the world outside the theater.[33] One can point to innumerable images in SF films which struggle—sometimes successfully, sometimes laughably—to exceed the anthropomorphic limits of the human imagination while still attempting to remain comprehensible.

A representative sampling of alien beings on the SF screen, for example, might include the image of the Martian "master mind" in *Invaders From Mars;* enclosed in its magically suspended transparent globe, it is an exotic head and upper torso around which its graceful tentacles curl like vines. Seen in close-up, the eyes in its wizened glowing face move in what seems a mechanical unison from side to side, while its expression remains frozen. The malevolent grace and silence of this alien can be contrasted to the busy comic strip activity of the Mutant in *This Island Earth,* "a clawed creature with an enlarged and exposed brain, apoplectic eyes and five interlocking mouths."[34] What it gains in menace, it loses in imaginative power for it is required to *do* too much and its shuffling activity defines it reductively in human terms as merely a movie "heavy." More provocative in its visual power, in its ability to make us truly wonder, is the final image of *2001:* the questionably human fetus of the Star Child in its amniotic sack suspended in black space above a revolving blue-green Earth, its vague eyes haunting because they are unfathomable.[35] The personal preference indicated here has not been accidental. If the totally imaginative visualizations of alien life forms in the SF film strive to dislocate us from the narrow confines of human knowledge and human experience, they best do so when they are virtually

This Island Earth (Joseph Newman, 1955). Publicity still. The alien mutant is reduced by his comic strip activity. (Universal)

silent and primarily inactive. (The alien creatures skillfully designed by Ray Harryhausen and followers are a case to be discussed later, as the images in which they appear are not aimed at removing us from a familiar context.) To give such imaginative visual realizations voice and function is to make them comprehensible and reduce their awesome poestry to smaller human dimensions; they exist most potently on the screen in a state of suspension, of pregnant possibility, of potential rather than realized action. Michel Ciment notes: "One of the weaknesses of science fiction is that it too often fails to

Star Wars (George Lucas, 1977). Alien life forms dislocate us from the confines of human experience when they are in a state of potential—rather than realized—action. (20th Century Fox)

break away from an anthropomorphic view of the cosmos. There are 100 billion stars in our galaxy and 100 billion galaxies in the visible universe, and one of the stock themes of science fiction is that of alien civilizations. But it is difficult to imagine these different worlds without falling back on human standards and thus making them ridiculous." [36] And Raymond Durgnat also suggests the problems inherent in creating truly alien beings: "It's hard enough to understand certain assumptions of the Samoans, the Balinese or the Americans, and all but impossible to empathize into the perceptions and drives of, say, a boa constrictor. How much more difficult then to identify with the notions of, say, the immortal twelve-sensed telepathic polymorphoids whose natural habitat is the ammonia clouds of Galaxy X7?" [37] This difficulty is perhaps also reflected in the relative lack of subjective camera shots in SF film which attempt to link us visually with nonhuman life. Previously, the use of such subjectivity has been discussed in reference to the subjective robotic vision which punctuates *2001, Silent Running* and *Westworld,* cinematographic instances which are quite powerful. But we might also point to the earlier vision of films like *It Came From Outer Space* (Jack Arnold, 1953). Here, the inadequacy of both 3D cinematography and a shimmering, quivering "whirlpool" superimposed over familiar sights to convince us that we were seeing through an alien's eyes and consciousness

Star Wars (George Lucas, 1977). The alien Wookie is reduced to anthropomorphic and comfortable size by his humanly comprehensible activity. (20th Century Fox)

is clearly apparent. And only slightly more adequate is the multiple vision of the insect-headed scientist in *The Fly* (Kurt Neumann, 1958), its impact caused more by the then-fascinating novelty of seeing multiplied images on the screen than by a sense that we were really seeing as a fly does. Attempts at stretching our perceptions by using a subjective camera to represent alien consciousness are relatively rare in SF film, probably because—dependent as they are upon the viewer's comprehension—such images must extrapolate from human vision and therefore cannot attain the inventive and speculative freedom they pretend to.

Less prone to anthropomorphic reduction is the studio-created geography of science fiction. Since it is usually not required to do anything but simply *be,* it is able to achieve a visual power which can last, if not over-done and over-used, through an entire film, maintaining our responses to it as alien and wondrous. Certainly, to this critic at least, the imaginative, if not completely prophetic, landscape of *Destination Moon* resonated more dramatically than the real moon televised from its own surface, a moon which turned out to be a dusty disappointment compared to the harsh images of a cracked, grayish-yellow "dried-up river bed which looked effective even though it has now been proved to have been a wrong guess." [38] Indeed, the craggy peaks, strange seas, swirling atmospheres, stark shadows, multiple moons, disquieting but breathtaking colors of other-worldly environments in SF film are powerful sights which stretch the imagination. Although, John Baxter writes, referring to *Forbidden Planet,* "Little is made of the landscape of Altair IV, with its green sky, cloud striped oversize moon and red earth," [39] little has to be made of it. We only need see it for its image to provoke wonder. More is made in the film of what Durgnat calls the "flowers-and-leopard sentimentality" [40] of Alta's (Anne Francis) humanly conceived Edenic playground, but its ability to take us beyond ourselves is minimal. In the same film, successfully attempting to stretch our conception of dimension to its limits, is the vast subterranean and abandoned urban landscape of the vanished Krels, buildings and generators and shafts dizzying in size and scope. Equally remote from earth-bound existence are the ravaged surface and strange light of Metaluna in *This Island Earth,* the bizarre and occasionally overworked Mars of The *Angry Red Planet,* and the post-Jupiter landscape of *2001,* all "mauve and mocha mountains, swirling methane seas and purple skies." [41] In the latter film, studio sets are not necessary to the creation of an alien and speculative landscape; color and optical printing have been used to camouflage the actual photographic content of the images (the Grand Canyon, Monument Valley, and the Hebrides Coast) so that what we see is like nothing we've ever seen before:

> Snowdrifts and floating icebergs lose their true color under layers of magenta and cyan filtration. They defy recognition, just as do the canyons and crags we should recognize from innumerable westerns. But intercut with strange sunbursts of light and continuously agitated by thrusts of the zoom lens, these sights seem the contours of another planet, or perhaps the anchor point of consciousness itself. [42]

The speculative, created geography of science fiction need not, however, extend its visualizations to outer space to evoke a sense of removal from the known world. *Fantastic Voyage* achieves its wondrously alien effects by taking us into the human body rather than out of this world; yet, regardless of the more than $3 million spent to realize anatomically correct sets, [43] we might as well be on another planet where anatomy no longer exists. In fact, although the plot and characterizations are generally cliched and banal, the film's visual conception is remarkably profound; here are our own bodies made alien and, paradoxically, antianthropomorphic. Our inside becomes the outside. Drawing a similar equation, Parker Tyler sees in the film what he calls "a great micromacrocosmic tension" and goes on to say:

The space-within exists—and must exist however consciously it be avoided—equally, co-extensively, with the space-outside. The science-fiction type of film, therefore, was bound to get around to viewing the interior of the body as an artifically constructed inner space corresponding with the real body's inner space, which in turn would be a trope for actual space: the "out there" space shared with all other men.[44] *

Despite the anatomical accuracy, the medical precision that went into the making of the film, it is illuminating to note the poetic rather than cooly descriptive language which has been used to describe its images. John Baxter aptly comments on the film's visual power: "Model sets like the white vaulted cathedral of the heart and the veiled jungle that is the scientist's brain touch, however lightly, the core of wonder that draws us back time after time to fantasy."[45] At one point in the film, the miniaturized travelers are menaced by a respiratory process we actually see

Fantastic Voyage (Richard Fleischer, 1966). The human body: the view we have of it is an impossible one. Inside becomes outside. (20th Century Fox)

* Woody Allen also sees internal space as external space in the "What Happens During Ejaculation" episode on his comic *Everything You Always Wanted to Know About Sex* (1972).

and they enter a brain which Luis Gasca describes as "an enchanted place ... with its iridescent and phosphorescent reflections emerging from a bluish shadow." [46] These phosphorescent reflections were achieved frequently in the film through a process John Brosnan describes as "painting with light." [47]

The human body in *Fantastic Voyage* truly belongs to that group of speculative images which are totally invented, for despite its anatomical and medical accuracy the view we finally have of it is an impossible one, a view not only impossible in perspective but in philosophical approach as well. Even though what we see is extrapolated or copied from actual scientific knowledge, the sets were, as well, "designed in a deliberately abstract fashion so as not to upset those with weak stomachs among the audiences." [48] And, director Richard Fleischer himself acknowledges the film's underlying speculative nature: "The whole thing was a product of the imagination and every interpretation of that imagination into realistic, technical terms had to be invented and manufactured." [49]

Perhaps less flamboyantly spectacular than *Fantastic Voyage*, but equally alien and disquieting is the almost continually abstract decor and design of *THX 1138* (George Lucas, 1971), a film which presents a totally different kind of visual speculation. The images consistently dislocate human faces and forms from their surroundings by using sets and compositions which subvert our ordinary awareness of size, dimension, and perspective. Originally a fifteen minute short conceived as "a lighting exercise" in which the filmmaker's aim was "creating an environment out of just film," [50] the exercise became an expanded feature film which visually dislocates the

THX 1138 (George Lucas, 1971). The wide screen is used like a canvas on which human forms are placed at vast distances and disturbing angles from each other. (Warner Brothers)

viewer as much as it does the characters from the known world. Using a wide screen, carefully selected color, and abstract composition, *THX* achieves its distancing effects by its evocation of a world which is so visualized as graphic art that it could not exist except in a frame. Through much of the film, a white vast background is shockingly punctuated by the discrete use of pure primary colors and black. Human beings—hairless and dressed in white clothing—show up against the white screen as disembodied heads and hands floating in limitless space, disconnected from a context and from themselves. Their own bodies are fragmented visually. Composition in the frame is just as disorienting; the wide screen is used like a canvas on which human forms are placed at vast distances and disturbing angles from each other. One responds to these images as to modern paintings, sculpture, graphic art, a work by Mondrian or Alexander Calder; their human content becomes almost totally absorbed by abstract form.

The kind of speculative image we see in *THX 1138* is fairly rare in science fiction; in fact it is fairly rare in commercial cinema of any kind. This is because it moves toward abstract art, toward form with a minimum of content which can be called narrative in the traditional sense. However, scattered here and there throughout the American SF film, there are moments of such abstraction. And there is one film made in the fifties which actually

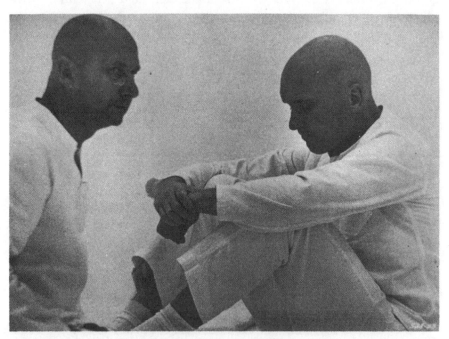

THX 1138 **(George Lucas, 1971). Human beings—hairless and dressed in white clothing—punctuate screen space. (Warner Brothers)**

2001: A Space Odyssey (Stanley Kubrick, 1968). The wide screen as an abstract canvas. (Metro-Goldwyn-Mayer)

Star Wars (George Lucas, 1977). The alien nature of symmetry. As abstraction, symmetry removes us from the "real" and random world. (20th Century Fox)

depends for its visual evocation of wonder, separation, and strangeness on the distancing power of abstract forms: *The Monolith Monsters* (John Sherwood, 1957). Here, an unknown element brought to Earth by a meteorite "grows" when it comes into contact with water. What we see in grandly isolated images on the screen are black, giant crystals which thrust out of the desert landscape like German Expressionist skyscrapers. Their growth is almost as painful to watch as it is beautiful, the forms geometrically exciting to the eye but representing a visual scream of splintering, shattering, stretching.

The Extrapolative

Similar to and yet also different from the invented or totally speculative images of SF filmmakers are those images of things in SF film which have an existence outside the movie theater but which—despite their reality—are visually denied to us because we humanly lack the physical ability to perceive them. Paradoxically, with the aid of fakery, special effects, model work, and mechanical devices, certain SF film images redeem portions of the physical world from the relative obscurity which their dimensions impose upon them. We know, for example, that there are planets in space, orbiting in some grand design, but our visual knowledge of them is generally limited to the unsatisfactory vagueness of the night sky or to a blurred photograph obscured by Earth's atmosphere in an astronomy book; even a clearly taken scientific snapshot cannot give us a sense of the magnitude of what's really out there. Similarly, we cough

The Monolith Monsters **(John Sherwood, 1957). The distancing power of abstract forms: giant black crystals like German Expressionist skyscrapers. (Universal)**

and sneeze enough to admit without doubt the existence of such things as viruses, but our visual knowledge of them is as remote as a handkerchief at such times is familiar. The SF film gives us images—even if manufactured—of the immense and the infinitesimal. Extrapolating from known and accepted science, these film images derive their power to induce wonder in the viewer not from the imaginativeness of their content, but from the imaginativeness of their stance and their scope. We don't marvel that there are such things as planets; we marvel at the fact that we can see them in a way which transcends our own human size and physical limitations. Those images which awe us, stun us, do so not merely because they seem meticulously authentic but because they alienate us from our corporeal selves, from human notions of time and space. It is in this sense that they are truly alien visualizations although based on known scientific realities.

The world "breathtaking" is therefore literally appropriate to such images as the Earth seen in its totality from space in *Destination Moon,* Mars and her surrounding planets viewed objectively at the beginning of *War of the Worlds,* the opening shots of *Forbidden Planet.* Speaking of the latter film, John Brosnan describes its marvels:

> The film begins with a sequence showing a flying saucer from Earth hurtling through space and entering an alien solar system. Here the eclipse of an enormous red sun is seen with the saucer silhouetted by the corona—a breathtaking panorama which is almost equal to the astronomical simulations in the later classic *2001: A Space Odyssey.*[51]

We are given through these images the visual scope of a god; as viewers we are no longer human. Speaking of *2001,* Stanley Kubrick says, "The mystical alignment of the sun, the moon, and earth, or of Jupiter and its moons, was used throughout the film as a premonitory image of a leap forward into the unknown."[52] Whether or not one finally accepts the mysticism of *2001*'s planets, moons, and monoliths, one has to agree that we do leap forward visually into the unknown by the transformation of our perception. There, before us, in the same frames, we can see all of the sun and the moon and the Earth, or all of Jupiter and its moons.[53]

As we are allowed to see the infinitely immense, so SF film also allows us to view the infinitesimally small. "In the mind of God there is no zero," says Scott Carey (Grant Williams) at the end of *The Incredible Shrinking Man* (Jack Arnold, 1957). While this film, despite its theme, derives its visual significance and power primarily from images highly dependent on a familiar world whose dimensions are clearly known to us (a world which will be discussed in those terms later), its main character's metaphysical discovery is akin to ours when, for example, we enter the hugely magnified

Silent Running (Douglas Trumbull, 1972). Images of planets, eclipses, suns, and moons remove us from out of our limited physical selves and give us the visual scope of a god. (Universal)

microscopic images of *The Andromeda Strain*. With our god-like vision, there is no zero. We watch the unknown alien "virus" grow under extreme magnification which almost totally fills the screen with what we cannot physically see at all under normal circumstances. Through electron microscopy and its magic, we discover the virus' crystalline form and watch it divide. We become incredibly sensitive to "the tremendous energies accumulated in the microscopic configurations of matter." [54] We are in the "reality of another dimension" which, however simulated, extrapolated from its base in fact, is "but a portrait—seen in a certain perspective—of the world in which we live." [55] That certain perspective, however, is definitely alien to us and SF film lets us assume it with authority. While it may be visually more god-like to enter the world of a virus, there is also power, albeit a trifle more secondary, to stretch our perceptions in the kind of close-up "documentary footage" of ant life inserted in *Them!* (Gordon Douglas, 1954). Removed from context, again in a film which visually moves us primarily by its manipulation of alien and familiar elements within a well-defined *mise en scene,* the close-ups of ants building and battling awe us not merely by their actions, but by our ability to visually penetrate into a world otherwise inaccessible to us. The SF film allows us to enter into the very circuitry of a computer or into the lethal interior of an atomic reactor and we become omniscient and omnipotent as gods.

I have attempted thus far to discuss those particular SF images which are obviously alien to us in either content and/or perspective. These kinds of images—introduced to amaze us—seem to stand alone in the films, deriving their poetic power from their very separation from a familiar context. Usually they—and they alone—must fill the screen to awe us. They are most effective in their lack of human association, alone in close-up and re-moved from a recognizable and reductive context or *mise en scene.* There-fore, at their most provocative, we see such images juxtaposed with other more familiar images, but usually not in the same frame with them. A SF film, however, cannot live by alien images alone. It goes almost without saying—but I shall say it anyway—that no narrative film, no fiction film, can sustain itself on visual surfaces which are completely and continuously strange and alien to either our experience or our mode of perception. We have to understand what we see and if what we see is unfamiliar, it must—to have meaning—be eventually connected to something we can compre-hend, to something we know. The SF film, although it strives in part to transcend the limits of human knowledge and imagination, is not aimed finally toward achieving total abstraction. There is, indeed, an urge toward abstraction contained in these alien images—and it is very much connected to a basic thematic concern common to all SF film: man and his relation-ship to the physical environment which surrounds him. Abstraction, itself, says one critic, "stems from the great anxiety which man experiences when terrorized by the phenomena he perceives around him, the relationships and mysterious polarities of which he is unable to decipher." [56] The SF film is concerned with this anxiety and reflects it, but not to a point of withdrawal from narrative into total abstract art; rather, it deals with this anxiety on a human as well as transcendental or formal level. The SF film is ever aware —thematically and visually—that we have to live in our own future, and that future, unknowable as it may finally be, is very real. The films are not interested ultimately in escaping from human connection, human perception, and human meaning into the realm of the avant-garde. Although they may contain many alien images, isolated for wondrous effect, images which evoke the "unknown" in all its scientific, magical, and religious or transcendental permutations, the films must obligatorily descend to Earth, to men, to the known, and to a familiar *mise en scene* if they are to result in *meaning* rather than the abstract inexplicability of *being*.

This prosaic urge brings us to a consideration of how the SF film tempers the awesomeness, the abstractness, the poetry of its isolate, alien, visual surfaces. The issue has been discussed peripherally but in some detail in the previous section on the "iconography" of the spaceship, its neutralization in some films·as an image of awesome visual effect, and it has also been alluded to in those remarks about the reduction of the strangeness of the alien Mutant in *This Island Earth*. There are three primary ways in which the wonder of alien visual surfaces in SF films can be subverted, bringing us back to a sense of comfortable familiarity with what we see. The first way is through repetition of the alien image so that it becomes familiar (and, unfortunately, in some cases contemptible). The second method is the humanization of the alien image so that we understand it rather than wonder at it. The third way is a deemphasis of the alien image by the camera in order to remove the viewer's attention from it. All three methods are used in SF film with the intent of bringing the alien image from isolation into an *active mise en scene* (activity being the visualization of understood cause and effect) so as to integrate that image back into human connection. As well, all three methods tend to coexist and commingle in the films rather than functioning

This Island Earth (Joseph Newman, 1955). **Three ways to reduce the alien: (1) repeat it, (2) humanize it, and (3) deemphasize it. (Universal)**

singularly, their end result turning our wonder to interest, our interest to comprehension and acceptance. (It should be emphasized, however, that interest and acceptance are not seen here as negative responses to the film image nor as some failing of the film image, but merely as responses which are different in kind from awe and wonder, from a sense of total dislocation and alienation.)

This process of change can be demonstrated, for example, in the use of the Korova Milkbar in *A Clockwork Orange* (Stanley Kubrick, 1971). The opening tracking shot back from an immense close-up of an "alien" face (alien because of our perspective, our lack of context, and the face's disorienting makeup and expression) to an almost completely static long-shot of the Korova Milkbar, composed as it is of bizarrely dressed "human" figures and sterile, white, nude sculptures, is truly wonderful. The image could hardly be more strange in its use of color (the black background seems to recede infinitely, denying yet also suggesting walls as does the lettering hung against nothing; and the human figures and sculpture are primarily white, accented and punctuated by bits of lurid violet and orange fluorescence). Also strange is the composition of the shot; the placement of figures emphasizes pools of disquieting space between their groupings. And the content of the shot, alien as it seems, is made yet more strange by its stillness; the human figures are almost as still as statues, the statues—human in form—are sculpted in attitudes of frozen motion.

The Korova's wonder becomes diminished, however, as it is repeatedly used as a setting. Our eyes become familiar with its plastic surfaces, its

A Clockwork Orange (Stanley Kubrick, 1971). The opening tracking shot back from an immense close-up of an "alien" face begins as contextless and disorienting (note the expression and makeup). (Warner Brothers)

A Clockwork Orange (Stanley Kubrick, 1971) Tracking back further, the composition becomes more abstract in design (note balance of milk and light and whiteness). (Warner Brothers)

color and light. As well, its wonder is reduced because it becomes humanized, it comes "to life" and is made to function (act) comprehensibly. The strange postures of the sculptures become defined in terms of furniture and vending machinery and finally the Korova is accepted by the viewer as a visual extension of the malt shop around the corner. It also becomes visually deemphasized as we understand its function; the camera shows us both itself and the Korova's clientele taking the Milkbar for granted, and also dwells less on its surfaces, moving instead closer to the characters (whose initial abstractness has been changed into human characterization through action and dialogue) so that the strange context becomes subordinate to their comprehensible interpersonal conflicts. The static Korova Milkbar we respond to with wonder in the opening shots is not the Korova Milkbar we've accepted later in the film; its initial unlimited possibility has been circumscribed and defined by its duration on the screen and by the familiar and comprehensible function it serves and by the very human activity within it. This process of lessening the visual wonder of science fiction is not limited, of course, to only visually reductive means. The alien images of the SF film can also be brought back down to Earth by way of music and dialogue, elements which will be discussed in the next chapter.

A Clockwork Orange (Stanley Kubrick, 1971). Further back, the *mise en scène* has not yet been defined by activity that will reduce it to the "malt shop" around the corner. Again, symmetry, lack of movement, imprecise depth, create wonder and awe and discomfort. (Warner Brothers)

A Clockwork Orange (Stanley Kubrick, 1971). The Korova Milkbar's wonder diminishes as it is repeatedly used. The strange postures of the furniture become functional, and we focus more on the human characters. (Warner Brothers)

The Alienation of the Familiar

We have discussed those SF films which, through their extensive use of studio-devised settings and special effects cinematography, strive to remove us from familiar experience and perception into the realm of the unknown, but which at the same time also attempt—for the sake of narrative, meaning, and relevance—to relate their alien images to human and familiar concerns. The result is visual tension, produced from two opposing impulses. The same visual tension can also be found in those SF films which are literally grounded, films which because of budgetary limitations and/or story line do not leave the Earth and its familiar terrain for distant galaxies, films which cannot or choose not to manufacture a totally alien environment or depend on elaborate special effects and creative machinery for their visual evocation of the unknown. These films, starting from home base and the familiar, strive not to bring us down to Earth, but to remove us from it in various ways, at the same time we remain visually grounded. The visual movement of such films is not toward a neutralization of the alien and abstract, but rather toward the viewer's alienation from the familiar and concrete. In some cases, that alienation is accomplished by disguising the familiar. John Baxter points out three spectacular instances in which Earth's environment, combined with a few special effects, was "framed in such a way that it appeared alien." He cites *Robinson Crusoe on Mars* (1964), in

Robinson Crusoe on Mars (Byron Haskin, 1964). The alienation of the familiar: Death Valley is transformed into the alien landscape of a hostile Mars. (Paramount)

which director Byron Haskin "chose as his setting the eroded nightmare of Death Valley" spiced by a pumpkin-colored sky; *Planet of the Apes* (Franklin Schaffner, 1967), part of which was filmed around Lake Powell; and *Marooned* (1969), in which John Sturges used Death Valley landscapes to represent not Mars, but the moon.[57] In other cases, however, the strange images of some high budget and most low-budget SF films are created from extremely ordinary visual content, less disguised than abstracted or distorted to evoke wonder. Such imagery may, additionally, cause anxiety because it hits us—literally—where we live, close to home. One might well echo Philip Strick and Peter Nicholls in their prefatory remarks to a National Film Theatre Bulletin announcing a series of SF films to be shown in London: "Although we have great affection for the familiar absurdities of low budget Hollywood sf, we feel that it's time that more credit be given to its positive achievements—the unfettered visual imagination, the creative use of already existing locations, the brooding landscapes, the deserts and deserted cities." [58]

Although there were many low-budget films best left to the kind treatment memory nostalgically provides them, films which feebly and laughably tried to imitate the more expensive spectaculars using one room, one dial sets and obviously rubber aliens, there are also a large number of films which deserve critical attention—those films we might call the *film noir* of science fiction. Quietly and grayly, they turn the familiar into the alien, visually subvert the known and comfortable, and alter the world we take for granted into something we mistrust. Using a minimum of special effects, if any, the films evoke wonder in their visual ability to alienate us from Earth's landscape and from human activity and from the people next door. But unlike the wonder generated by inherently unfamiliar images (in content and/or scope) which is often exciting and exalting in quality, the wonder created by these smaller films is ultimately depressing in its implications, its pessimistic vision. Although he hasn't linked the terms to any particular hierarchy of films within the genre, Parker Tyler, in one of his more lucid paragraphs, has discussed the optimism of big-budget science fiction and the pessimism of low-budget science fiction, using psychologically apt terms: "The science-fiction genre, in or out of film, is destined (with a fate now much realized) to cope with that combined spatial megalomania and spatial paranoia that I define as mankind's oldest known sort of self-harassment." [59]

In these low budget SF movies the viewer is not confronted with the alien as something "other" than himself or as something "away" from his world, nor has he the exhilarating ability to see the physical world as a god might see it (an ability which could serve as the filmic fulfillment of "spatial megalomania"). In such movies, we are not gods although our perceptions are, indeed, transformed. Indeed, it is our security in the power of being human which is visually undermined (causing a definite sense of "spatial paranoia"). The wonder we feel at such films is the wonder of being totally suspended in limbo; we are visually denied the comfort of a familiar and anthropomorphic Earth and we no longer have the power to reach the stars.

Subversion of the Landscape

Inherent in the big-budget SF film which moves toward the neutralization of its many alien images is a visual aura of confidence and optimism. The strange is conquered—not just in terms of the plot, but also in terms of the visual movement of the film itself. The infinite is introduced and made finite, the unknown is made familiar. The cold vastness of impersonal space, the terror of man confronting the universe and the void—out there—is diminished through an increasing movement away from abstract presentation of wonderous imagery toward its integration with the known and human. This positive visual movement is informed by the somewhat smug and optimistic belief in infinite human and technological progress and by a view of the unknown as a beautiful undiscovered country (no neighbor to Hamlet's) which holds only minor terrors and creates minimal anxiety because it is, in visual fact, ultimately discoverable and conquerable. In movies like *Destina-*

Star Wars **(George Lucas, 1977). Big-budget SF film is visually optimistic, believing in infinite human and technological progress. (20th Century Fox)**

Destination Moon (Irving Pichel, 1950). Man's jargon, technological ac-complishments, banal competence, and Tom Swiftian enthusiasm has robbed the infinite of its ability to terrify. (United Artists/Eagle-Lion)

tion Moon, Riders to the Stars (Richard Carlson, 1954), *The Conquest of Space* (Byron Haskin, 1955), man has always slipped into his rocket as though it were a new automobile. His jargon has been reassuring; his tech-nological accomplishments, banal competence, and Tom Swiftian enthusiasm has—within the protective armor of his starship—robbed the infinite of its ability to really terrify us, and reduced its blank impenetrability to the di-mensions of a highway.

Those films which take us "out there" into space or to other planets via the magic of special effects are visually optimistic. They reassure us in their very view of the alien and strange as something "other," as something separate from man and his personal domain, *our* planet. We're out there because all earthly terrain has been challenged and conquered and there is nowhere to go but—literally and metaphorically—up and away. This opti-mism is also apparent in those films which bring the "other" here. The aliens fighting on earthly battlegrounds fight not just against men but against the planet itself; Earth is on our side. Earth and Man are an organic unity, a known quantity, working together to repel the alien "other." The Martians of *War of the Worlds* are killed not just by God's wisdom, but by Earth's germs; the very atmosphere rebels against such unscrupulous intrusion. In these films, our cities and traffic and technology, our churches and national monuments all give an anthropomorphic—and therefore reassuring—face to our planet. They suggest that we and the very ground we walk upon are ultimately bound together in a symbiotic relationship, harmoniously entwined in some metaphysical lovers' embrace.

At the same time these films which celebrated Man and his works and the whole concept of infinite possibility were being made (the fifties through the early sixties), imaginative and financially hampered filmmakers were pulling the ground out from beneath our complacent feet; in their films Man's previously harmonious marriage to the landscapes of our planet ended in divorce. In search of cheap locations which were "neutral" enough to admit the introduction of the extraordinary and fantastic into what was, after all, a real and familiar world, such filmmakers as Jack Arnold, John Sherwood, and Gordon Douglas discovered the desert and the beach. What happens in their films (and the films of others who staked out similar territorial rights) is that the extraordinary and fantastic—the monsters and mutants and alien invaders—become virtually subordinate in their ability to evoke awe and wonder to the impressive visual power of the terrain itself. What creates the terrifying wonder and pessimism in these films is not primarily the giant ant or spider, not the Creature, not the alien invader—all of which appear in this group of films either fairly infrequently or in shadow or are not seen at all because they are technically inferior to their more expensive relations. Rather, what evokes awe and terror is the terrain of Earth itself. Viewing those dark and brooding seascapes, the dull wet sand and the surf crashing crazily against the outrageous and indefinable geometry of towering rocks, seeing the unshadowed and limitless stretches of desert punctuated by the stiff and inhuman form of an occasional cactus or the frantic scurrying of some tiny and vulnerable rodent, the spectator is forced to a recognition, however unconscious it may remain, of Man's precarious and puny stability, his vulnerability to the void "right here" as well as "out there," his total isolation, the fragile quality of his body and his works, the terrifying blankness in the eyes of what he thought was Mother Nature.

As opposed to those imaginary other worlds created on a studio set or those real urban worlds so filled with the outcropping of our achievements that they appear anthropomorphic, the desert and the beach exist as the receptive breeding ground or hiding place for those things which threaten to destroy us and thus become hostile areas of a formerly nurturing and anthropomorphic Earth. Working inversely from those movies which optimistically reduce the infinitudes and uncertainties of space to a view seen from an intergalactic automobile, the films which show us the "other-ness" of the world in which we actually live expand the finite and certain limits of a car on a highway winding through the desert or along a lonely stretch of sea-coast road into a journey through an infinite and hostile void. When the land which has nurtured us threatens us, we are truly lost in space. What such films as *It Came From Outer Space, Them!, Creature from the Black Lagoon* (Jack Arnold, 1954), *Tarantula* (Jack Arnold, 1955), *Beast with a Million Eyes* (David Kramarsky, 1955), *Invasion of the Body Snatchers* (Don Siegel, 1956), *The Monolith Monsters, The Space Children* (Jack Arnold, 1958), and *Most Dangerous Man Alive* (Allan Dwan, 1961), tell us is that the Earth is not a part of us, it does not even recognize us. These films—in whole or in part—take us away from our larger structures, our cities and skyscrapers which normally break up the disturbing blankness of the horizon. Our civilization and its technological apparatus is at best a small town set on the edge of an abyss. Watching these films with their abundance of long shots in which human figures move like insects, their insistence on a fathomless landscape, we are forced to a pessimistic view of the worth of technological progress and of man's ability to control his destiny.

It Came From Outer Space (Jack Arnold, 1953). This film and other low-budget SF of the fifties take us away from the cities and skyscrapers that break up the disturbing blankness of the horizon. (Universal)

113

We are shown human beings set uncomfortably against the vastness and agelessness of the desert and sea, are reminded by the contrast that land and water were here long before us and our cities and towns and will be here long after we and our artifacts are gone. We see ourselves—normal, human, incredibly mortal—against an unblinking and bare landscape that refuses any anthropomorphic sweetness with which we strive to endow it.

In *It Came from Outer Space,* the camera scans a desert in which a row of telephone poles and the men working on the wires appear ineffectual in breaking up the endless wasteland and the empty sky. The men doing their jobs, trying to impose limits on an expressionless and terrifying expanse of space, seem to unconsciously recognize the futility of their attempt to make an impression on the desert. One of them voices the uncertainty and discomfort we already feel from the images on the screen: "You see lakes and rivers that aren't really there, and sometimes you think the wind gets into the wires and sings to itself." The desert is deceptive and the wind sings, not to man, but to itself. People go into the desert and don't return or they return transformed in some way by the experience: the little girl stumbling out of it in shock in *Them!,* the "taken over" small town folks of *Invaders from Mars,* the hired man in the unfortunate, but still fascinating, *Beast with a Million Eyes,* the gangster in *Most Dangerous Man Alive.* In *Beast with a Million Eyes,* the camera, at the film's beginning, lets us peep into the desert (which we shall see more extensively later on) through a curtain of safe and civilized foliage while the narrator talks about the strangeness and evil of place: "It has to do with a feeling you get when you think about what's out there beyond the grove." The desert nurtures and protects the alien, the mutant; in this setting which—like the beach and sea, and less frequently the Arctic—has experienced every form of evolving life, nothing is strange. The giant spider of *Tarantula* or the ants in *Them!* look normal in such a context; it is only in comparison with Man and his works that they seem huge and grotesque. The house isolated in the desert in *Tarantula* is visually doomed when we see it; it cannot possibly survive against so straight and vast a horizon and it doesn't, whereas the mutated animal organisms seem immediately at home. In bleached sunlight, a man and a woman stand in the desert, minute against a fathomless sky and an ungeometric, uncivilized outcropping of rocks, their automobile parked diminutively by the side of a quasi-road; they stand uncomfortably and the man says, "Every beast that ever crept or crawled the earth began here. All this was once an ocean. You can still find seashells out there." [60] As far as the desert is concerned we could all be "a pair of ragged claws, scuttling across the floors of silent seas." [61] It remains connected to the primordial past and thus makes the present acutely uncomfortable.

As well, the earthly landscape of the seacoast with its beaches and caves can be powerfully transformed into an alien environment as in *The Space Children,* a film which is a bit logically inoperative and, therefore, often dismissed without regard for its visual surfaces. A rocky seacoast and beach harbor an alien power (something which starts out as a provocatively glowing pebble, but which grows into a ridiculously glowing brain). Only the children in the area know of its existence and it telepathically commands them to sabotage a missile on a military base at which their fathers work. The power is more laugh-provoking visually than it is terrifying; what is terrifying, however, is the landscape. Only the children in the film possess any connection with the desolate environment, unaware of the implications of its frightening limitlessness, but even their connection to it seems one of morbid and visually controlled fascination. There are no happy beach scenes, children romping in bright warm sunlight; the film's images show us a beach and an ocean gray in a flat, bleak light by day, or dangerously dark and dank by night. The children are constantly seen clutching sweaters, picking up jackets, protecting themselves physically as they silently serve what's hidden in one of the caves. *Creature from the Black Lagoon* opens "as a camera prowls through writhing mists and half-glimpsed landscapes; the sea rolls endlessly to the horizon, and as it washes on a dark and empty

The Space Children **(Jack Arnold, 1958). Publicity still. In this film, the landscape and the children's relation to it are far more chilling than the alien invader. (Universal)**

115

beach, formless footprints are seen leading from the water up into the darkness." [62] Possibly aeons later, we see the Creature, this "evolutionary dead end" in the shimmeringly beautiful but finally unfathomable Black Lagoon. The pastoral loveliness of the water's surface is transformed by the camera to a "primal sink" [63] in which the Creature is seen as graceful, sensuously and powerfully swimming, at home in an environment in which man looks ridiculously gawky in flippers and oxygen mask. Like the desert and the seacoast, "the lagoon is a place . . . of clarification and terror." [64] Its depth throws Man—and the viewer—into an awareness of his isolation, his essential homelessness. This homelessness, this feeling that Man is no more than a transient on the planet, is visually realized in many of the films where the characters are seen as not even strong enough to set up permanent dwellings on the hostile land. The family of the little girl who has stumbled off the desert in *Them!* was living not in a house but in a trailer which we see demolished, its personal belongings and furniture strewn about on the sandy ground as so much straw in the wind, broken and ravaged. The general store which is raided for sugar by the ants is made of boards, rickety and full of cracks; not only do we hear the wind blowing through the chinks in its poor armor, but we see the sand insinuating its way in to coat the counters and the floor, already starting a process of erosion which will eat away all traces

Creature from the Black Lagoon **(Jack Arnold, 1954). The Black Lagoon's pastoral loveliness is turned to a "primal sink," a place of both "clarification and terror." (Universal)**

The Thing (Christian Nyby/Howard Hawks, 1951). Subversion of the landscape: the frozen and hostile world of the Arctic in which human geometry is chillingly at odds with the landscape. (R.K.O./Winchester)

of Man. In *Creature from the Black Lagoon,* the characters live in a boat, fragilely floating on the surface of an unknown world. In *The Space Children,* the children and their parents live in little mobile homes, a trailer park on the brink of infinity; the lights in the windows—seen against the bleakness of the terrain and the blackness of night—are only the smallest candles lit against this chaotic and incomprehensibly alien void here on Earth, a world made out of once-familiar things.

Films visualizing the terrain of Earth as alien and hostile have been made in locations other than the desert and beach, although not as frequently. The Arctic has effectually given us the frozen and hostile world of *The Thing* (Christian Nyby/Howard Hawks, 1951); the long-shot of the men physically describing a circle on a vast field of ice in an attempt to discover the dimensions of a buried space vehicle is awesome not because of what's beneath the ice, but because their diminutive achievement of geometry is so chillingly at odds with the landscape. The beginning of *The Beast from 20,000 Fathoms* (Eugene Lourié, 1953), also takes advantage of the Arctic as a hostile background for the discovery of the Rhedosaurus, which will proceed to produce a different kind of visual power when it arrives in Coney

Island. The swamp and jungle have threatened us much less effectively, however, and have been used with even less frequency than the Arctic in SF film; they seem to belong more to the landscape of the horror film than they do to science fiction: *The Leech Woman* (Edward Dein, 1960), or *Frogs* (George McCowan, 1972). They have not been particularly useful in evoking that sense of the void which gives the low-budget film its uniquely devastating visual quality. The swamp and the jungle—however alien to those of us who are used to pavement beneath our feet—are too leafy, too obstructed, and constricted to allow us that sense of limitless and unconquerable space that can be visually evoked by the desert, the sea, and the Arctic, that sense of rootlessness and impermanence which awes and terrifies us all. Here it might be interesting to note that as long as the "other" is on the desert, on the beach, or in the water, it is almost always indestructable. As long as it is connected with the landscape which supports it, Man cannot successfully subdue it. That previously anthropomorphic union between Man and his physical environment has been changed to show a union of hostile forces. Man can only conquer in his own small enclaves. The giant ants are killed in city drains, not in the desert; the "Thing" is electrocuted indoors, not destroyed on the frozen wasteland of Arctic ice; the alien power in *The Space Children* can return, unharmed, from whence it came since it has made no move to leave the cave on the beach; the Creature is safe as long as he remains in the Lagoon.

There is yet another type of visual subversion of a familiar landscape in SF film which should also be considered here and which is not confined to low budget films: the transformation and alienation of the city. There are images in certain SF films (most often those dealing with postatomic holocaust) which show us emptiness on a scale which is psychologically as well as visually awesome. These films depend for their visual power not on a grand battle between man and alien forces in a familiar and active urban context, but rather on a subversion of that context's familiarity. When we think of the city, when we see it in "real" life or even in most movies, it is bristling with activity, people, traffic, motion. To see it robbed of that motion (which is, after all, a visual sign of life) is to see it as something devastatingly strange, to see it "as if some robot camera had continued to unwind film and photograph the world without man's help." [65]

In *Five* (Arch Obler, 1951), we enter, with the heroine and villain, an empty canyon whose walls are skyscrapers, whose floor is punctuated by static and forlorn automobiles distraughtly angled; nothing moves but the car in which they slowly ride, and a skeleton stares out at them from a window. *On the Beach* (Stanley Kramer, 1959), shows us a submarine crew trying to find the source of a signal from a radioactively dead America. The men wander in an empty San Francisco only to "discover the source of the

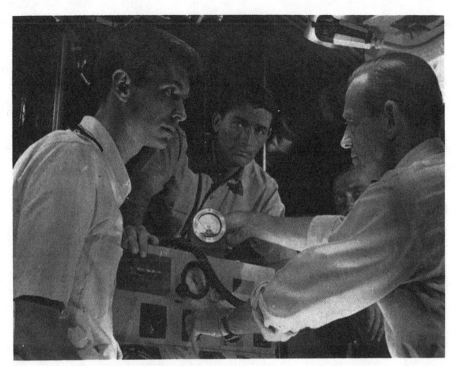

On the Beach (Stanley Kramer, 1959). One of many films featuring the inactive, dead city. (United Artists)

signal, the random tapping of a morse key by a bottle caught in a window blind; the final, horrifying irrelevance." [66] (And a Coke bottle, no less.) This dead stillness, this emptiness, is continually explored by the camera in *The World, the Flesh and the Devil* (Ranald MacDougall, 1959), which roams through New York City, down Wall Street, around the United Nations building. Cars eternally stalled on a bridge, newspapers blowing down the street as if to mock animate existence—these are recurring images in the postholocaust cities of science fiction from the fifties through the seventies. Different than the visual impact of the photographed action of disaster, this is the still and silent "garbage of disaster": [67] the Statue of Liberty literally brought low in *Planet of the Apes,* the razed and time-encrusted Radio City Music Hall marquee and the subway station of its sequel *Beneath the Planet of the Apes* (Ted Post, 1970), or "the empty city, the untended houses, the corpse-filled hospital beds" [68] in *The Omega Man* (Boris Sagal, 1971).

The city, then, is as susceptible to the void as the small town sitting on the edge of the desert or by the sea. "Film photography of a world untenanted by man (the streets of a modern city . . .) brought to men themselves, the spectators of this fantasy, an awareness of their own self-created

The Omega Man (Boris Sagal, 1971). The still and silent "garbage of disaster." (Warner Brothers)

world nominally, technically, and finally divorced from their participation. Man had made this world no longer 'his,' insofar as he was foreseeing the time when mankind would have no hope for survival, become virtually extinct." [69]

The Dehumanization of Humans

Visual subversion of the familiar, of course, is not limited solely in subject to the landscapes or cityscapes of science fiction. The same negative imaginations which alienated the viewer from his beloved and anthropomorphic Earth were also the imaginations which changed filmdom's "friendly people next door" into the cold and passionless alien beings who invaded so many low-budget movies. Although certainly less visually startling and physiologically amazing than the assorted flamboyant aliens and slimes created through the use of expensive special effects, the "taken over" human figures of the low-budget SF film make up in their power to disturb us what they lack in the power to astonish. While we may react with varying degrees of detached wonder to invading Martians or Metalunan Mutants who are distinctly seen as "other" than ourselves, our responses to those aliens clothed in our own familiar skins are another matter entirely. We expect unnatural behavior from something seen as unnatural, alien behavior from something alien. What is so visually devastating and disturbing about the SF films' "taken over" humans is the *small*, and therefore terrible, incongruence between the ordinariness of their form and the final extraordinariness of their behavior, however hard they try to remain undetected and "normal."

Most of the films which subvert human form and behavior—make of them something unknown—depend for their visual and emotional effectiveness on the contrast between the most dully normal, clichéd, and commonplace of settings and the quiet, minute, yet shockingly aberrant behavior of the invading aliens who pose as just plain folks. Thus, the setting of nearly all such films is small-town America, a community which is as familiar, predictable, snug, and unprivate as a Norman Rockwell magazine cover for *The Saturday Evening Post*. In such a world, against such a background, the smallest deviation from the norm, from ritual and habit, from warm, friendly, social—and even eccentric—Americana will carry the visual force of a Fourth of July fireworks display, if not a space-age nuclear detonation. What is chilling about the films, what causes our uneasiness, is that they all stay right at home threatening the stability of hearth and family, pronouncing quietly that nothing is sacred—not even Mom or Dad, nor the police chief, not even one's own true love.

In *Invaders From Mars,* the first to be "taken over" are a little boy's father and mother, then a little girl, and next the chief of police. (As in the majority of such films, we do not see the actual process of transference from alien body to human, although the gimmick is revealed: a red crystal embedded into the base of the victim's neck accomplishes the transformation.) *It Came From Outer Space* has the protagonist's girlfriend among those "taken over." The brilliant *Invasion of the Body Snatchers* transforms families (a little boy flees from home and hysterically maintains that his mother isn't his mother anymore), authority figures, friends, and, finally, the heroine whose passionate humanity has been cooled by the aliens while she sleeps. *I Married a Monster from Outer Space* (Gene Fowler, Jr., 1958), carries the threateningly successful charade into the nuptial bed. And *The Day Mars Invaded the Earth* (Maury Dexter, 1962), presents us with the final and cinematically singular perversion of familial togetherness: a scientist and his family are "taken over" in an atypical finale, the end of the film revealing them "incinerated by the Martians' rays and their ash silhouettes flushed down their empty swimming pool, while their simulacra drive off in the family car." [70]

Much of the attraction of these invisible invasion films has been attributed to their metaphorical realization of the *angst* of modern man living in a technological, bureaucratic, and conformist society. More than any other

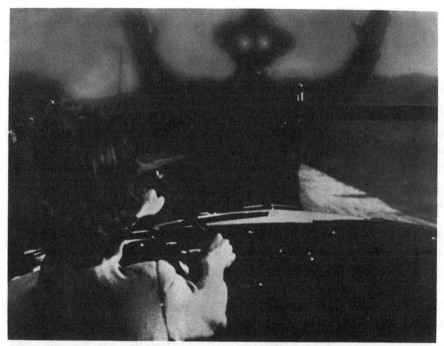

It Came From Outer Space (Jack Arnold, 1953). The subversion of the human—the alien invasion in which humans are "taken over" creates visual paranoia. (Universal)

aspect of the SF film, the plot device of being "taken over" has commanded the serious attention of critics of both film and popular culture. Thus, for example, the protean *Invasion of the Body Snatchers* has prompted various political and social analyses which are, as well, relevant to even the worst of the alien "infiltration" films. (Briefly, for those readers unfamiliar with the film, *Body Snatchers* tells the story of a town invaded by aliens who take over humans while they sleep, aliens who after having grown to maturity—inside giant seed pods—look like their human counterparts but are really emotionless simulacra.) Ernesto Laura feels "it is natural to see the pods as standing for the idea of communism which gradually takes possession of a normal person, leaving him outwardly unchanged but transformed within." [71] Brian Murphy bases the film's appeal on its convincing atmosphere of paranoia: "the image of people, your postman, your policeman, your wife, being taken over by an alien force was rendered with horrible and frightening conviction." [72] Charles Gregory writes: "Made in 1956 in the middle of the decade, peopled by men in gray flannel suits, the silent generation, the status seekers, Senator Joseph McCarthy, and lonely crowd, Siegel's science fiction thriller was a cry of frustrated warning against the conformity and uniformity of a society that was blissfully living in the best of all possible worlds."[73] Susan Sontag goes beyond this one film to generalize about the significance of being "taken over," depersonalized, in all the films of this type. She views being "taken over" as "a new allegory reflecting the age-old awareness of man that, sane, he is always perilously close to insanity and unreason"[74] and she also sees in the films the playing out of the ambiguous appeal of pure reason. And Carlos Clarens looks at such films thus:

> The ultimate horror in science fiction is neither death nor destruction but dehumanisation, a state in which emotional life is suspended, in which the individual is deprived of individual feelings, free will, and moral judgment . . . this type of fiction hits the most exposed nerve of contemporary society: collective anxiety about the loss of individual identity, subliminal mindbending, or downright scientific/political brainwashing.[75]

Amid all this critical activity, one might also note that there is a definite emotional appeal to the idea of being "taken over" which goes beyond the inherent attractions presented by the pod-psychiatrist in *Invasion of the Body Snatchers* and which is echoed in all the other films as well: "Love, desire, ambition, faith—without them life is so simple." That added emotional attraction is "no more responsibility." Being "taken over" can be likened to being drafted, to having to follow orders. "Taken over," we cannot be held accountable for our crimes—passionate or passionless.

In the heat of all the critical fires stoked by the varied significance of pods and Martians and other assorted aliens who insinuate themselves under our skins, it is quite easy to forget that all the discussion starts from a visual base, from images which, after all, are quite another thing than ideas. It is interesting, and just, that Don Siegel, director of *Invasion of the Body Snatchers,* although keen on the "message" about people as pods, speaks most convincingly in visual terms; he moves from the abstract concept to the visually concrete:

> To be a pod means that you have no passion, no anger, that you talk automatically, that the spark of life has left you. Remember the scene in the movie in which Kevin and Dana walk down the street pretending to be pods? He tells her to walk normally, blankly, react to nothing, but she can't help letting out a gasp when she thinks a dog is about to be run over in the street. In a world of pods who don't care if a dog dies, her humanity betrays them.[76]

> What I thought was quite delicious was our playing with the fact that as a pod you don't feel any passion. So, when he comes back to the cave and she falls, he tries to kiss her awake in a delicious non-pod way but she's a limp fish and he knows immediately that she is a pod.[77]

Invasion of the Body Snatchers (Don Siegel, 1956). When you're a "pod" you don't feel any passion. Miles is not able to kiss Becky back to humanity; she has been "taken over" by the aliens. (Allied Artists)

What is visually fascinating and disturbing about the images in films like Siegel's *Body Snatchers* is the way in which the secure and familiar are twisted into something subtly dangerous and slyly perverted. Looking at the small town America of the film mentioned is like looking at Andrew Wyeth's paintings; the subject matter is familiar, ordinary, but one experiences a tension which seems to spring from no readily discernable cause, a distortion of angle so slight as to seem almost nonexistent, but so great as to set the teeth intolerably on edge. Those aliens in the films who have "taken over" human bodies behave so nearly correctly that their primarily quiet distortions of human behavior are like a slap in the face. One cannot laugh at such almost perfect performances; the "straight" and "trusted" characters who fill the screen in their purposefully gray and dull way do not act in a manner so crude or obvious as to parody human behavior. As viewers, we are forced into an extremely active role watching these films, a role not often demanded of us by movies; we are seduced by the minimal activity and novelty of what's on the screen into an attentive paranoia which makes us lean forward to scan what seem like the most intentionally and deceitfully flat images for signs of aberrant alien behavior from the most improbable of suspects. In an excellent monograph on violence and genre films, Lawrence Alloway indirectly suggests that *suspense is nothing happening.*[78] If this is so, the films we've been discussing could hardly be more suspensful and engaging for most of their duration—and this is not meant ironically. The fact that so little happens in a "movie" makes us, as viewers, exceedingly suspicious and watchful.

What gives the aliens away? As Siegel has pointed out by his examples, it is primarily a matter of *negative* behavior, of *not* doing something: a gasp not gasped, a kiss not returned. For most of the various films' duration, then, we sit attentively watching ordinary people being ordinary, so pointedly ordinary at times that they appear finally as wooden as the aliens and create an extra visual tension—not only can't we tell who *has* been "taken over," but we also can't tell who *hasn't* been "taken over." Thus, the films' flat angles, uninspired camera movements, and downright unimaginative cinematography seem finally purposeful in creating a *mise en scene* in which a drumming insistence on the ordinary creates extraordinary tension. In the films, it is an absence of response, a nonaction, we are told to watch for, a rather inverted and disturbing movie-going experience in itself. To see things "not happen" one has to watch the screen very carefully, indeed—and, in the few cases where the alien "human" actually does something revealing (the

Invasion of the Body Snatchers (Don Siegel, 1956). The creation of paranoia: for most of the film's duration we attentively watch ordinary people being ordinary. (Allied Artists)

125

presence of action, rather than its absence), it is extraordinarily shocking no matter how small the action is nor how deemphasized it seems to be in the *mise en scene*. We cannot miss it, however "hidden" it is, for we have been compelled to watch those familiar images on the screen with the eyes of a hawk—and to distrust them with the heart of a paranoid.

John Baxter gives examples of both the active and passive aspects of the "take over" films in a discussion of Jack Arnold's *It Came From Outer Space:*

> ... Arnold cleverly uses disturbances in behavior to convey mood. All those people who have been "taken over" behave in a way slightly but eerily out of key; the two truck drivers, glimpsed in town by Putnam and cornered in an alley, emerge from the shadows *holding hands,* while one of the men, his attention drawn to the blazing sun, looks up and stares unblinkingly into it. When Putnam faces his girl on a windy hillside at dawn, she stands untroubled by the chill desert wind, while he must pull up his collar and flinch against its bite. Economically we are told that there is something outside our experience, a "different-drummered" world beyond our own.[79]

It Came From Outer Space (Jack Arnold, 1953). A recurrent image is a loved and trusted person staring coldly into the camera or into off-screen space. (Universal)

We are told in these films that, indeed, there is something outside our experience—but we are also shown that the "something" is inside our skin. The intimacy of the threat is what causes us to respond with discomfort, if not downright anxiety. The films are rife with images of mothers and fathers, good doctors, average nice-guy truck drivers, telephone company linesmen— as well as images of little girls and boys and even a faithful dog (the latter

The Manchurian Candidate (John Frankenheimer, 1962). The "take over" films of the fifties transformed into the surreal paranoia of the sixties. The "aliens" are now Communist brainwashers, and Mom is the Arch-Villain. (United Artists)

is transformed in *Beast with a Million Eyes*) who finally do not act in ways merited by such usually sacrosanct roles. The major recurrent image in these films is that of a loved and trusted person staring coldly into the camera or into off-screen space, ignoring the protagonist's distastefully human, emotional display of concern or love. Visually, then, the films are heretical. The familiar characters we see on the screen and to whose roles we respond with complacency are not what they appear to be. And, because the image attempts to deceive us, no familiar person or activity finally escapes our scrutiny and our suspicion. The smallest gestures of the most innocent characters become suspect; nothing and no one can be taken for granted. Mother, father, husband, wife, child, neighbors, civil servants, must be watched for signs that they are, under the surface skin—invaders. We cannot automatically believe what we see. Thus, these films visually—as well as thematically —suggest that to trust and believe in other people (even those nearest and dearest and most familiar to us) is ridiculously naive and self-destructive; the way we watch the films—suspiciously—is the way we should watch each other, and "healthy" paranoia is made to seem a reasonable and self-preser-

Dr. Strangelove: or How I Learned to Stop Worrying and Love the Bomb **(Stanley Kubrick, 1964). Publicity still. The human is transformed and distorted into the alien with lenses, angles, lighting, and stylized performance. (Columbia)**

128

vational alternative to trust. (It is interesting to note here that what is implicit in these films—most of them made in the fifties—is explicit by 1962 and John Frankenheimer's *The Manchurian Candidate*. This political SF film, made when pessimism and chic disenchantment became big business, is bizarrely comic at times in its blatant revelation of Mom as Arch-Villain and its visual device of having the brainwashed "taken over" men remember their communist captors as little old ladies at a garden club meeting.)

Another means of transforming the human into the inhuman, the familiar face into an alien physiognomy, depends less on cinematic passive-aggression (that suspense created by "nothing happening") than it does on an actively aggressive and flamboyant use of filmic elements like lighting and/or distorting lenses. In a film like Stanley Kubrick's *Dr. Strangelove: or How I Learned to Stop Worrying and Love the Bomb* (1964), the distortion of human faces and bodies is used to create a black comedy; the film deals with the insane inevitability of some high-placed madman pushing the button which starts a thermonuclear war. The "evil" and "mad" characters are lit so grotesquely as to suggest they have just stepped out of *The Cabinet of Dr. Caligari* or an old Universal Studios horror film made in the thirties. Their gothic treatment is funny because it is incongruous with their more modern milieu (an up-to-date air force base) and their contemporary problems and idiosyncracies. As characters who evoke the German Expressionist cinema by virtue of the angles at which they're photographed and the lighting which makes their faces grotesque, both General Jack D. Ripper (Sterling Hayden) and Dr. Strangelove (Peter Sellers) are out of visual step with the style of the backgrounds in which they move, the characters with whom they interact. Their look is twenties cinema (the thirties at the latest), while the look of the backgrounds and most of the other characters is fifties: a gray and two-dimensional image capturing flatness with unimaginative and non-horrific light.

Obvious distortion juxtaposed with flat and gray images is also combined to fine effect in John Frankenheimer's *Seconds* (1966), a film in which James Wong Howe's use of distorting lenses conveys not humorous incongruity but, rather, chilling paranoia. *Seconds* is the story of a man who would like to start life over again and is able to pay for a spatial, occupational, physical, and hopefully spiritual "nose job." The protagonist (Rock Hudson) gets his second chance, but cannot, finally, escape himself; his "rebirth" is only a superficial one—and he blows his new life and his new "cover" and becomes an embarrassment to his corporate rejuvenators who must, at last, eliminate him. Cinematographer Howe uses a fish-eye lens to distort human forms into horrendous grotesques which evoke both paranoia and a sense of the mutability of flesh itself:

In the climactic scene, the central note of the hero's awareness is that

129

Dr. Strangelove: or How I Learned to Stop Worrying and Love the Bomb (Stanley Kubrick, 1964). In contrast to the Gothic visual treatment of madmen Strangelove and Ripper, the look of the military is fifties—gray, two-dimensional, unhorrific. (Columbia)

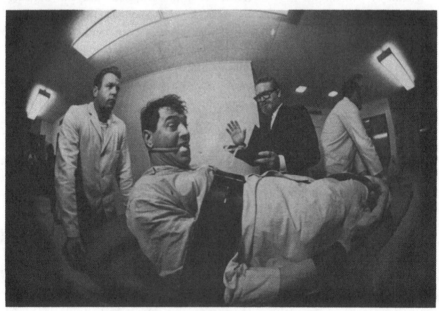

Seconds (John Frankenheimer, 1966). Cinematographer James Wong Howe uses a fish-eye lens to distort human forms into horrendous grotesques. (Paramount)

there is no escape. Hence it is fully appropriate that the hands of the medical assistants who strap him down should be monstrous, utterly nonhuman. Nor should it bother us that their arms, similarly close to the camera and wildly exaggerated as to size, are themselves as large as all the rest of their bodies. What we see here is not the real world, but the subjective insight of a beaten man, overwhelmed by irresistible, diabolic strength.[80]

Human beings are not the only familiar subjects transformed in the SF film, made strange and new through visual subversion. *Soylent Green,* for instance, is at its best when visually convincing us that the staples of life we take for granted today are completely unknown to all but the most influential and wealthy inhabitants of New York City in the year 2022. Two scenes (excerpted from the unpublished screenplay and used in the film) establish how a visual treatment can make us wonder at something which normally wouldn't cause us to bat an eyelash. The first takes place at night in a place called Brady's Market; the *mise en scene* is thus described:

Soylent Green (Richard Fleischer, 1973). The film is at its visual best when convincing us that small things (a tomato, running tap water) are wondrous and strange. (Metro-Goldwyn-Mayer)

A man with a shotgun sits guard just inside the door. Against one wall there are bins containing not more than a half dozen each of items like bread, apples, lettuce, celery, onions. There are some shelves with jars, not cans, of preserved fruits. There is an old refrigerated case with glass doors revealing some bottles of milk and small cubes of butter. Mr. Brady, nobody's fool, and all of these goods are protected by a wire mesh rising from the counter dividing him from his customers. It looks more like a pawnshop than a black market grocery store.[81]

In this setting, when we finally do see a small piece of beef (the script says it is "unappetizing by our standards"[82]), it is—or was in the only mildly inflated days of 1973—as alien to us as it is to the girl who is paying $279 for a small bag of groceries. Later, the film's protagonist, a detective named Thorn (Charlton Heston), is so entranced with the taken-for-granted sensual pleasures of a middle class bathroom that it is impossible for us to look at the bathroom in the film as a familiar place:

> ... Thorn almost reverentially turns on the sink taps. The water cascades out. He lets it run over his hands for a moment. He spots a piece of soap. Smells it, then experimentally tries it on his hands. After rinsing off the lather, he again smells his hands in some wonder. Then he cups his hands and splashes it on his face, hair, neck.[83]

Soylent Green may have its moments, but like many big-budget, color, SF films starring Charlton Heston (the rich man's Richard Carlson), the visual subversion of familiar images seems only a peripheral concern, a way station on the road to bigger and better and more shocking or spectacular revelations. The very dramatic and technical impulse toward visual extravagance and leisure which compose the artistically rich blood of the big-budget SF films results in a film style completely antithetical to the economic anemia which keeps the low-budget films so utterly and rigorously dependent on their visual use of a familiar world. Therefore, despite its occasionally effective transformation of the familiar, *Soylent Green* seems to visually meander among its various cinematographic options in contrast to the visual insistence and single-mindedness of a low-budget SF film like Jack Arnold's *The Incredible Shrinking Man*. The latter film's entire visual movement is toward a transformation of the absolutely familiar into the absolutely alien, and this is accomplished with an economy of means Martin Rubin justly feels transforms "functionalism into the poetry of the mundane."[84]

In *The Incredible Shrinking Man*, we are forced by the slow process of Scott Carey's (Grant Williams) miniaturization to constantly reevaluate our responses to the ordinary and normal, to the animate and inanimate. John Baxter, for example, points to the changing role of the family cat "from

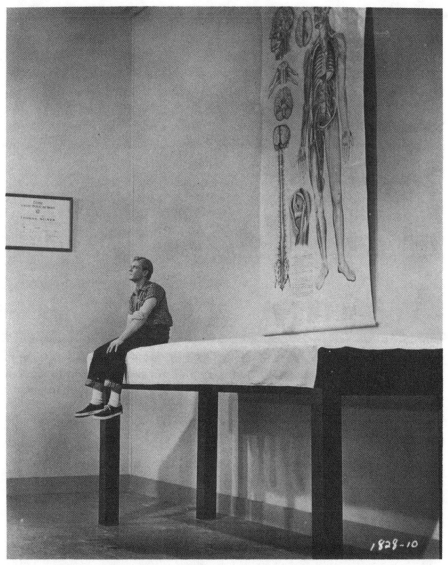

The Incredible Shrinking Man (Jack Arnold, 1957). The film's entire visual movement is toward a transformation of the absolutely familiar into the absolutely alien. (Universal)

prop to companion to menace." [85] Scott's wife and brother become increasingly less sympathetic, their humanity dwindling as they physically loom larger on the screen until they are obliterated by a kind of visual synecdoche: a huge foot on the cellar stairs. It is fascinating and indicative of the film's entire visual emphasis that the cat and the spider who are Scott's antagonists become more personalized than either Scott's wife or brother. But, as Martin

The Incredible Shrinking Man (Jack Arnold, 1957). We are forced to reevaluate our response to the ordinary and normal. The family cat, for instance, changes in function from "prop to companion to menace." (Universal)

Rubin notes, what causes even more wonder than these animate "monsters" are the film's mundane objects, which take on entirely new meaning without having to change their appearance.[86] (Physically, of course, they do change size, and are the result of art directors Alexander Golitzen and Robert Clatworthy's suitably proportioned sets, as well as effectively used back projection and optical effects.) Rubin also draws a parallel between the way in which the film makes us newly aware of the ordinary and what is called New Realism in modern art (e.g., Warhol's Campbell Soup can): "A lawnmower . . . could almost be a Ready-Made by Duchamp. A coffee can, a pin cushion, a drop of water, the corrugated surface of wood . . . to resemble an exhibit of ultra-realistic modern sculpture."[87] *The Incredible Shrinking Man* is, perhaps, paradigmatic in its ability to totally alienate us—and its protagonist—from a customary taken-for-granted environment. Despite its somewhat gratuitous and metaphysically upbeat ending ("In the eyes of God, there is no zero"), visually the whole film moves us pessimistically and existentially away from the supposed security of human relationships, the comforts and connotations of "home," into a totally vast, unstable, and non-

The Incredible Shrinking Man (Jack Arnold, 1957). The cat and spider as Scott's antagonists become more personalized than either his wife or brother. (Universal)

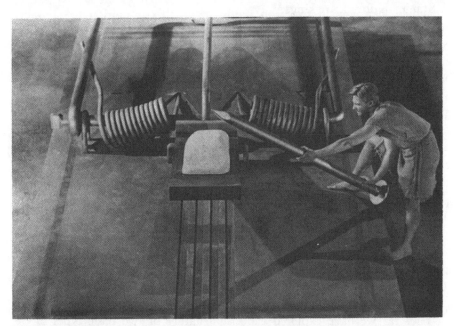

The Incredible Shrinking Man (Jack Arnold, 1957). What causes even more wonder are the film's mundane objects. As with Warhol's Campbell Soup Can, we are forced into a new relationship with the ordinary. (Universal)

anthropomorphic universe. As Carlos Clarens has pointed out, the film "introduced a very different type of fear into the dark solitude of movie houses, not instant annihilation but a gradual inexorable descent into nothingness."[88]

Although there will always be exceptions, in the final analysis it is the low-budget, black and white, SF film which has created a definite and sustained *visual style* arising from its subversion of the familiar. It is unfortunate, however, that because the films are so visually quiescent, so deceptively flat, many film critics have seen not a style, but rather a lack of style. Martin Rubin, for example, while admiring *The Incredible Shrinking Man,* not only fails to make a distinction between low- and big-budget science fiction, but also seems to see the SF films' visual success as highly dependent on the *lack* of talent and imagination of their directors:

> . . . science-fiction films are best served by bland or mediocre talents. For instance, a Wellesian director would have overinflated this film and compromised its sense of the ordinary with shadows and angles, while a more accomplished stylist of almost any other order would have softened it too much--such attitudes are better off in the horror film . . . the genre is best represented by efficient and functional technicians like Gordon Douglas and Joseph Sargent. In such a stylistically blind (and bland) world, one-eyed directors like Arnold, Don Siegel, and Stanley Kubrick are kings.[89]

Clearly, Rubin sees SF film style paradoxically deriving from its very style-lessness, its lack of "personality." And certainly, if one equates flamboyance with style, the low-budget SF film does, indeed, lack style. But if one sees visual style as a specific cinematic way of looking at the world and as a specific way of responding to it, then the low-budget SF film has style enough to spare. The combination of inexpensive settings and unexpressive actors with a special effectless and relatively confined *mise en scene* has resulted in a group of films which have at their worst made mediocrity mildly interesting, and at their best have created memorably bleak, pessimistic, and poetic visions of a fragile and precarious Earth inhabited by equally fragile and hollow men.

The Alien and the Familiar: The Aesthetics of Collision

Thus far we have explored the visual nature of two basic types of SF film, each, generally speaking, antithetical to the other and each visually communicative in its own unique way. Where the more solvent color science fiction extravaganza is confident and optimistic in its "I came—I saw—I conquered" visual movement (a movement which creates and then subdues the extraordinary), its lower budget counterpart is marked by a relentless pessimism reflected in a constant visual affirmation that, indeed, each man *is* an island, isolated and alienated from even the most familiar of people and places and things (a visual movement which surrenders to and then destroys the ordinary).

There is, however, a third kind of SF film which seeks a middle ground —a sort of cinematic demilitarized zone—between visual optimism and visual pessimism. In fact, this type of SF film is principally dependent for its power upon its ability to achieve visual neutrality, to evenly balance both its alien and familiar content—its fantasy and realism—in the same frame, so that we are amazed by their togetherness and their collision, by their compatibility and their incongruence. In these films "the poetry . . . radiates from the bombardment of the familiar by the unfamiliar." [90] Most often, however, that poetry is climactic rather than constant, the films' major visual movement a kind of photographic foreplay, a teasing and tickling of the viewer's anticipation of and desire for the final collision and bombardment of opposite elements in the same frame.

Thus, in such films as *The Beast from 20,000 Fathoms, The Amazing Colossal Man.* and *Earth vs. the Flying Saucers* (to name only a random few in the grouping) the visual movement is from *montage* to *mise en scene,* from unremarkable fragmented editing of separate shots to the long take and a climactic collision of previously isolated elements in the same frame. The suspense in these films is generated not merely by the literary question of whether the monster or aliens can be stopped and mankind saved, nor is it prompted only by an anticipation of cathartic disaster; a great deal of our rising curve of excitation is based on a cinematic teasing of our desire to see "everything" in one uncut long shot, to see what we know is unreal and impossible made real—authenticated—by its presence in a real and familiar context which has been photographed in a manner reserved for actual and real happenings, uninterrupted by either art or commentary. The rhedosaurus in *The Beast from 20,000 Fathoms* is remarkable primarily in its visual relationship to Coney Island and the roller coaster; abstracted in closeup, fragmented by editing, it might as well be an ordinary lizard.[91] *The Amazing Colossal Man* is no big deal (is, in fact, just another actor: Glenn Langan) until he strides through a recognizable Las Vegas and we see him remove and wear a giant crown which has topped one of the casinos. The flying saucers of *Earth vs. the Flying Saucers* are memorable not for their static symmetry, but for their aggressive action in long shot, their attack against a Washington, D.C., defined by its monuments and landmarks and by its realistic appearance on the screen. Ray Harryhausen, who engineered the special effects for the film, explains the realism:

War of the Colossal Beast (Bert I. Gordon, 1958). This sequel to *The Amazing Colossal Man* attempts to set the giant against a familiar landscape, but lacks the original's amazing specificity of place, its setting in Las Vegas. (American International)

Many shots were of the real buildings in Washington. We, of course, did have model duplications for the destruction sequences but our budget didn't permit high-speed shooting so the collapse of the buildings had to be animated frame by frame. That meant that each brick was suspended with invisible wires and had to change position with every frame of film. Dust and debris were added later. It was something I would never do again.[92]

Whether or not such painstaking work was done again is another story, but the urge toward this kind of authenticity is certainly relevant here.

At this point, it is interesting and quite apropos to note that in his famous essay "The Virtues and Limitations of Montage," film theorist André Bazin used fantasy films as examples to demonstrate how the illusion of realism can be achieved or destroyed by the editing decisions made by the filmmaker. Much of what he has to say about the use of *mise en scene* or the long shot and long take to "authenticate" a fiction could be well applied to the visual thrust of this last large group of science fiction films, films which move from the fragmentation of editing (*montage*), from separate shots in which neither humans, city, nor Creature are particularly amazing, toward the spatial unity, maximized "reality" and wonder of the long shot and long take which reveals humans, city, and Creature together in one frame (*mise en scene*). The plots and visual progression in such films move toward that one climactic moment when "those elements previously separated off by montage" [93] are brought together in the same frame so that what has until that moment been kept imaginary and unwondrous is presented with "the spatial density of something real." [94] Thus, the climax of this third group of SF films is a moment in which a spatial relationhsip—not merely a Creature—is revealed: the giant octopus created by Ray Harryhausen for *It Came From Beneath the Sea* (Robert Gordon, 1955), wrapping its tentacles around San Francisco buildings and destroying the Golden Gate Bridge; Willis O'Brien's *The Black Scorpion* (Edward Ludwig, 1957), tangling with a helicopter and an express train in Mexico; *The Deadly Mantis* (Nathan Juran, 1957), finding refuge in a tunnel under the Hud-

The Black Scorpion (Edward Ludwig, 1957). Fake looking in close-up, this "scorpion" gains power and poetry only when it is restored to the *mise en scène*. (Warner Brothers)

son River; Harryhausen's Venusian "Ymir" wrecking Rome and battling an elephant in *20 Million Miles to Earth* (Nathan Juran, 1957). In reference to his work in this last film, Harryhausen said: "In designing it we used all the Roman ruins and monuments, including the real Colosseum. The creature was matted into the real scenes." [95]

What we move toward, thirst for, in such films, what fulfillment we find in them is in the cinematic realization of an *imaginary action* occurring in what seems to be documented *real space*. As Bazin points out: "If the film is to fulfill itself aesthetically we need to believe in the reality of what is happening while knowing it to be tricked." [96] The fictions of these SF films and their ability to give us pleasure "derive their full significance . . . from the integration of the real and the imaginary." [97] The creature, in other words, was matted into the real scenes. What is so satisfying in the visual climax of such films is not simply an act of destruction, of wrecking, and the catharsis and aesthetic pleasure which Susan Sontag suggests is the result of being able to "participate in the fantasy of living through one's own death and more, the death of cities, the destruction of humanity itself." [98] Catharsis, loosely defined as it is these days, can be brought about by films which have nothing to do with science fiction. And wrecking, with its scatological satisfaction, is also not unique to science fiction (witness the whole concept of the demolition derby and the spate of "disaster" films

20 Million Miles to Earth (Nathan Juran, 1957). Imaginary action in "real space." (Columbia/Morningside)

140

which show us ocean liners overturning, skyscrapers tumbling or ablaze).
There is, however, a satisfaction which is uniquely derived from the SF
film, which arises from the combination of those two antithetical words—
"science" and "fiction." The satisfaction comes from seeing the visual integration of actual and impossible in the same frame, from the filmmaker's
ability to make us suspend our disbelief at the very moment we are also
wondering, "How did they do it?"

Both the creation and the release of emotional tension in these films is
equally brought about by the cinematic introduction and resolution of a
visual and perceptual paradox: the coexistence of the real and the fake in
the same frame, the same context, the same moment of screen time and
viewer apprehension. Most often scorned, and defined primarily by the
Creature whose singular iconic fate seems to have been its confrontation with
urban civilization, this group of SF films under discussion moves toward a
simultaneous collision and collusion between what is real and what is faked,
between what we know to be a fact (Washington, D.C., in *Earth vs. the Flying Saucers* or Rome in *20 Million Miles to Earth*) and what we know to
be a fiction (those flying saucers and the Venusian Ymir).

The wonder, then, which is caused by this simultaneous visual collision

When Worlds Collide **(Rudolph Maté, 1951). The collision of the real and
the imaginary in the same frame. New York is inundated by a tidal wave
as a roving planet moves toward Earth. (Paramount)**

141

and collusion does not necessarily arise from the "aesthetics of destruction
. . ., the peculiar beauties tо be found in wreaking havoc, making a mess,"
as Susan Sontag suggests it does.[99] The mess is only contributory to the
wonder, and not the source of it. Certainly, images of destruction are peculiarly pleasing and satisfying to watch on the screen, but they are not
dependent upon the juxtaposition of the real and the fake for their aesthetic
effectiveness. A volcano erupting in a documentary gives us similar aesthetic
satisfaction as Tokyo toppling in *Godzilla*. The wonder of this last grouping
of SF films arises from a more particular visual source than destruction itself,
a source dependent upon a juxtaposition which creates *incongruence,* "the
same special, deliberate incongruity we see in surrealist paintings . . . the
kind of incongruity which makes one stare and stare and stare because of
the confusion of emotional associations attached to different objects placed
in the same visual frame."[100] Thus, demolition, destruction, and wrecking
are not essential to the wonder generated by the incongruent content of the
images on the screen. The toppling of national monuments by flying saucers,
the squashing of automobiles by alien reptilian feet, aesthetically pleasing as
they may be in their destructiveness, are finally a flamboyant demonstration

Reptilicus (Sidney Pink, 1962). Although we find aesthetic pleasure in
destruction, that pleasure is also the result of seeing a flamboyant demonstration of incongruence in action. (American International)

of incongruence in action; the mere fact of action is a Q.E.D. to a proposition already proved more quietly: the coexistence and equivalence of the real and the imaginary in the film frame. Destruction is not a necessary element of the wonder we feel; *The Amazing Colossal Man* amazes us quietly by inspecting a woman's slipper of giant proportions which has been atop a Las Vegas casino, by being absorbed in his own concerns while he towers over a city whose actual size and landmarks are known to us.

The wonder which we feel at the incongruence of elements within the frame is also critically enhanced by its flat presentation, a presentation which has been seen less as a condition of our amazement than as an aesthetic joke. Surely, what finally adds to our amazement is the camera's eerie and inhuman *lack* of amazement. The incongruence is accepted and contained with the utmost blandness by the camera, the camera which not only rejects the hysteria of motion and the emotionalism of angles but which faces the incongruence with such documentary coolness, such bizarre placidity, that one wonders at the implacability of its stare as much as one wonders at the subject of its gaze. The blandness of the camera's view is incongruent with what it is viewing and an extra element of incongruence is thus added to the content of the image. It is odd, then, that those very few critics who have noticed the neutral flatness of the camera vision have pejoratively

20 Million Miles to Earth (Nathan Juran, 1957). The camera's eerie and inhuman lack of amazement. (Columbia/Morningside)

evaluated it as a demonstration of "bland and mediocre talents" [101] or as a recurring accident rather than as a definite style used—consciously or unconsciously—in connection with specific subject matter in the most rigid and classically conventional manner possible.

Frank McConnell, for instance, is one of the few critics who acknowledges the visual nature of such films and correctly assesses their effect: "the remorselessly plain camera angles of these movies insist on the same vantage for humans and monsters; and therefore inadvertently project flat visual equivalence between the 'normal' and the freakish which is finally a devastating reduction of humanistic perception." [102] What is disturbing about McConnell's acute analysis, however, is that he sees the effect of the insistent cinematography, and the resultant reduction of humanistic perception, as something negative. Might not the lack of imagination McConnell sees demonstrated by the flat vision of the camera, the "reduction of humanistic perception," as readily be seen as positive, as an expansion of perception beyond the human, as—indeed—inhuman but in being so also offering us an imaginative alternative to the way we "normally" view the freakish. Finally, the impassive third-person camera eye, in its flatness, its balanced and symmetrical attention to both the real and the imaginary, creates a wonder which is unique. It arises not from the visual transformation of the alien into something known as

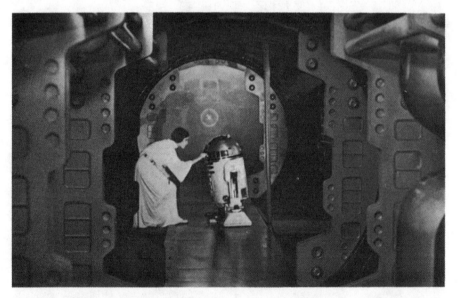

Star Wars (George Lucas, 1977). The impassive third-person camera eye, in its flatness, its balanced and symmetrical attention to both the real and the imaginary, creates a wonder unique to science fiction. (20th Century Fox)

144

The Beast from 20,000 Fathoms (Eugene Lourié, 1953). The Creature films simultaneously evoke the security and safety to be found in objectivity and the terror created by such apocalyptic indifference. (Warner Brothers)

does the optimistic visual conquest of big-budget science fiction. Nor does it arise from the conversion of the ordinary into the alien as does the pessimistic visual subversiveness of low-budget science fiction. Rather, this third group of much-maligned SF film balances and equates the ordinary and the alien in a vision neither humanly optimistic nor pessimistic.

To some viewers, the films of this group are not worth the watching. And it is finally true that in most of them we are treated or subjected (depending on one's response) to fragmented images which only at the last gain visual significance in *mise en scene,* to plots and images which are the most rigidly repetitious and conventional of all science fiction films from their first montage of news casters to their last surveillance of the wreckage. To some, those few moments of wonder are not worth waiting for. But the wonder is finally generated and the vision (like the techniques used to create it) is finally paradoxical in its simultaneous cinematographic evocation of the security and safety to be found in objectivity and the terror created by apocalyptic indifference. Susan Sontag begins her now-classic essay "The Imagination of Disaster"; "Ours is indeed an age of extremity. For we live under continual threat of two equally fearful, but seemingly opposed, destinies: unremitting banality and inconceivable terror." [103] What is unique about this last group of SF films is that its visual style demonstrates simultaneously both the unremitting banality and the inconceivable terror.

145

3

The Leaden Echo and the Golden Echo: The Sounds of Science Fiction

I remember once hearing an apocryphal story about a man, unfamiliar with English, who thought that the most beautiful, musical, romantic and mysterious word in our entire language was "cellador." He had slurred together two extremely ordinary and less than beautiful words—"cellar" and "door"—to come up with something which sounded rather like the name of a magical Arthurian isle or the heroine of an Edgar Allan Poe poem. I have always hoped that the gentleman in the story never did learn sufficient English to suffer the literal disenchantment which knowledge and comprehension of our language would have caused him.

In science fiction (SF) cinema, perhaps the quintessential equivalent to "cellador" can be heard in *The Day the Earth Stood Still* (Robert Wise, 1951). It is a single magical line of dialogue spoken by actress Patricia Neal to a giant faceless robot: "Gort, Klaatu barrada nicto." This sentence, through its internal rhythmic and grammatical structure, creates not only music but also an extraordinarily imaginative resonance. The meaning of the sentence in its cinematic context is simultaneously accessible and elusive; the words and their order achieve a most delicate balance between sense and nonsense, between logical communication and magical litany.

In the film's context, we understand the line generally but cannot grasp it precisely. Gort is the name of the robot, Klaatu the name of the alien visitor to Earth who has been shot and who has instructed the woman to say the words to the robot should anything happen to him. We may understand that the sentence is a command and in some way is meant to deter the robot from retaliation for Klaatu's death. It may also suggest some course of action to the robot, for Gort is later seen mechanically "resurrecting" Klaatu

The Day the Earth Stood Still (Robert Wise, 1951). "Gort, Klaatu barrada nicto" is a linguistic reaching-out that takes us beyond the limits and literalness of Earth-bound language. (20th Century Fox)

whose body he has recovered. But what "barrada" and "nicto" actually mean, what parts of speech they are, remains a mystery. Is "barrada" a verb perhaps, "nicto" a negative, a noun? "Gort, Klaatu barrada nicto." One line of dialogue in a film otherwise emphatically comprehensible. Although there are a few other instances of alien language in the film, it is this particular line which lingers. The words themselves are wondrous for they let us speculate endlessly, they resonate. And—unlike other such dialogue— these words are spoken to an alien by a *human*. That linguistic reaching out takes us, even if only briefly, beyond the literal and limited boundaries of Earth and Earth-bound language. It is our "cellador."

In all American SF cinema, only one film has seriously attempted to give us a spoken and, more importantly, a *sustained* language equivalent to its wondrous visual images—and it is certainly not coincidental that the film and the language were adapted from a novel, *A Clockwork Orange* by Anthony Burgess. In his 1971 film adaptation, Stanley Kubrick has retained and made sound of the visual rhythms of Burgess' invented language, Nadsat. Spoken by protagonist Alex and his droogs (friends), the mixture of Anglicized Russian with comprehensible English is onomatopoeic, rick and lush, coarse, Elizabethan, and definitely wondrous. Nadsat infuses the film with strangeness and tension, complementing or in contrast to the images we see on the screen, the colorless speech of other characters, the music on the soundtrack. Nadsat, particularly as spoken by Alex (Malcolm Mc-Dowell) in a manner which Pauline Kael pejoratively dismisses as "arch," [1] is more than a futuristic tongue, a sign of linguistic change, a gimmick; it is a song and an attitude, a celebration of sound itself and a new way of look-

147

A Clockwork Orange (Stanley Kubrick, 1971). To date, the only film that has seriously attempted to use a spoken and sustained language equivalent to its wondrous imagery. (Warner Brothers)

ing at, describing, and thinking about what our own eyes perceive in every-day contemporary English. We deal with Nadsat not only as an alien language, but also as the expression of a foreign *mind*—therein the wonder lies. Ironically, but understandably, Anthony Burgess—with due respect to *Clockwork* as a film—has written about the adaptation: "The light and shade and downright darkness of my language cannot, however brilliant the director, find a cinematic analogue." [2] What is ironic is that Burgess has chosen *visual* terms to describe the written language of his book—and equally ironic is the fact that the success of that language in the film is in its sound, its being spoken aloud by a human voice which can indeed lighten it, shade it, darken it with menace. What is significant about the language of the filmed *Clockwork Orange* has little to do with its literary qualities or the fact that it is adapted from written literature. Rather, the significance and impact of Nadsat in the film arises from the fact that it is *not read*, but *spoken* and *heard* as a truly wondrous, part-human, part-alien tongue. Making up one's "rassoodock," "tolchocking" victims, "peeting vino," using one's "glazzies," seeing things as "horrorshow" or "ultraviolent," recognizing "gorgeosity"—this is not literature in its filmed state (nor less than literature either, as Burgess would try to convince us) [3] but spoken, expressive, and

A Clockwork Orange (Stanley Kubrick, 1971). "Nadsat" is more than a futuristic tongue. It is an attitude, a foreign language, the expression of an alien mind and sensibility. (Warner Brothers)

living language. Its spoken combination of unfamiliar nouns, verbs, and adjectives, common English, and poetic, surprising, and punning portmanteau words is vital to the film's creation of an alien consciousness and sensibility. In its achievement of this creation through spoken language, *A Clockwork Orange* is unique in SF cinema. As Philip Strick observes of the film, "it is the first sustained success on film of what science fiction writers (notably Heinlein) have long used as a necessary element in describing plausible futures." [4]

"Gort, Klaatu barrada nicto" is an isolated line of wonder in an otherwise primarily dull, if intelligent, linguistic context; its imaginative resonance is, indeed, enhanced by its relative isolation. Nadsat, on the other hand, is an alien language which we as viewers and listeners *learn* as it is sustained for the film's duration and parsed by linguistic and visual context. Both these films are successful in moving language beyond the feeble futuristic gadget-naming of most SF films (i.e., the "Interociter" of *This Island Earth* [Joseph Newman, 1955]; or the "quanto-gravitetic hyperdrive and postonic transfiguration" of *Forbidden Planet* [Fred Wilcox, 1956]). Unfortunately, however, both *The Day the Earth Stood Still* and *A Clockwork Orange*—in their attempts to create alien dialogue that *is* alien—are exceptions to rather

149

than the rule.[5] They are only two films in more than two decades of SF films, two decades of films certainly not recognized by even the most ardent SF buffs for their adventurous treatment of alien or, for that matter, human dialogue.*

Surely, one of the most disappointing elements of SF cinema is dialogue. How can a genre which so painstakingly tries to awe and surprise us with imaginative images seem so ignorant and careless of the stiffness, banality, pomposity, dullness, and predictability of its language. This lack of imaginative dialogue in the SF film has been consistently noted by film critics with either affectionate condescension or hostile interest since the genre arose in full force in fifties America. Penelope Houston, in one of the earliest articles identifying and describing the genre, wrote: "One does not mind if space travel oversteps the bounds of the scientifically likely, provided that it does so with imagination. But Hollywood is perhaps not the starting point for such journeys. The shiny, gadget-crammed rocket is dispatched into a universe that comes straight out of the comic strips, and the Brooklyn boy or the chorus girl, greeting a new planet with a 'Gee! We're here!' scarcely seem fitted for the tradition of a Columbus."[6] Susan Sontag in her "The Imagination of Disaster" says: "The naive level of the films neatly tempers the sense of otherness, of alien-ness, with the grossly familiar. In particular, the dialogue of most science fiction films, which is generally of a monumental but often touching banality, makes them wonderfully, unintentionally funny."[7] And Brian Murphy, discussing monster movies of the fifties, attempts to relate the weak dialogue to the decade in which the films were made and, as well, suggests the crux of the aesthetic problem posed by SF dialogue:

In the Fifties, prose itself became horrifying, and the response was, certainly not poetry but, more and more prose; and the more scientific, the more it sounded like computerized jargon, the better, the more reassuring.

One cause of this general weakness of monster movies is the poverty of the language. Poverty of language turned the U. S. moon flights into bores because no one, except a few journalists, could think of any compelling way to talk about them. There is a similar aesthetic problem in monster movies: they deal with interesting problems and even Great Issues, but it is nearly impossible to remember anything that is said in them.[8]

Suggested here are two major reasons for the presence of weak dialogue

---

* These films have since been joined by *Star Wars* (George Lucas, 1977), which uses alien speech and translates it via subtitling. The languages are fascinating but the translations reduce their poetic resonance considerably, creating comedy instead.

in SF films. One is that it is almost a condition of the genre, part of the form itself. The banality, the laconic and inexpressive verbal shorthand and jargon, the scientific pomposity, are needed to counterbalance the fear (of both falling and flying) generated by the visual image which takes risks and is unsettling. How do we reconcile the visual sight of a rocket launch (all fire and thrust and movement) with the verbal reduction of that image to an "A-OK. We have lift off." How do we reconcile the awesome visual poetry of Kubrick's *2001: A Space Odyssey,* for example, with its tedious half-hearted dialogue which barely approaches prose. Murphy would see this reductionism as necessary, as evidence that a terrifying (even if wondrous) world is under control, reduced through containing and controlling jargon to human size and manageable predicament. Susan Sontag would see the juxtaposition of grand image with small talk as an attempt to "normalize what is psychologically unbearable, thereby inuring us to it," [9] a case of the word neutralizing the image. Indeed, the idea that small talk and big images are *necessary* screenmates—are, in fact, a definitive element—of SF cinema is not at all untenable. Certainly, the verbal limitations of the genre reflect the visual tensions discussed in the previous chapter: the tension between those images which strive to totally remove us from a comprehensible and known world into poetry and those images which attempt to bring us back into a familiar, reassuring, and prosaic context. The American SF film, no matter how abstract individual images may be, finally grounds itself in comprehensibility, in its necessary commerciality, and dialogue helps ground it. The jargon and banality Murphy identifies as a reassurance the fifties' viewer, in particular, needed and wanted perhaps can be more generally identified with the aesthetic tensions and essential contradictions of the genre. Therefore, the history of the SF film up to the present can lead one to expect that more often than not the more wondrous and alien the image, the more usual and Earthly the spoken word.

The other suggested reason for the poverty of language in a great deal of SF cinema confronts a crucial artistic problem. How *does* one talk in a compelling way about things which are conceptually magnificent, visually exciting, but linguistically dull or difficult, abstract or reductive. How, for example, can an observation, explanation, or description of the approaching roving star Bellus and its planet Zyra in *When Worlds Collide* (Rudolph Maté, 1951), match in any way its visualization. The observation and description are only a pale approximation of the image and an explanation removes the emotion contained in the magic of seeing what we see on the screen. Companion music may be of the spheres, capturing the emotion we feel in response to natural forces, but scientific dialogue tends to stay on the ground, emotionless and imageless. The language of science, after all, is scientific—formulaic, abstract, abbreviated, a jargon which is cooly functional and essential to quick and clear communication. It is also a language which strives toward the most objective unemotional communication possible and is therefore—in its straightforward manifestation—totally unimaginative.

Ironically, part of the problem at issue here can be dramatically illustrated by a brief interchange in *Marooned* (John Sturges, 1969), a film which Pauline Kael appositely (though in terms of the genre, uncomprehendingly) described as having "a script that sounds as if the author had never met a human being." [10] The implicit contradiction between the empirical scientific method and the human imagination occurs in a nonscientific conversation between the three astronauts trapped in "Ironman One," a space capsule orbiting the moon. They are all exhausted, all hopeless of rescue, and one of them, Buzz (Gene Hackman), nearly hysterical. The calmest of the three, the least emotional, is Stoney (James Franciscus) who, to pass the time and perhaps calm the other two men, remembers that all three of them had taken a psychological test in which they were shown a blank piece of paper and then asked what they saw. Stoney reminisces that he was the only one of them to answer, "A blank piece of paper." "No imagination?" one of the

Marooned **(John Sturges, 1969). The film's script has been criticized because it "sounds as if the author had never met a human being." (Columbia)**

Destination Moon (Irving Pichel, 1950). The first SF film with dull, unemotional, and reductive language, which very well may authenticate the fiction of its premises and imagery. (United Artists/Eagle-Lion)

other trapped astronauts asks him. "No," Stoney says. "Devotion to truth."

Poetic imagination and scientific truth are verbal enemies in a great deal of SF films. One might suggest, however, that because of the average viewer's inability to understand the technical language of science, like the man who found poetry in "cellar door," he too will find beauty in the language's mystery, poetry in its inaccessibility. But that seems not to happen in most cases in which the scientific jargon is presented straightforwardly (scientists and technicians talking shop in films including *Destination Moon,* [Irving Pichel, 1950]; *Magnetic Monster,* [Curt Siodmak, 1953]; *Riders to the Stars,* [Richard Carlson, 1954]; *Earth vs. the Flying Saucers,* [Fred F. Sears, 1956]; *Countdown,* [Robert Altman, 1968]; *Colossus—the Forbin Project,* [Joseph Sargent, 1969]; *Marooned;* and *The Andromeda Strain,* [Robert Wise, 1971]). The language of science, designed to be exclusive rather than inclusive, eschews resonance. Poetry and mystery never have a chance against the reductive excess of competence, efficiency, assurance and flatness which sounds across the screen. Imaginative flights of rhetoric (if they appear at all in such SF films) tend to be regarded by both characters and viewer suspiciously, manifestations at best of fatigue and stress, at worst of psychosis.

Another reason for the dull, unemotional-ergo-inhuman language in many SF films is that in laboratories, around space installations, in and about scientific haunts and allied institutions, there is, in fact, dull language; it's authentic, real. In a space station orbiting the Earth, an astronaut talks about "cleaning house"; in military discussions of human casualties, euphemisms like "hair mussing" are used. Both are verbal evidence of an inadequate or inappropriate response to the actual stimuli. The first instance would perhaps be a touching demonstration of inadequate response had it not been delivered with such cheery aplomb. The second instance is a sample of what Stanley Kubrick has called "statistical and linguistic inhumanity." [11] But, however one interprets or feels about this kind of language which subdues experience, it is *authentic*—and it is authenticity toward which the SF film strives. This is not merely a case of pathetic fallacy. We cannot forget that while the science and/or technology and/or problem in all SF films may be credible, possible, or even probable, it is never actual. Therefore, dull and routine language by remaining dull and routine may very well authenticate the fiction in the films' premises or images. (Personally, I would enjoy seeing someone create an SF film in which all the science, technology, and problems were real, but in which the emotions and language were fictitious; I envision a scene of white-coated lab researchers crying hysterically, chanting mumbo jumbo, or hugging themselves in excitement and speaking, perhaps, Middle English over their centrifuges as they demonstrate a fictional empirical method.)

As of now, the dull and flat language of reality is often used to create credibility and lend a documentary quality to SF cinema. Thus, Neil Hurley, a theologian and film critic, is prompted to ask: "Is it possible that men will become more neuter and less human as they immerse themselves in technology?" [12] And a Columbia University student can accurately say to *Mademoiselle* magazine which featured an article on science fiction: ". . . staggering things are being done by boring, bland people. Who wants to talk to one of the astronauts? This is an age of exploration that beggars Drake, but there aren't going to be any more gallant Lindberghs setting out alone." [13] The language of science and technology is antiromantic and thus anti-individualistic; it does not express personality and consequently it is antiheroic. Who, indeed, wants to talk to *one* of the astronauts? The astronauts are a team hero, speak a team language which brooks no romantic self-consciousness. The astronauts exist plurally, not singly, outstandingly, as did Drake and Lindbergh. Pauline Kael, in her negative review of *Marooned,* misses the point when she asks: "Who in his right mind would cast the three leads with Gregory Peck, Richard Crenna, and David Janssen, when anybody can see they're all the same man?" [14] The dull language, the flat intonations of SF film are exceedingly democratic in their reductive capacity, their ability to efface personality. Yet while this creation of a corporate consciousness, a group protagonist, is quite appropriate to the *public* concerns of science fiction, it also has to be recognized that the resultant lack of differentiation destroys the dramatic concept of character and, as well, the traditional relationship between the screen hero and the film viewer. Thus, while remaining stylistically true to its social and public concerns (its democratic preoccupation with the group or team and with anti-individualistic, impersonal language), the SF film can—and often does—offer the viewer less than a satisfying *dramatic* cinema experience. Aesthetically, the dull and flat language in the SF film creates and destroys simultaneously.

Obviously, there are many SF films in which the dialogue is less flat and banal than it is overblown, overly explanatory, overly metaphysical and self-important. All of us can remember lines from films, lines which are memorable because their aphoristic quality makes them seem self-conscious, unreal, and, consequently, funny. Again, these effects can be caused by a demonstration in inappropriate response. Take, for example, an interchange between two soldiers in *The Beast From 20,000 Fathoms* (Eugene Lourié, 1953). In a visually thrilling climax, the army is battling a trapped prehistoric Rhedosaurus in an amusement park, trying to kill it by firing radioactive isotopes into a wound in the beast's throat. One soldier says to the other in the heat of the fray: "Every time we let one off I feel like I'm writing the first chapter of the new Genesis." And his companion responds without turning a hair or batting an eyelid: "Let's hope we're not writing the last chapter of the old!" The general impression one gets from such dialogue is that when it isn't funny, it's "talky," "unrealistic"—words which sum up the feeling we have that nobody talks like that. The sudden attention paid to grammar when something "philosophical" or "intellectual" is to be said is mind boggling in its regularity; it's as if filmmakers assumed that Truth comes only in complete oracular sentences and in paragraphs rampant with parallelism.

In the *Planet of the Apes* film series, for example, there are many, many instances of effective dialogue which is not naturally spoken—an aesthetic distortion which shall be discussed at length later in this chapter. However, in the same films it is also not unusual to find sections of dialogue which are rendered "straight" and which are pretentious in their portentous phrasings, their thinly disguised spelling-outs and explanations which supply too much information and interpretation. Michael Wilson's screenplay of the first film, *Planet of the Apes* (Franklin Schaffner, 1968), contains this "normal" conversation between Taylor, the astronaut time traveller (Charlton Heston) and Dr. Zaius, the senior scientist orangutan (Maurice Evans), a conversation which appeared more or less intact on the screen:

Taylor: From the first, I've terrified you, Doctor. And in spite of every sign that I'm an intelligent being who means no harm, you continue to hate and fear me. Why?

Zaius:
Because you are a man. And you were right—I have always known about man. From the evidence, I believe his wisdom must walk hand in hand with his idiocy. His emotions must rule his brain. He must be a warlike animal who gives battle to everything around him—even himself.[15]

And the weight and insistance of the following dialogue spoken by the ape General Ursus in Paul Dehn's screenplay for *Beneath the Planet of the Apes* (Ted Post, 1970) certainly scotches the satiric possibilities of the material.

Gen. Ursus:
I do not say that all Humans are evil simply because their skin is white. But our Lawgiver tells us that never will they have the Ape's divine faculty for distinguishing between Evil and Good. Their eyes are animal, their smell the smell of the dead flesh they eat. Had they been allowed to live and breed among us unchecked, they would have overwhelmed us. And the concept of Ape Power would have become meaningless; and our high and splendid culture—would have wasted away and our civilization would have been ravaged and destroyed.[16]

Planet of the Apes (Franklin Schaffner, 1968). Astronaut Taylor and Dr. Zaius in serious conversation. "Straight" dialogue is often portentously phrased and overly explanatory or didactic. (20th Century Fox)

Conquest of the Planet of the Apes (J. Lee Thompson, 1972). **Heightening the racial themes of its predecessors, the film was rarely satiric. It was, with great seriousness, full of aphoristic language: "Evolution before revolution." (20th Century Fox)**

In Dehn's last *Apes* screenplay *Conquest of the Planet of the Apes* (J. Lee Thompson, 1972), which continues the racial themes of the earlier films with more insistence, the following "straight" and "typical" interchange occurs. Caesar, the chimpanzee rebel and savior (Roddy McDowall) is discussing the oppression and servitude of his fellow chimps and comparing it to the glorified servitude to the state by which the black MacDonald (Hari Rhodes) has been bound, and against which he is now considering rebellion.

Caesar: Which are you fighting? The cruelty or the captivity?

MacDonald: First things first, Mr. Caesar. Evolution before revolution. Until there's kindness, there won't be freedom.

Caesar: Some say until there's freedom, there won't be kindness. Some say there won't be freedom, until there's power.[17]

This last example typifies the sound of purportedly "significant" dialogue in the SF film. It contains the alliteration ("cruelty or captivity") which perhaps signals the listener that literature—something worthy of being written down—is being spoken. It has not only an aphorism ("evolution before revolution"), but also the literary playfulness which shifts words and meanings while retaining similar structure and rhythm (the freedom/kindness lines).

The *Apes* series' dialogue cited is a big-budget, example of what seems to be a more frequent occurrence in the low-budget SF film—strained seriousness, talkiness, literariness (we hear the words as if they were written down rather than spoken aloud). It is, after all, logical that the low-budget films, deprived of special effects and consequently grand flamboyant images, would try to locate their "science fiction-ness" in the spoken word. A small image seems to command big talk (the obverse example of the same kind of tension discussed earlier which exists between the wondrous image and reductive dialogue). Those big-budget exceptions to this general rule seem to arise less out of aesthetic necessity than a self-important sense of purpose: an awkward and self-conscious desire to use the didactic possibilities of science fiction combined with a misguided compulsion (based on an assumption of audience stupidity) to make the visually or intellectually obvious perfectly clear. Thus, even in so visually lush a film as *Zardoz* (John·Boorman, 1974), embarrassments of dialogue may still occur, as when a character portentously states: "The gun is good, but the penis is evil."

The incidence of inflated dialogue, however, is much higher in the low-

Zardoz **(John Boorman, 1974). Even so visually lush a film may have overbown and pretentious dialogue: "The gun is good, but the penis is evil."**

budget, visually spare SF film than in the lavish SF production. Obviously, when in doubt about dialogue, when sceptical of spoken polemic, the SF filmmaker with lots of money can rely on his visuals. Highly successful SF film is marked, in fact, by its paucity of dialogue rather than its poverty of language or its flights into poetry. There are only forty-three minutes of dialogue in *2001: A Space Odyssey,* a film 138 minutes long.[18] Much of *Silent Running* (Douglas Trumbull, 1972) is silence itself; the film's visuals evoke, call for silence much as did the images in the earlier *Robinson Crusoe on Mars* (Byron Haskin, 1964). While it is a fact that many low-budget films availed themselves of similarly isolated characters bereft of companionship, characters foraging through a deserted metropolis where they didn't have to say a word to anyone, the images (as discussed in the previous chapter) in such postcatastrophe films were startling and wondrous and their visual power could be depended upon. Confined, however, to more conventional settings, the low-budget film was not able to rely on the power and novelty of its images and confidently lapse into silence. Therefore, those low-budget SF films which attempted to do something beyond formula dialogue (scientific jargon, bland romance, "To hell with radiation, let's go," [19] adventurousness) tend to be talky and literary, tend toward profoundly grammatical dialogue. Nowhere is this more evident than in an ambitious but cramped low-budget film whose reach far exceeded its grasp, *Creation of the Humanoids* (Wesley E. Barry, 1962).

Creation of the Humanoids has the most limited and unprovocative sets one can think of: an apartment living room, halls of various sizes, a restaurant. In contrast, Jay Simms' dialogue, often quite witty, is dense and quotable—so much so that watching the film is an experience akin to reading rather than to viewing. It is almost as if the poverty of the image had been decided upon—chosen—in order to leave the screen image purposefully bare, static, and dull so that the content and configurations of the dialogue could be easily apprehended. The film is, finally, located in its stilted (as spoken) dialogue. The lines often look quite good on the printed page, but aloud they slow down pace and rhythm to a crawl, a monotone composed of short complete sentences of approximately equal length spoken by human voices which fall with each period and rise with the beginning of each new sentence. The following is a sampling of the kind of dialogue which attempts to sound "science fiction-y" and profound to make up for the impoverished image it accompanies:

"Mankind is a state of mind. Man is no more nor less than he thinks himself to be."

* * *

The animal develops a brain and the brain destroys the animal."

* * *

"I'm circuited to be logical but not to offend. This sometimes presents an insoluble problem."

* * *

"We fall in love when we see some part of ourselves reflected in another person."

* * *

"A man may have his leg amputated. Is his soul decreased?" "Then I have a soul?" No. Only the memory which includes the faith that there is a soul." [20]

The stilted, stiff sound and cadence of such sentences indicate the problems of dialogue in the majority of SF films, low budget or big budget. Certain critical questions are raised nearly every time a character opens his mouth to speak seriously. For example, is stiffness an inherent quality of what is spoken in seriousness and not couched in specific scientific jargon which needs only to be taken on its own terms. Is such stilted speech purposefully employed—if not all that effectively—to create a sense of something alien and, perhaps, futuristic? Is it because we, ourselves, don't speak constantly in complete sentences in common parlance that the characters in such films do? Is banal language and reductive jargon intended evidence of future dehumanization, de-emotionalization, or is it evident of a lack in the screenwriter's imagination? Is stilted speech and aphoristic rhythm an imagined quality of superior men in the future or a literary pretension of the screenwriter in the present? Obviously, if a film provokes the uncertainty reflected by these questions, the dialogue and the movie have a problem. This problem is echoed by what Parker Tyler has to say about science fiction which, perhaps, is twice as true of the SF film than it is of SF literature: ". . . the sad thing about science fiction . . . is that it has not developed a method in film or on the printed page to distinguish convincingly between *de*humanization and *super*humanization without landing back (thud and bump) with the grand old sentimental clichés that have always worked with juvenile adults and adult juveniles." [21]

The Transformation of Spoken Language

Certainly, even some of the most minor and unoriginal SF films have evidenced an awareness of the clichés attached to the dialogue of the genre. In an otherwise most traditional space adventure film *The Angry Red Planet* (Ib Melchior, 1960), a spaceship lands on Mars for the first time. Aboard, as a member of the crew, is Sam, a character who provides comic relief (cf. the similar characters and function of astronaut Dick Wesson in

Forbidden Planet (Fred Wilcox, 1956). Often a comic character—like Cook Earl Holliman—can illustrate the genre's reflexive awareness of its own inadequate clichés. (Metro-Goldwyn-Mayer)

Destination Moon and cook Earl Holliman in *Forbidden Planet*). Sam is genuinely funny in his rueful awareness of the conventional inadequacy of SF language. "Well," he says to his fellow crew members, "Shall we go out and claim the planet in the name of Brooklyn?" This line apologetically, self-consciously, and humorously echoes not only Penelope Houston's earlier cited criticism of the genre's "Gee! We're here!" comic strip dialogue, but also the deadly serious and sentimental pomposity of the line uttered by the spaceship commander (Warner Anderson) in the seminal *Destination Moon:* "By the grace of God and in the name of the United States of America, I take possession of this planet!"

Sam's shrewd self-awareness in *The Angry Red Planet* was, unfortunately, an isolated incident. He became cute and wisecracky and the film relied heavily on lines not meant to be comic at all: "We're all afraid of the unknown." But what is interesting about Sam's single lapse into self-consciousness is that it demonstrates that humor, parody, and satire can transform SF dialogue into a highly *adequate* response to unconventional situations without transforming the language and the words at all. If the form (humor, parody, satire) allows that the dialogue *is* ridiculous, than that dialogue can function comically on purpose instead of comically by accident. The dialogue can remain conventional in a comic climate or it can be flattened and blunted into an exaggerated blandness for the purpose of parody and satire. Jargon, banality, pomposity, all can be made to function as self-conscious *alternatives* to jargon, banality, and pomposity.

Humor, Parody, and Satire

Unlike SF literature, there have been few instances of SF comedy on the screen. Although there are many films which use science fiction satirically, and there are a few parodies of the genre and numerous comic scenes within otherwise serious films, the incidence of gentle comedy—comedy whose goal as defined by its premises and its dialogue is amusement rather than Swiftian instruction—is relatively rare. There are only a handful of films which gently fool with SF elements in a sustained and self-contained comic climate. (For various reasons, Americans have tended to regard anything scientific quite seriously, a fact which perhaps helps explain our penchant for satire.) *The Twonky* (Arch Obler, 1953), was one such charming comedy based appropriately on a short story by Henry Kuttner, an SF writer whose forte was humor. The film's premise centered around a television set possessed by a spirit from the future who proceeded to run its owner's (Hans Conreid) life. *The Atomic Kid* (Leslie H. Martinson, 1954), on the other hand, took genre elements like a radioactive human mutation, mixed in spies, and starred Mickey Rooney and Robert Strauss to only a fair comic effect, reminiscent of Abbot and Costello and the Three Stooges films which could as easily play out their plots and crack their verbal jokes in haunted castles, Switzerland, or Venusian jungles.[22] And, surely, one of the pleasantest SF comedies ever made was the Walt Disney production, *The Absent-Minded Professor* (Robert Stevenson, 1961)—a film which presented the world with antigravitational "flubber" and gave Fred MacMurray a part to which he was finally suited.

162

Have Rocket, Will Travel (David Lowell Rich, 1959). The Three Stooges could as easily play out their plots and crack their jokes in haunted castles, Switzerland, or Venusian jungles. (Columbia)

The Absent-Minded Professor (Robert Stevenson, 1961). In a publicity still, an Air Force jet is juxtaposed with a "flubber-activated" Model T. A rare instance of SF comedy. (Walt Disney/Buena Vista)

There are only a handful of such SF films which are amusing without being vicious or condescending to their subject matter. And there is, perhaps, only one SF film of recent vintage which can truly be called a "gentle" comedy.* The film (misunderstood and roasted by critics seeking parody and satire) is *Doc Savage* (Michael Anderson, 1975), and it brings to the screen the hero of Kenneth Robeson's series of pulp novels about the

Doc Savage (Michael Anderson, 1975). Doc Savage, the Man of Bronze, takes himself and his mission seriously in this SF comedy. (Warner Brothers)

---

* Now *Star Wars* can be added to the small list of SF films which established a primarily comic climate and which are humorous rather than satiric.

"Man of Bronze." The most satiric moment of this film could hardly be called stringent: when Doc smiles in close-up, a point of light sparkles like a rhinestone in one of his eyes. The film otherwise takes its hero straight (and its villains, too); the characters are funny in terms of *their* world and context, not ours. Thus, Doc can convince the heroine (and even those of us wordly wise in the audience) that his lack of response to her verbal and chastely physical protestations of love is a necessary sacrifice to the preservation of the world's well-being. Our laughter at the scene is not directed at the characters, but at our past comic-book experience, our lost innocence and belief in the heroicness of heroes. The film (produced and co-written by SF veteran George Pal) is amusing without being cruel to its characters and without suggesting a sneering omniscience behind the camera.

Science fiction parody is also rarely seen on the screen in any sustained form. The problems of aping conventions and dialogue which themselves often border on the ridiculous in their straight and serious forms of presentation seem insurmountable and peculiarly attached to science fiction. Horror films have been parodied successfully from the genre's beginnings; contemporary parodies that come to mind are Roman Polanski's *The Fearless Vampire Killers* (1967), and Mel Brooks' *Young Frankenstein* (1975). Gangster films have had their conventions, dialogue, and iconography mimicked to humorous excess from *Brother Orchid* (Lloyd Bacon, 1940), to *Some Like It Hot* (Billy Wilder, 1959), and beyond. And Westerns have been the most vulnerable targets for parody; *Cat Ballou* (Eliot Silverstein, 1965), *Support Your Local Sheriff* (Burt Kennedy, 1969), and *Blazing Saddles* (Mel Brooks, 1974), are only three examples chosen from many. The SF film, however, has seemed to attract few filmmakers interested in parodying the genre's form, conventions and dialogue. Perhaps the reason is, as previously mentioned, the tightrope of credibility which science fiction walks in its undistorted state, a state already strained by its very seriousness and solemnity. Perhaps, as well, the attractions of using science fiction for satiric purpose are too great for a comic bent of mind to stop short at parody. At any rate, there are few SF parodies on the screen: *The Monitors* (Jack Shea, 1969), which made fun of SF plots, robots, future societies; *Flesh Gordon* (Howard Ziehm & Michael Benveniste, 1972),[23] which was a skin flick hilariously molded around the Flash Gordon serials, and fully and lovingly aware of genre conventions from special effects to dialogue; and *Dark Star* (John Carpenter, 1974), a film which fully utilizes a broad range of generic elements for comic effect (space exploration, monsters, dialogue, conventional relationships between characters, technology, and special effects) in what its director has called *"Waiting for Godot* in space."[24] The marvelous and funny Woody Allen is responsible for two other attempts at SF parody, one as successful a genre parody as

165

Flesh Gordon (Howard Ziehm & Michael Beneviste, 1972). A skin-flick hilariously molded around the Flash Gordon serials. A true SF parody. (Mammoth)

Dark Star (John Carpenter, 1974). An SF parody that its director has called *"Waiting for Godot* in space." (Bryanston Pictures)

either *Flesh Gordon* or *Dark Star*, and the other less dependent on the genre for its humor than on the cultural, political, and religious habits of its viewers.

Although it is only the final segment of Allen's episodic *Everything You Always Wanted to Know About Sex* (1972), the self-contained dramatization of a male body *in coitus* struggling to sustain an erection and achieve emission is a marvelous and telling parody of science fiction. In the film's climactic episode, "What Happens During Ejaculation," Allen uses the firing of a rocket as a metaphor for the ejaculation of a sperm (played by a sceptical and reluctant sperm-paratrooper Allen who says, "You hear rumors about this pill these women take"). A great deal of the humor arises from the use of SF convention, dialogue and technical jargon; "the body's vital organs are operated by white-overalled technicians at flashing electronic consoles." [25] What is so consummate (no pun intended) about the parody is the inherent recognition it has of the surrogate sexuality of the concentrated effort and tension and release of shooting rockets into space, "getting one's rockets off," so to speak. In a complimentary "serious" scene in *Marooned,* as the rocket lifts off, all the technicians in the NASA control room stand at their consoles, look at the big TV screen, and chant "Go! Go! Go!" in ascending and rhythmic crescendo. The connection between the basic asceticism of male characters in science fiction in their relationships with women, and their constant orgasmic release in a giant public and communal effort which transcends the earthbound corporality of flesh, is made a central, if underlying, idea in Allen's film which finally comments

167

on the SF film as much as it does on sexuality. Unfortunately, Allen's feature length SF parody *Sleeper* (1973) is somewhat less successful in utilizing the genre as the source of its humor than *Everything You Always Wanted to Know About Sex,* although the film is quite successful on other grounds. *Sleeper's* futuristic setting allows Allen to use the jump in time to make jokes about and create gags around current issues and concerns, most of which are dependent upon the characters' inaccurate identification or placement of various artifacts or pictures of people with which we, the audience, are familiar; history in the future tells Allen that the old civilization was destroyed "over 100 years ago, when a man named Albert Shanker got his hands on a nuclear warhead," and that "Norman Mailer donated his ego to the Harvard Medical School." Allen, as the main character thrust

Sleeper (Woody Allen, 1973). The futuristic setting allows Allen jokes about current issues and concerns. (United Artists)

into the future, confidently misidentifies and muddles the material goods and heroes of his *own* culture in a demonstration of our grab bag absorption of stimuli around us in our own time: he remembers Charles de Gaulle as "a famous television chef." (The premise is set up when in the year 2173, Allen is awakened after 200 years from his cryogenic bed looking rather like a baked potato in tin foil.) At any rate, there is little attempt in the film to deal with the genre itself as the primary *subject* of the parody; its SF elements are strewn through the movie indiscriminately and generally used for gag value, for one-line or one-routine jokes which are funny but which don't fully reflect on the genre (although there is a wonderfully funny scene in which a futuristic kitchen appliance malfunctions and an instant pudding becomes a giant, blob-like, and hostile mass which must be beaten into submission with a broom). *In Everything You Always Wanted to Know About Sex,* in contrast, the SF film was as much a *subject* of the parody as was sex.

Obviously, spoken dialogue is only one element in the creation of SF comedy, parody, and satire. But what concerns us here is the transformation of ordinary and conventional SF dialogue by the manner in which it is treated into something other than its banal and conventional self. The ridiculousness of context, the garnering of too many conventional SF elements

Invasion of the Saucer Men (Edward L. Cahn, 1957). Invaders from outer space in a teen-oriented "C" movie, a classification of films now considered "camp." (American International)

169

into one film to purposefully strain and finally overload credibility, change conventional dialogue in such low-budget and teen-oriented "C" pictures as *Invasion of the Saucer Men* (Edward L. Cahn, 1957), and *Invasion of the Star Creatures* (Bruno VeSota, 1961). In the former film, Steven Scheuer notes in his guide to films on TV: "Cool kids spot some invaders from outer space. Script kids the horror films."[26] The film uses a lovers' lane as the aliens' landing site. And the "saucermen" have contrived the most grotesquely funny way of killing their victims—they inject alcohol into their veins to bring on a fatal case of the DTs. In the latter movie, "a couple of soldiers discover plant-like creatures who are in control of a group of sexy Amazons. The plot goes haywire from here."[27] In these films the dialogue is transformed by ridiculous premises and by a rather adolescent self-consciousness which results in "cute" jokes, mild pokes at scientific talk and the repetition of classic *SF cum horror* film lines about tampering with the unknown. These last low-budget film excursions into questionable humor are obviously a great deal less significant than they are numerous, appearing endlessly and repetitiously in their various guises on Saturday afternoon television (programming for the family known to be not at home).

The form of SF film in which ordinary dialogue is transformed most pointedly, successfully, and significantly is not comedy, parody, or senseless and undirected spoof. It is satire, a form of humor and instruction which has a natural affinity for the utopian or dystopian worlds of science fiction—literature and film. Through extrapolation, through the creation of a time and/or place not present, science fiction allows the distance necessary for satire to function. We, as viewers of film, for example, can be shown ourselves in the present, in the here and now, with our cultural, political, and social eccentricities, manias, and phobias, our appalling idiocies—only we are shown ourselves *now* under the thin guise of *then* or *when*. Ordinary dialogue spoken by ordinary people in an extraordinary setting, place, or situation points out either the extraordinary inadequacy or the extraordinary inappropriateness of language, both finally dangerous in their reduction of the human and humanistic. The displacement which is an inherent quality of the genre offers the filmmaker a ready-made "otherness" in his point-of-view, a vantage point from which to look at humanity from a great spatial and/or temporal distance and to find its ordinariness not only extraordinary, but also horrifying. Thus, Stanley Kauffman can aptly observe that it seems as if *Dr. Strangelove: or How I Learned to Stop Worrying and Love the Bomb* (Stanley Kubrick, 1964), "has been made, quintessentially, from the viewpoint of another race on another planet or in another universe, observing how mankind, its reflexes scored in its nervous system and its mind entangled in orthodoxies, insisted on destroying itself."[28]

Dr. Strangelove, a black comedy about a nuclear crisis fatally initiated by

Dr. Strangelove: or How I Learned to Stop Worrying and Love the Bomb
(Stanley Kubrick, 1964). A film located as much in its language as in its
imagery. Note the juxtaposition of action and printed word, the terrible
irony the shot communicates. (Columbia)

a paranoid general, is certainly one of the first American films to openly
flaunt the scientific and military and political limitations of language. It is
one of the first American films to juxtapose the serious smallness of genre
movie dialogue and "real" institutional conversation with the ironic
grandeur of an annihilation which language cannot either prevent or contain. The word—created by the military, scientific, and political minds of
our time—is not only absurd and comic; in *Dr. Strangelove* it is revealed
in all its reductive and therefore destructive insanity. All the bizarre sur-
realism of irreconcilable language and event in *Dr. Strangelove* rejects
sanity and common sense, and it suggests that we not only have no freedom
from fear, but, more horribly, we have no freedom *to* fear, that "fear" itself
has been stripped from our vocabulary, replaced by words euphemistically
comforting and lethally irrelevant. *Dr. Strangelove* is an SF film which is
based on inadequate human response revealed in horrifying inappropriate
inhuman dialogue, and it is the first modern American SF film satire to use
openly, even brazenly, the mordancy of black humor then already apparent
in contemporary American literature (i.e., *Catch-22*). And, most interesting
in its relation to the literary concerns of the sixties, *Dr. Strangelove* is a film

which is located at least as much in its language as in its images; for despite the sophistication and occasional heaviness of its photographic content (the wit in the editing, the "black and white straight-on" Howard Hawks' look of the bomber scenes, the hysterical angles and Karl Freund lighting of General Jack D. Ripper, etc.), the film relies heavily on the verbal, on literary ironies created by the contrast between the way we humans speak about what we do and what we actually do. As Judith Crist observes: "For this is the way the world will end, in a welter of mechanical failures, human bloopers, jargon and gobbledygook." [29]

Thus, in *Strangelove,* General "Buck" Turgidson (George C. Scott) urges an all-out nuclear attack on the "Ruskies" in language so reductive and bloodless that it is simultaneously comic and horrific. "I'm not saying we wouldn't get our hair mussed. I am saying only ten to twenty million people killed, tops, depending on the breaks." Or: "It is necessary to choose between two admittedly regrettable but nevertheless distinguishable postwar environments: one where you've got twenty million people killed and the other where you've got one hundred and fifty million people killed." The U.S. President (Peter Sellers) breaks up a fight between a Russian diplomat and American general with a language able only to express the logic of madmen: "Gentlemen, you can't fight in here! This is the War Room!" And a list of items contained in the survival kits of a B-52 bomber crew, when read aloud in a regionally accented but unemotional monotone by the captain "King" Kong (Slim Pickens), creates a chain of relationships which are surreal and horrendous in their random incongruous couplings. The list, read aloud, "covers the whole range of human emotions, noble and vile, from the life-preserving aids to the lust-satisfying ones; it contains, among other things, a .45 pistol, ammunition, four days' emergency rations, one hundred dollars in rubles, nine packs of chewing gum, lipsticks, nylon stockings, and prophylactics." [30] General Jack D. Ripper (Sterling Hayden) creates a psychosis out of catch-phrases one finds in places like *The Readers' Digest* ("communist infiltration," "fluoridation of the water") with a type of rhetoric endemic to antivivisectionists and health-food freaks ("purity of essence," "precious bodily fluids"). And American morality filtered down to the ordinary soldier (G.I. Joe via Alfred Lord—"Ours is but to do or die"— Tennyson, and Korea) is totally unreasonable in its deference to rote learning and its lack of differentiation; soldier "Bat" Guano (Keenan Wynn), in the midst of terminal chaos, refuses to shoot a Coke machine in order to get change for a phone call which may save the world from atomic catastrophe. Indignantly, he responds to Group Captain Mandrake's (Peter Sellers) request: "That's private property!" Then, having obtained the change for Mandrake, in a resurgence of moral indignation Guano tells him as he enters a phone booth to telephone the White House, "Try any *preversions*

Dr. Strangelove: or How I Learned to Stop Worrying and Love the Bomb (Stanley Kubrick, 1964). Publicity still. Language is only able to express the logic of madmen. (Columbia)

in there, I'll blow your head off!" We are given in *Dr. Strangelove* a world which is "suffering a total disruption of communication. The chief area of communication that has broken down is, of course, in human sanity."[31] But that breakdown in sanity is revealed by the disparities between action and language, event and response; each lacks connection with the other, suffers from isolation in its own continuum. To borrow a conceit from Norman Kagan (who used it to describe the misapplication of patriotism in the film), the language of *Dr. Strangelove* is "misinterpreted and misapplied so many times in so many ways that it seems a sort of logical mistake, like a round square or four-corner triangle, or, even more, a short circuit of the nervous system, an intellectual epilepsy, meaningless and lethal." [32]

Equally flamboyant and broad as *Dr. Strangelove* but less controlled in its satiric thrust is *Wild in the Streets* (Barry Shear, 1968), a film fashioned by American International, a production company shrewdly and commercially attuned to the times and quick to exploit the topical. Focused around a youth revolution and government take-over, *Wild in the Streets* was "a film which combined SF with another of the studio's specialities, the 'teenage sex musical, in a one-off collage of sensuality, revolution and mad humour." [33] Unlike the single-minded indictment in *Dr. Strangelove*, *Wild in the Streets* takes pot shots at most everything: war, youth, old age, TV and the media, politics, etc. As Joseph Morgenstern says in a perceptive review of the film: "It is nothing substantial and everything urgent, and most of all it is an infinitely extensible shoe that fits white youth, Black Panthers, Red Guards, John Birchers, the poor, the disenfranchised, the powerless, anyone and any group cursed with want and doubly cursed with not knowing what to want." [34] The unselective satire in the film is seen by Patrick MacFadden as "one of the more swinish examples of the new paranoid style. In shoveling one more group into the snakepit for those you-love-to hate, it may have outdone itself." [35] The "new paranoid style" which informs *Wild in the Streets* springs—as did *Dr. Strangelove*—from an atmosphere in the sixties which affected drama, fiction, and film, a kind of sour and pessimistic misanthropy which found its expression in gallows jokes, in what has since come to be called black humor. Such humor can be savage and unsparing and it is most often intellectual, calling for the mind to appreciate its construct rather than trying to make the belly laugh. It depends on incongruence and the viewer's recognition of disparity (and thus assumes, even at its most heavy-handed, a certain amount of viewer intelligence). Thus, in *Wild in the Streets,* which traces pop singer Max Frost (Christopher Jones) in his rise to the Presidency of a youthocracy and the United States, there is much humor in the dialogue based on the irony created by incongruence. As a multimillionaire pop singer, Max is surrounded by, among others, "a Black Power drummer (author, the script says, of the best-selling *Aborigine Cookbook*)" and "a fifteen-year-old Yale law grad" [36] who speaks like both a precocious brat and an Ivy League prig. Shelley Winters, playing Max's abandoned-for-good-reason mother, sees her long gone son on TV and after checking his image against an old snapshot, chortles, "I'm a celebrity!" And a TV newscaster looks out from the screen and intones with the proper solemnity of crisis journalism, "Three matrons in Orange County have died of heart attacks from watching the riots on television." As Renata Adler notes:

The writing (by Robert Thom, on the basis of his own short story) if often marvelous. There are some monotonous, ringing banalities spoken by the young, but there are other lines: when the liberal senator (played with power-corrupt cool by Hal Holbrook) visits Miss Winters to complain that her son is paralyzing the country, she answers with the dignity of any up against the wall mama. "Senator," she says, in what might be a slogan for our times, "I'm sure my son has a very good reason for paralyzing the country." [37]

It is, however, in Stanley Kubrick's *2001: A Space Odyssey* that the transformation through incongruence of ordinary dialogue achieves its height. The incongruence between the quality of the dialogue and the events (seen in images) which provoke it is so vast as to produce irony, satire, and, at times, uneasiness. We are made constantly aware of the growing inadequacy and weakness of human speech—and, as a corollary, the probable underlying weakness and pallor of human emotions not up to finding or creating suitable verbal expression. As previously mentioned, there are only 43 minutes of dialogue in a film which is long enough to have built into itself an intermission. The paucity of dialogue creates an interesting effect; since characters speak so infrequently, when they do open their mouths it seems natural to expect something significant to come out, something saved up, something important or informative. The characters' silence creates a pregnant expectancy when their lips finally do part, but what is delivered is puny, weak, unfulfilling, stillborn. As Clive James points out in a fascinating piece on the film:

> ... there is more beauty to be seen but less ability to respond to it; all gains lose. Not only can verbal poetry not hope to compete with visual poetry in the film (a very sound cineaste position); the film is about a time when verbal poetry has actually ceased *trying* to compete. It is no longer a contest. Perhaps the process begins with specific selection of emotionless men for space, but Kubrick suggests that it soon becomes a general cultural change. [38]

In *2001* we have none of the comic strip broadness of *Dr. Strangelove*, no insistance on surreal incongruence. The satire is quieter and more ominous in its closeness to present reality, the way we do respond *now* with banality and jargon to the marvelous. The center of the most obvious satire aimed at language is Heywood R. Floyd (William Sylvester), the scientist/official who arrives at the orbiting space station with the pleasant but bored expression of a businessman making a biweekly trip to Kennedy International. The other characters (although they are hardly individualized enough to be called characters in a traditional sense) whose poverty of language is crucial to the film's irony are the two astronauts, Bowman (Keir Dullea) and Poole (Gary Lockwood). In an article entitled "The Comic Sense of

2001: A Space Odyssey (Stanley Kubrick, 1968). Heywood Floyd, the scientist/official who arrives at the orbiting space station with the pleasantly bored expression of a businessman. (Metro-Goldwyn-Mayer)

2001," F. A. Macklin focuses on the way language and scientific jargon function satirically and are brought to our attention transformed not by content, but by context.

When Floyd gives his remarks at the briefing the satire of the inept language fairly leaps out. It is trite and inarticulate. But it is not Kubrick's (or Clarke's) inadequacy; it is the characters' inarticulateness, their loss of language. A parade of meagre "well's" fills the air. Halvorsen, who introduces Floyd, starts out, "Well,..." He sticks his hands in his pockets. If this were done once, one might assume that it didn't matter. But this stance and feeble language are the imprint of the scene, the exposing of dullness.

If the audience hasn't recognized what Kubrick is exposing about language, he reemphasizes the pathetic quality on the craft when he has one man say, "That was an excellent speech you gave us, Heywood." "Certainly was," affirms a second man. The irony is explicit.

If one is aware of Floyd's and his compatriots' satiric demeanor, it is easy to recognize the similar identity of the two astronauts on the spaceship, *Discovery 1,* Frank Poole and David Bowman.... On TV there is their interview with a TV interviewer. "How is everything going?" Again language fails. Poole offers trite sanguinity. "Marvelous." Bowman is less enthusiastic. "We have no complaints." Then there is the labored production from Poole's family. His mother, who is a teacher, says "Frank, you're a big celebrity in the second grade." His father cries: "We wish you the very happiest of birthdays." They sing *Happy Birthday.* Frank lies limpish with his sun glasses, sunning himself under a sunlamp.[39]

Macklin goes on to point out that the irony is deepened by the human

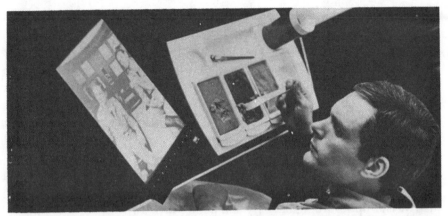

2001: A Space Odyssey (Stanley Kubrick, 1968). Astronaut Bowman watching himself in a TV interview. In a voice without texture or emotion, Bowman answers a question about their status: "We have no complaints." (Metro-Goldwyn-Mayer)

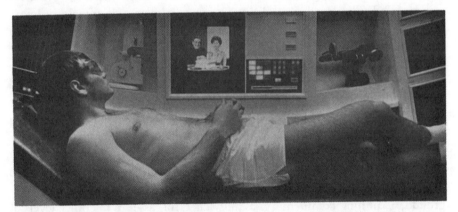

2001: A Space Odyssey (Stanley Kubrick, 1968). Another failure of language and emotion. Frank Poole's parents sing "Happy Birthday." (Metro-Goldwyn-Mayer)

qualities conferred on HAL, the 9000 computer which eventually malfunctions. HAL's voice is ripe and soft whereas Bowman's and Poole's have no texture. In comparison to the astronauts, creating the context which emphasizes the lacklustre and mechanical quality of human speech spoken by humans, HAL—in the first part of the flight—can almost be regarded as a chatterbox, a gossip, emotional.

In *2001*, whenever someone speaks we are consistently made aware of how our language—and, therefore, our emotions and thought patterns—have not kept up with either our technology or our experience. We no longer have the words, or the imagination, to describe our universe (let alone anyone else's). As Penelope Gilliatt notes: "The citizens of 2001 have forgotten how to joke and resist, just as they have forgotten how to chat, speculate, grow intimate, or interest one another. But otherwise everything is splendid. They lack the mind for acknowledging that they have managed to diminish outer space into the ultimate in humdrum, or for dealing with the fact that they are spent and insufficient, like the apes." [40] In *2001*, Kubrick has allowed ordinary speech to reveal itself in all its pathetic and comic limitations; by making us see the banal as banal, Kubrick has transformed the banal into the significant. Thus, ordinary language spoken by visible human characters is distanced for our inspection and, perhaps, our instruction. There is no need to change linguistic structures or to "invent" a new way of speaking; we end up regarding banality and jargon with awe.

Displaced Voices

Apart from satire, as well as in conjunction with it, there are other instances in SF film in which ordinary human dialogue may remain ordinary yet transcend itself and become new and different. Human dialogue spoken by nonhumans makes us regard the words from a nonhabitual stance; we listen freshly. The example which first comes to mind is, of course, the talking machine: the computer HAL in *2001,* or the "sexy" disembodied public address system voice in *The Andromeda Strain* which piques the sexual interest of one of the scientists and which is later reported to belong to a 63 year old lady in Omaha. Philip Strick mentions the talking mechanical policemen in *THX 1138* (George Lucas, 1971), "their heads glowing chromium, their voices glowing too, with mellow tones of reassurance." And Strick goes on to say of the film's omnipresent machinery: "In the background, a running commentary, blandly cheerful, assesses tolerance levels of men being 'conditioned', genially gives the statistics of the latest disaster, and answers a steady stream of calls for advice with the phrase 'What's wrong?', spoken as though nothing ever took more than a few seconds to put right." [41]

One remembers, too, how pride becomes a comic eccentricity of Robby the Robot in *Forbidden Planet* (Fred M. Wilcox, 1956); a human trait transposed to a nonhuman being and evidenced by human dialogue creates an incongruence to which we respond with wonder.* It is not surprising, then, that in *2001* "HAL is deliberately made into a repository of the old stock of human emotions so carefully drained out of his scientific minders.

---

* A variety of human traits (including the capacity for friendship) are conferred upon *Star Wars'* "See Threepio," a golden fussbudget of a robot, and "Artoo Detoo," who communicates in whistles and whirrs rather than in English but who still manages to convey a mischievous sense of humor and an inordinate amount of human cowardice.

Forbidden Planet (Fred Wilcox, 1956). Displacement of speech to machine creates an incongruence to which we respond with wonder. (Metro-Goldwyn-Mayer)

He keeps omniscient control, gives counsel, shows curiosity, awards praise. His voice suggests he exists to serve, but the certitude of his responses creates a suspicion that he intends to dominate. "Intends' is itself an emotive word in this context." [42] HAL's voice is even ambiguously suggestive enough to cause Joseph Morgenstern to describe the computer as carrying on "like

Star Wars (George Lucas, 1977). Displacement of speech to machine. C3P0 is a golden fuss-budget of a robot with an English accent. (20th Century Fox)

an injured party in a homosexual spat."[43] Another reviewer echoes by calling HAL "effetely histrionic."[44] Indeed, HAL's "death scene"—his dismantling by Bowman—is the most emotional in the film. It is even more disquieting in its effect on the viewer in contrast with Poole's human death which has left us relatively uninvolved, unaffected emotionally. As Walker says, "The scene induces deep discomfort among many who watch and listen to it. Indeed, it is the only one in the film to engage one's sympathies on behalf of a character. And the fact that the character consists of a bug-eyed lens, a few slabs of glass, and a dissociated voice is the best possible tribute to Kubrick's success in creating a mechanical artifact more 'human' than the humans."[45] This humanity arises out of the transposition of ordinary human speech and inflection (trivial, banal, jargon-y) to a machine. This anthropomorphism allows for human weakness and cliché to function exotically—as a sign of both the machine's possible "otherness" (its potential and fearsome autonomy) and its attractive and dependent vulnerability. Thus, what results is the "bitter-sweet quality" Macklin ascribes to HAL's "death."[46] The machine attempts to reason and wheedle and then to beg for its "life":

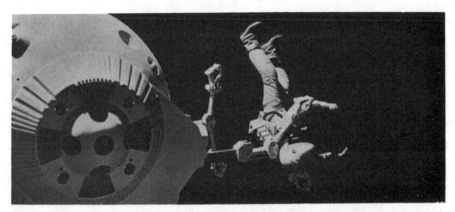

2001: A Space Odyssey (**Stanley Kubrick, 1968**). **Compared to HAL's death, Poole's human death is relatively uninvolving. The machine is more human than the human. (Metro-Goldwyn-Mayer)**

> "Look, Dave, I can see you're really upset. You should sit down calmly, take a stress pill, think things over. I know everything has not been quite right with me . . . I feel much better now, I really do. I know I've made some very poor decisions lately, but everything is back to normal."

And as Bowman starts to pull out the individual components of the memory bank, HAL's "brain cells":

> "Dave, stop. Will you, stop, Dave. Stop, Dave. Will you stop, Dave. I'm afraid, Dave. Dave, my mind is going. I can feel it . . . I can feel it. My mind is going. There is no question about it. I can feel it. I can feel it. I can feel it . . . I'm afraid.
>
> Good afternoon, gentlemen, I am a HAL-9000 computer. I became operational at the HAL plant in Urbana, Illinois, in 1992. My instructor, Mr. Langley, taught me to sing a song. It's called *'Daisy'*. . . . 'Daisy, Daisy, give me your answer true. I'm half crazy . . .'." [46]

And HAL's voice slows to a mechanical stop to be replaced by the cheerfully noncommittal voice of Hewood Floyd who mechanically explains the Jupiter's mission. Nothing HAL says is, in itself, remarkable. What is remarkable is that he says it. That human voice talking about feeling, its almost mystic presence unseen but heard, buried somewhere in the solid state memory units, contained, trapped—that voice and emotion move us. For a machine aspiring to or achieving humanity strikes us as incredibly poignant —a feeling generated, of course, by our own insular and limited moral and emotional imagination.

Computers and robots, however, are not the only nonhuman hosts for human speech. Animals, although as yet used less frequently, will do almost as well in putting distance between our language and ourselves. The most obvious example is the entire *Planet of the Apes* series. In an interview, Franklin Schaffner (director of the first film in the series) relates how 20th Century Fox was worried into making makeup tests "just to see if a monkey walked into a room where there was a man, and they started speaking a common language, whether anybody would pay attention to what they were saying." [47] Obviously, audiences paid attention. Human speech from the mouths of chimps, gorillas, and orangutans need not be any more remarkable in content to amaze us than the ordinary words also spoken by machinery. Abstracted from the human body, human speech (with all its emotional and intellectual content) sounds and, of course, looks different and comments upon itself and our relation to it. As Schaffner indicates about his film, *Planet of the Apes*, "Hopefully, it worked on the level that you were sitting and watching a simian society functioning, and it occurred to you, suddenly that you were in a hall of mirrors, looking at yourself." [48]

In *Escape from the Planet of the Apes* (Don Taylor, 1971), for example, the actions and dialogue of chimps Zira and Cornelius in a particular mon-

Planet of the Apes (**Franklin Schaffner, 1968**). **Displacement of speech to animals. (20th Century Fox)**

182

tage sequence are comic and interesting only because chimps are acting and responding like humans to human situations. Replaced by humans, the sequence would have no interest, no meaning, no irony. The two chimps have travelled backwards in time from 3955 to 1973, escaping the Earth's destruction in their own time. After they reveal they can talk, there is a montage sequence which shows them, world celebrities, coming to terms with culture in the United States. They are guests of the Beverly Wilshire Hotel in Los Angeles and their suite is decorated with cellophane-wrapped gift baskets of fruit and flowers. We see them outfitted in Earth clothing (briefly modeling the garments in a way somewhat reminiscent of fashion interludes in films of the thirties and forties). Zira takes a bubble bath. She is asked to speak at the Bay Area Women's Club about women's liberation. "A marriage bed is meant for two," she says. "But every damn morning, it's the woman who has to make it. We have heads as well as hands. I call on man to let us use them." [49] Cornelius is taken to a prizefight and deems it "beastly" in an ironically more-human-than-human response. We are told by newscasters that both were present to dedicate a new jungle ride at Disneyland. And the montage ends when Zira visits the Museum of Natural History, turns a corner to face a huge stuffed gorilla, and faints. In response to the assumption that she fainted from shock at the unexpected and emotionally upsetting confrontation with one of her own kind, stuffed, she responds: "Shock, my foot. I'm pregnant." The charm and humor of the entire sequence lies in its ability to distance us from our own culture, but in a gentle enough fashion for us to laugh at ourselves in comparative comfort, to admire Zira's feisty personality, so full of pepper, so . . . human!

Another film which puts human speech into an animal body is *The Day of the Dolphin* (Mike Nichols, 1974). Unfortunately, the film leaves its quiet SF mooring and sails off into a sea of cliché and melodrama specifically associated with genres other than science fiction: flamboyant but predictable spy and assassin stuff which allies the movie more closely with James Bond films than with the concerns of science fiction. The fascinating premises upon which the film rests and their treatment in the beginning seem reduced halfway through the movie to the wrong kind of questions. We find that the film asks "Can one dolphin prevent the other dolphin from planting a bomb on the underside of the President of the United States' yacht?" The more interesting questions that the film asks at its beginning, questions which are indeed the province of science fiction (i.e., "Can man teach dolphins to talk and communicate with man? What is the affinity between man and dolphin, two intelligent creatures whose environments are so essentially foreign to each other?"), those questions are dropped. Despite its failure to explore its own possibilities, *The Day*

Planet of the Apes (Franklin Schaffner, 1968). Zira, the chimp-heroine, who later stands up for women's rights in *Escape from the Planet of the Apes*. It's not so much what she says but that she—a chimp—says it. (20th Century Fox)

of the Dolphin has moments of grandeur, moments when the viewer responds with awe to wondrous images which suggest alternative ways of looking at the world: George C. Scott as scientist in what amounts to a sexual water ballet between human male and female dolphin. As well there are moments in which the sound of human dialogue coming from

184

an animal's mouth moves us emotionally to a great degree. Both dolphins, Fa and Ba, speak only on the most rudimentary level. Their limited vocabulary and simple sentence structure (when they do speak in sentences—which is seldom) is calculated in its simplicity, its resemblance to the verbal progress of human children, its evocation, therefore, of total and poignant innocence. Unlike the talking primates in the *Planet of the Apes* series, the dolphins function neither comically nor satirically. We regard them in worried earnest; the viewer cares about their innocence and believes in their voices. Their sound is a shrewd amalgam of thin reediness (all scrawny-legged child with skinned knees) and slightly abrasive bird cry. The resultant effect is to appeal to our aural memory of both the known and vulnerable and of the alien; we are reminded of human children and birds which, like dolphins, live in an environment essentially alien to humans although visible and of this Earth.

What is most interesting about *The Day of the Dolphin* in terms of the SF film is not the particular movie itself, but the possibilities it suggests for the future. What the film proves—almost in spite of itself—is that human speech coming from the mouths of animals need not be funny. The film medium can allow for the same credibility which SF literature has long enjoyed. And "talking" animals on the screen need not function only satirically to be believed. Obviously, a speaking dolphin does not remind us of the cartoon characters we watched as children; it is therefore easier to accept the sound and image of a talking dolphin without concrete preconceptions based on our past Disney experiences. A talking dog, however, might be much more difficult for us to accept seriously, bred as we all are on Disney's Pluto, Lady, or Scamp. Our ingrown memories of anthropomorphic cartoon canines may be too involved with having seen ridiculous imitations of human action and gesture. (One can imagine the artist moving his mouth in the mirror in pain and surprise so that Pluto can respond humanly to a cartoon hurt.) On the other hand, the dolphins are kept nonanthropomorphic to a large degree; they do not move their snouts (or muzzles or whatever it is dolphins have) to conform to the movements of human lips. And they are, in their dolphin-ness, less human and more credible. It would be nice to think that the SF film could sustain serious animal characters as does SF literature, that, for example, a successful and moving film could be made with material of the kind treated by Clifford D. Simak in *City* in which dogs *do* talk seriously, sitting around a fire telling only half-believed legends about when there were such things as men. One such attempt has been made with partial success in *A Boy and his Dog* (L. Q. Jones, 1975). Based on a novella by SF writer Harlan Ellison, the film creates a major canine character who—despite his misogyny—is quite as winning as he is convincing.

Thus far, we have been dealing with the transformation of ordinary dialogue into something alien and new through distancing—a dramatic device which moves us to a fresh inspection of the familiar. Parody and satire distance us from our language by emphasizing its discrepancies; films with machine or animal "characters" distance us from our language through its displacement. Most frequently, however, the transformation of ordinary dialogue in the SF film is dependent upon neither discrepancy nor displacement. It is, instead, dependent upon quite the opposite: a ritual enactment of familiar and appropriate rhetoric in an expected and completely circumscribed and delimited setting.

The ritual dialogue to which I am referring occurs throughout SF cinema in radio broadcasts, news telecasts, public speeches, and in scientific slide and/or documentary presentations within the film. A lack of emotion in the voice or color in the rhetoric can be accepted as conventional behavior on the part of "objective" reporters. A newscaster's urgency can be seen as simultaneously real and synthetic. We watch public figures speak a special unprivate language which is both realistic in its broad familiarity

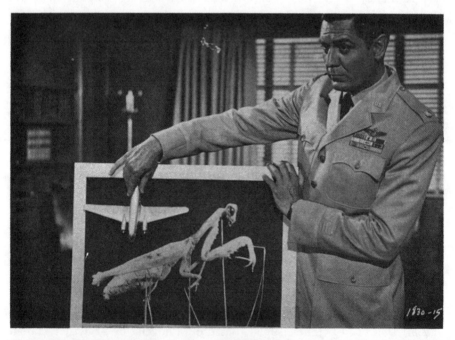

The Deadly Mantis (Nathan Juran, 1957). Dialogue as ritual: the scientific presentation, an instance of speech framed by the context of a well-defined public event. (Universal)

and yet leaves room for the assumption that the character can speak otherwise if he chooses—in other situations. Thus, ritual dialogue is not mocked for its inadequacy, its inappropriateness, or its banal and repetitive qualities. In the SF film, it can be seen as having a function and place in the film's social order which, once that dialogue is understood to be limited, is necessary and beneficial to the culture which is created by man in a crowded and urban environment. After all, a speech is a speech—and a newscast a newscast. Neither is an ordinary instance of common human interchange and yet each in our culture is common and, therefore, ordinary. Neither offers us pleasure by virtue of its novelty or originality of form or rarity of incidence. Rather, we are comforted and soothed by their sameness, by their common unnaturalness, by their containedness. What we respond to with perpetual wonder of a comfortable kind is speech *framed*—by a podium and a microphone, by a TV camera, the radio, by maps or slide chains, by flashbulbs, by the rectangle of the TV console itself. Most of us viewers are still technologically naive enough to appreciate the magic of media. In most SF films the newscast serves a dual function, one practical and the other almost mystical. Obviously, in the traditional SF film, the news montage of a single newscast or of broadcasting personalities from around the world serves to compress the film's narrative in terms of time and space, to supply necessary narrative information economically, and to act as a cinematic conjunction between scenes of dramatic intensity. As well as serving this practical function, the news montage also seems to act simultaneously as a ritual affirmation of the global community (there is a white magic in that electronic unity caused by catastrophe), and as an almost sinister reminder of the literal and figurative power of the media (a black magic capable of electronically creating and shaping public opinion and/or hysteria).

Used positively or negatively (and often both ways in a single film), the media plays an important role in the SF genre. Its use is a convention, a familiar signpost that the film is of the world, of and about society, and masses of people. One does not see newscasts in even contemporary horror films, for the concern of the horror film is moral, its sphere is small, its characters isolated in their mortal struggle which is of an ultimately private nature.

There is, however, one exception that comes to mind and which loosely pretends a connection with science fiction. *Night of the Living Dead* (George Romero, 1968), is a black comedy, a moral fable in which all virtue is singled out and rewarded with death. The film is really a horror film, based on an extremely flimsy and cursorily dealt with SF premise: radioactive material brought back to Earth by a space vehicle of some kind converts the recent dead into flesh-craving ghouls who roam the

Night of the Living Dead (George Romero, 1968). A horror film based on a flimsy SF premise, the movie grimly reverses the usual function of radio and TV in SF films. (Continental)

isolated countryside in groups, scavenging for human food. The ghouls lay siege to a farmhouse in which a disparate group of people have gathered, their only source of information at first a radio and then a repaired television set. The prominence and treatment of the TV set in *Night of the Living Dead* is fascinatingly apropos here and deserves some consideration even though the film is more a horror than SF film, for the TV set's treatment mocks the prevalent function of the media in most traditional SF films and therefore illuminates it.

In a deadly quiet and parodic reversal of radio and TV appearances in traditional SF films, the radio and TV in this film demonstrate a total lack of connection with the characters in peril. Yet, throughout the entire film—despite the TV's bad advice, its lack of relevance to the situation and characters we, as viewers, are involved with—the film's characters, in traditional SF fashion, believe implicitly what the radio and TV tell them. A young husband tells his wife they must leave the shelter of the farmhouse for the "protection center" in Willard "because the TV said so"; following such advice leads to their deaths. The deciding factor in a violent argument concerning the superior shelter and safety of either the basement or the main floor of the farmhouse is that the TV set is upstairs. The repair of the set is treated with relief, as if it were an event equivalent to rescue itself. Interestingly, ironically, despite the characters' extreme dependence on it, the TV is visually emphasized as something from a world other than the one in which the characters are fighting for their lives. Apart from the content of the newscasts, the way in which the set itself is photographed is drastically at odds with the cinematography of the rest of the film. It is shot straight on, centered symmetrically in the screen, while everything else in the film is viewed from either grotesque or uncomfortable angles. And, although the entire action of the film only occurs one night from dusk to dawn and over a small localized geographic area, the exterior news scenes on the telecasts seem shot in daylight while the action we watch at the farmhouse occurs in darkest night. (It's certainly possible, considering the low budget of the film, that this discrepancy in continuity was entirely accidental, yet it enhances the vast gap between experience raw and experience framed and transformed by the media.)

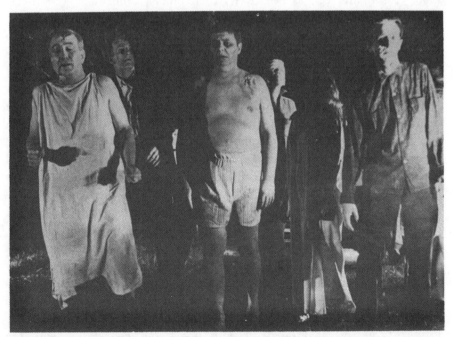

Night of the Living Dead (George Romero, 1968). **Mordant fun is made of the media's uselessness, inappropriateness, and capacity for exploitation. (Continental)**

The content of the telecasts are essentially traditional to SF film: information and coverage of action elsewhere. Yet here, mordant fun is made of the telecasts' uselessness, their inappropriateness, their capacity for exploitation under the guise of moral and noble motives. A radio newscaster, in bulletin-fashion and with an apparent professional immunity to horror, intones with just the barest edge of EXTRA enjoyment to his voice: "These ghouls are eating flesh! Repeat. They are eating flesh!" (As if one might miss the message the first time.) And the telecasters are calm in their sterile studio settings as they talk about atrocities like they talk about the weather, "protection center" locations superimposed on the bottom of the screen like temperatures around the country. We see TV coverage ("filmed reports") of senators and public officials hustling to and fro in Washington, D.C., in a flurry of ineffectuality, men taking immense pride in their loss of sleep, overcaffeinated nerves, and ability to organize meetings. A local sheriff (who turns up later to kill, in a grossly stupid act, the film's nominal hero, the last survivor of the night in the farmhouse) is televised with a mob of volunteer vigilantes eager to kill ghouls; "Kill the brain and you kill the ghoul," he says complacently, secure in the rhythms of his own slogan. In direct contrast to the treatment of the media in the most traditional SF films, the radio and TV in *Night of the Living Dead* are seen as negatively, even fatally, influential. The magic of the media is, indeed, black. For the public is totally credulous and trusting while the media is electronic, apathetic, and finally immune to private experience. (In a way, private experience is at the crux of the horror film and, therefore, it is appropriate that as a horror film *Night of the Living Dead* should reject the publicness of the media as irrelevant.)

The traditional SF film, on the other hand, pictures the media as more than responsible and committed to good, *public* good. Radio and television are, indeed, powerful, but the magic they perform is white. Television, for example, repeatedly creates a brotherhood of catastrophe, a United Nations of disaster, an electronically uplifting Family of Man. It informs positively, it reassures, it even tells us what to do. The very cant of newsmen indicate "things" (from giant locusts to flying saucers) are, if not under control, at least under advisement. In *Them!* (Gordon Douglas, 1954), for instance, when the giant ants are found nesting in the sewers of Los Angeles, the panic-stricken citizenry are soothed and instructed by the media, which is treated with no trace of irony. "An announcer goes on the radio and the television air waves to utter a sentence which echoes through all the monster movies and which, indeed, echoes through all the Fifties: 'Your personal safety depends upon your cooperation with the military authorities.'" [50]

The news montage sections of *Earth vs. the Flying Saucers* (Fred F.

Sears, 1956), seem self-contained episodes of reasonable and credible rhetoric in a film which—despite its grand special effects—deems ordinary such dialogue as: "If it lands in our nation's capitol uninvited, we don't meet it with tea and cookies." A line of dialogue like that is hard to take seriously although, in context, it's certainly intended to be. A news report, however, even a pompously phrased one, is far more acceptable because we relate to it on its own terms, in its own frame of reference. In addition to news reports, the force, the magical powers inherent in television (and in some cases radio) is revealed in this film as it has been in others by the fact that the aliens (and in a few isolated instances, God; see *Red Planet Mars,* Harry Horner, 1952) can appropriate it at will, spreading disembodied threats around the world in ever-widening circles of the kind that used to emanate from radio-towers in newsreel animated diagrams. The aliens in *Earth vs. the Flying Saucers* prefer to take over the Earth without war. After a few skirmishes with uncooperative American military Earthlings, a show of power seems appropriate. The whole world gets the message via radio-TV (we see that conventional global montage of people tuned to their sets, listening or watching): "Look to your sun for a warning. There will be eight days and nights of meteoric convulsions." In subsequent telecasts we hear sober but calm commentators report over footage of the affected weather around the world, weather which has resulted in catastrophe, and totally affected transportation and communications (except, of course, the magically immune radio and TV).

Another kind of ritual reportage with familiar and unemotional rhetoric occurs with a certain stately dignity at the beginning of *The Deadly Mantis* (Nathan Juran, 1957). This is the "documentary" exploration in which maps, charts, diagrams, planetarium drawings, or film strips and slides are graced with measured explanations by someone paternally comforting (see Edmund Gwenn in *Them!*) and/or of cultured voice. For example, the voice at the beginning of *The Deadly Mantis* intones: "For every action, there is a reaction" while we see a map of Antarctica and watch a volcano erupt. We then visually shift to the Arctic where a glacier starts to break up, the glacier in which the Mantis has been embedded for aeons. Similar to this presentation and even more worthy of mention is the resonant opening of *War of the Worlds* (Byron Haskin, 1953), in which Sir Cedric Hardwicke's narration sonorously tells us about the doomed Martian civilization over glorious astronomical paintings of the planets by Chesley Bonestell.

The usual mode of ritual dialogue is, however, the television newscast and montage, and it is present in far too many SF films to mention, usually appearing in conjunction with an equally economical and communicative montage of newspaper headlines. In general, the newscast is used as an economical way of compressing information or expressing emotion which, if stated by characters in an unframed situation, would sound talky or unnatural or funny. Thus, in *The Angry Red Planet* a newscaster can rhetorically express emotion about the survivor of the crash of a rocket returned from Mars in terms of "the prayers of a grateful nation." Or in a strangely fascinating horror/SF amalgam *Queen of Blood* (Curtis Harrington, 1965), a newscast featuring coverage of the first visitors to Earth from another galaxy tells us, in a totally natural informational context, that the year is 1990 and that the first moon landing occurred twenty years before. This kind of ritualistic transfer of narrative information works on a credible, acceptable level—particularly when contrasted to "normal" interchanges: "They may be some sort of intellectual insects" or "One should not be shocked by anything we find out there."

In these traditional SF films, the media function ritually and conventionally, and are viewed positively. Unlike those in *Night of the Living Dead,* the newscasts in these films are not really reflexive, commenting ironically upon their own function in the films. There are, however, many SF films which do question the use to which the unquestioned power of the media is put—while still using that power cinematically and narratively to frame and ritualize otherwise untenably phrased dialogue, or to supply otherwise unavailable information. This general mistrust of the media and its attendant authoritative rhetoric is primarily a phenomenon of the films of the sixties and seventies, by which time the novelty of TV had worn thin and its more sinister security capabilities and its ability to deceive had become apparent. Yet it is interesting to note that the fifties' film which perhaps set the standard for all traditional film telecasts and news montages to follow, *The Day the Earth Stood Still,* also attacked the media's penchant for sensationalism.

The Day the Earth Stood Still is a cautionary tale which points again and again to human pettishness as the major cause of human misery and aggression. Obvious but intelligent, the film tells the story of an alien visitor to Earth who assumes a human identity in order to accomplish his mission of ending Earth wars forever, a task finally less altruistic than space-preservational. "The man from space loses himself in American society, passing through a world of boarding houses, radio news flashes, the FBI, witch hunts, the Pentagon, and cops." [51] At one point, the *incognito* Klaatu (Michael Rennie) is part of a group of curious people milling about the landing site of the alien spaceship. Approached by a microphone-toting reporter looking for "newsworthy" public response, Klaatu (alias Mr. Carpenter) starts to talk about the danger of "fear replacing reason," but he is "cut short by the reporter impatient for scare comments." [52] The film directly charges the press with irresponsibility in its preference for sensationalism over sanity; we are shown a credulous public through which vibrate waves of fear and hysteria periodically amplified and accelerated by the media. The rhetoric which sways and frightens and titillates a pliant and trusting populace is seen as potentially lethal and those newsmen who cut off reason and promote fear are shown to be dangerous to the public welfare. The film, however, true to both its own reasonableness and the fifties fascination with the comforting authoritative aspects of the media, finally seems to separate the lunatic irresponsibility of roving reporters in the park and those telecasts and radio broadcasts which frame and ritualize "great events."

The Day the Earth Stood Still initiates the traditional news montage from the film's beginning—and in its functional and effectively persuasive editing perhaps sets the standards for subsequent instances in other movies. Near the opening, we get a series of broadcasts in many languages, a montage which creates a global simultaneity of experience and human response. Newscasters (i.e., Walter Winchell and Ernie Pyle) who are world famous for their individual brands of rhetoric and delivery tell us about the spaceship in orbit around the Earth; this type of montage is also repeated after the spacecraft lands in Washington, D.C. The effect of these rapidly cut, rapidly spoken sequences is not only to convey information, but also to create authenticity, tension, and urgency. We are constantly reminded, as well, that this is a global affair. The prime function of these broadcasts, however, is to economically and credibly convey public opinion, public reaction, and we are conditioned from the beginning to regard them as authentic barometers of world feeling. These two fairly lengthy news montages early in the film set the stage, the pace, the credibility, and the topicality of the film. Because of their length, detail, ritually persuasive rhetoric, and their internationality, they also condition us to accept as authentic shorter broadcasts and newspaper headlines later in the film. Most of what we learn about public reaction to the visitor and spaceship and the events which follow throughout the rest of the movie comes from newscasts and newspaper and magazine headlines and the almost choral reaction to them of the small group of people in the boarding house where Klaatu has taken up *incognito* residence. Our willingness to accept these brief news flashes and their boarding house response as a microcosmic reaction of the world as a whole is created by the credibility, the ritualistic authoritativeness of the two early news montages showing the same stories being broadcast in the same way throughout the world. Finally, then, despite its pointed attack on the sensational and exploitative practices of the media, *The Day the Earth Stood Still* depends a great deal—and positively so—on the authority of the media to persuade us of its own credibility.

The media, particularly television, also function ritualistically in the SF films of the sixties and seventies—but the ritualism, the rhetoric, the authoritative power of the media is seen as neither comforting nor informative. Television is seen negatively, viewed as something sinister in its bland persuasiveness, its ability to frame and thereby authenticate the banal, the deceptive, the dangerous. Often in these later films, the rhetoric of TV is only implicit and the visual images of monitor screens on the screen carry a weight unshared by spoken and ritualized dialogue. In *Seven Days in May* (John Frankenheimer, 1964), for instance, TV screens are omnipresent but for the most part they function silently. In this film about the uncovering of a planned military *coup d'etat,* "television monitors turn a grey unwinking gaze on every action: the Pentagon is littered with them, repeating images along silent corridors, reflecting the suspicious, disturbed nature of life among the technological wizards." [53] The 1974 adaptation of Michael Crichton's novel *The Terminal Man* (Michael Hodges), effectively uses a hospital's closed-circuit TV screens to chillingly multiply its computerized Dr. Jekyll/Mr. Hyde protagonist into a visual metaphor of sterile and inhuman conformity—a kind of electronic cloning.

Although TV monitors work effectively as silent and visually expressive icons in such films as *Seven Days in May, The Manchurian Candidate* (made two years earlier by Frankenheimer), *THX 1138,* and *The Groundstar Conspiracy* (Lamont Johnson, 1972), they also function ritually in the same films in relation to dialogue, commenting upon it and serving as the excuse for its stilted quality. "Speechifying" in such films is a public ritual performed more for cameras than for crowds. One such instance is a press conference held by the Secretary of Defense in *The Manchurian Candidate;* the scene is filled with shots of action repeated on monitors in miniature, filled with a sense of public performance. The dialogue framed by the TV monitors and the ritualization of expression (the press conference) functions both naturally and unnaturally, straight and ironically. Frankenheimer also uses speech making as an integral part of the "message" dialogue, the polemic, of *Seven Days in May.* Gerald Pratley, in his book on Frankenheimer, admires the director's "use of 'speeches' given by the President. Scoffed at by some as 'respectable, liberal lines,' they are delivered by March [Frederick March who plays President Jordan Lyman] with complete naturalism at times when they are logically called for, and with great honesty and conviction. They restate familiar principles perhaps, but they need to be said again, even if we have heard them before." [54] Whether or not one feels inclined to agree with Pratley's admiration of and justification for the President's dialogue, one can read between the lines a certain naive belief (one, I think, we all irrationally and secretly share) that the President doesn't talk like the rest of us, that even in the most private moments words

THX 1138 (George Lucas, 1971). The director sees his futuristic and sterile world as an "intercom" society. (Warner Brothers)

from his mouth find a patriotic, public cadence and rhythm appropriate to his exalted station.

In *THX 1138*, television and public voices are separated from each other, but linked by implication. In a stream-of-consciousness interview with Lawrence Sturhahn, director George Lucas describes the world of his film:

> ... we are being watched constantly ... the very strange reality in our environment, between us and the make-believe world television brings into our houses ... and alienated society ... we are losing humanity, you know.[55]

> ... one of the mechanical principles is that of intercom dialogue, and the fact that people are separated—like it's difficult to communicate into a telephone ... try to tell somebody how to thread a needle over a phone ... we've kind of deviced through the barriers, between people and between things. So you have to communicate via intercom, that is one of the things in the society of the film. ...[56]

Intercom dialogue, itself a form of ritual language, while not always linked to TV monitors in *THX 1138* is the outcome of a culture dependent upon the media for the interpretation and containment of experience. In this film, speeches and rhetoric unattached to human bodies fill the sound track, seem to emanate from corridors, phone booths, confessionals, and black walls.

The Groundstar Conspiracy, perhaps because it is the most visually ordinary of the antimedia films discussed here, is the least subtle in its polemic, its instructional dialogue. The film is, indeed, cautionary and—as Richard Schickel says in his review—"encourages us to spare a serious thought or two, in this instance for the security mania of government agencies, expertly personified by George Peppard as the guy in charge of catching spies hanging around a space research facility doing work so avant garde that the script breathes scarcely a word about its mission." [57] Peppard, playing Tuxon, is the fair-haired quasi-villain who speaks a clipped hard dialogue which is so emotionlessly programmatic that it chills. "If I had my way, there'd be a bug in every bedroom in the country," he says with absolutely no prurient interest whatsoever. And to his military companions (who speak, of course, in ritual militarese) : "Yes, gentlemen, I tap my own phone, too." Asked by one of the only two humanly emotional characters in the film, "Isn't there privacy anywhere?", Tuxon responds like an automaton programmed to display a frightening self-confidence about what is absolutely right: "No. Murders are planned in private. Sabotage, and revolution are planned in private. I would put my own family in a spotlight naked to protect this country." Everyone in the film—with the exception of two people—speaks a ritual language dictated by their profession; their rhetoric is, therefore, unnatural but convincing. The military speak conventionally (General: "This whole thing would never have happened if the Air Force had been in control of the whole thing."). Tuxon, as demonstrated, speaks as if everything he said was being overheard, tapped, and taped. And a governmental press secretary talks in the language of the rhetoric he passes on for public consumption: "I'm sort of a governmental disc jockey. I sell dreams to the public, lies to the press." This dialogue is framed and made credible by the film's emphasis on the institutional (public buildings, hospitals, etc.), on the public person who functions in full view of the world, who is monitored by hidden microphones and television cameras. The appearance of stilted and even cliché-ridden dialogue is thus made comprehensible in context. And, as well, it becomes new and fresh, infused as it is with sinister overtones.

Liturgy

There is one last major way in which spoken dialogue in the SF film

Planet of the Apes (Franklin Schaffner, 1968). Ordinary speech is transformed into liturgy throughout the *Apes'* series. There is liturgical dialogue ranging from invocation to nursery rhyme. (20th Century Fox)

can be significantly altered so that it transcends the familiar and ordinary. Closely linked to the ritual rhetoric created by the presence of the media and its attendent conventions in SF film, is something we might call liturgic dialogue. Liturgic dialogue can be best identified by its striking resemblance to verbal instances of public worship: invocation, litany, prayer, chant, and sacred song. What is significant about the effectiveness of such dialogue in SF films is that it is treated almost as music; its cadences and rhythms are extremely important in creating a sense of the alien. As well, this kind of dialogue functions through repetition (overt and latent) and its ability to communicate itself within the film as an oral tradition which is simultaneously public and sacred without necessarily being religious. In fact, the sacredness of such dialogue seems to arise out of its public-ness, its ability to unite a community by virtue of its being known to all.

The *Planet of the Apes* series is rife with such liturgic dialogue ranging from invocation to nursery rhyme. In the first film, Cornelius (Roddy MacDowall) reads to his fellow chimps, orangutans, and gorillas from "Sacred Scroll 23, 9th Verse":

Beware the beast man, for he is the devil's pawn. Alone among God's

197

primates, he kills for sport, or lust or greed. Yes, he will murder his brother to possess his brother's land. Let him not breed in great numbers, for he will make a desert of his home and yours. Shun him. Drive him back into his jungle lair: For he is the harbinger of death![58]

And in *Beneath the Planet of the Apes,* both religious and secular liturgy appear. Driven underground, human mutants see "The Bomb" as a "Holy Weapon of Peace" and worship before it, chanting, "I reveal my Inmost Self unto my God!" as, in unison, they peel off their "faces" to reveal hideous scar tissue beneath.[59] In secular play, children also avail themselves of liturgy:

> Ring-a ring o' neutrons,
> A pocketful of positrons,
> A fission! A fission!
> We all fall down.[60]

This kind of children's jingle which functions liturgically and with a certain contextual poignance is used for satiric purpose in *The Monitors* (Jack Shea, 1969). The film depicts a futuristic nonviolent United States, run by a robot-like yet pleasant group of young men wearing leotards and bowler hats who call themselves the Monitors. Agents of another world overseen by their chief Jeterex (Shepperd Strudwick[61]), the Monitors and their polite good deeds need to be "sold" to the American public like detergent. Thus, jingoism and the media combine in the film to create a comic liturgical motif: a series of TV "spots" or commercials in which citizens of all social classes, nationalities, and educational backgrounds extol the Monitors' virtues, each preceded and followed by a recurrent short and simple jingle dealing with the Monitors and their ability to bring happiness. (The jingle also seems to fill the streets, emanating from public address systems everywhere.) Such public acts of worship as the incantations and sacred songs attendant to the selling of material goods and politicians is soundly spoofed in *The Monitors.* Yet, comic as they are, the musical "spots" also recur often enough to create an alien atmosphere. They do, indeed, punctuate the film regularly with comic content which is framed; various familiar personages make cameo appearances in the commercials: Alan Arkin as a garbageman, the late Senator Everett Dirksen reading Scripture, band leader Xavier Cugat holding a Chihuahua, and others. In fact, as Howard Thompson notes in his review of the film, "At times, considering the endless, peek-a-boo calvacade of guest comedians, it suggests that the Marx Brothers—and their sisters, cousins and aunts— had been turned loose on George Orwell's *1984.*"[62] Yet, each individual appearance is framed by the jingle which because of its frequent repetition functions liturgically within the film's total structure.

Most instances of liturgic dialogue in the SF film, however, are less pointedly obvious than those in the *Planet of the Apes* series and less bizarre and comic than those in *The Monitors*. In fact, most liturgic dialogue is exceedingly simple, so simple that we, as viewers and listeners, absorb it without notice as part of a conventional *mise en scene*. Such dialogue usually arises in a context in which a group of men are publicly and unconsciously worshipping technology, acknowledging through their behavior the religious and/or magical nature of the fruits of science, unconsciously but rhythmically making obeisance to machinery. Such worship occurs in the SF film in nearly every NASA control room, in nearly every computer control center in which the checking of equipment, the routine question and response required by a team effort at one task, takes on the rhythms, cadences, and religious orchestration of litany and chant. Human voices combine in patterns which suggest sacred ritual as individuals respond "Check" or "Systems Go" to the high priest's call for perfection. Indeed, "the dashboard paraphernalia and control dials become as potent and dominant as icons and sacraments—faith is placed in technical efficiency." [63] Groups of men verbally intoning their faith can be seen in films from *Destination Moon* on, among them *Countdown* (Robert Altman, 1968), *Marooned, The Andromeda Strain,* and *Westworld* (Michael Crichton, 1973), to name only a few. And, in fact, in one scene in *Marooned,* the liturgy becomes quite primitive and prominent: the rescue spaceship has to leave Earth through the eye of a hurricane and as it rises, so do the men in NASA control; standing at their consoles they chant in unison like tribesmen asking the gods for good crops, "Go! Go! Go!" Reason is chucked for rhythm, and science is epiphanetically revealed as just a neater form of religion and magic.

The Word as Image

Thus far, the major concern of this chapter has been to explore and describe the various ways in which spoken dialogue in the SF film may be transformed into something fresh and wondrous while still remaining spoken and comprehensible. At this point, however, before going on to discuss the aural but nonverbal functions of music and sound effects in the genre, it seems appropriate and pertinent to discuss a related phenomenon peculiar to the SF film: the transformation of the prosaically verbal into the poetically visual, the transformation of the word into the image, the heard into the seen.

Certainly, the printed word seen on a movie screen is not unique to

SF cinema. Newspaper headlines have given us narrative information in every kind of film; we've read letters over characters' shoulders and glanced at Top Secret documents. We've looked at "Wanted" posters and seen billboards and signs comment ironically or appositely on the situations or feelings of a film's characters. And, quite bluntly, we've been told, in print, where, via the screen, we have physically got to. But in none of these instances has there been an effort to create an aesthetic transformation of something usual into something less usual. Except for the purpose of ironic comment, most films other than SF which use language visually do so for economy's sake, for narrative compression. No where does one have the feeling that the print we are looking at is meant to be beautiful in its form, in its graphic appearance and color. It is only the SF film (and fairly recent SF film, for that matter) which has created a visual poetry composed of letters, words, numbers, and formulae—originally meant to be spoken aloud or read in a book, but made magical, made runic by their transformation into something seen and unspoken on a screen.

Perhaps it is merely a personal fancy unshared by other viewers, but it has always seemed to me that an unspoken word *seen* on the screen (unless prosaically attached to the familiar print experience of a newspaper or a

Five (Arch Obler, 1951). A postnuclear holocaust film in which print transforms language into visually ironic counterpoint. (Columbia)

magazine) is pregnant, swollen with possibility; meant to be heard, the words are instead silently read and the tension created by their absence of sound seems to me almost palpable. I am speaking less of the kind of quietly and narratively functional silence created by photographed print in a postnuclear-holocaust film like *Five* (Arch Obler, 1951), than I am of the tensely palpable silence amplified by print in *2001: A Space Odyssey, The Andromeda Strain, Westworld,* or *Zardoz.*

In *Five,* the print's soundlessness (its lack of articulation into spoken language) arises out of the film's narrative context and functions ironically and sometimes laboriously rather than aesthetically. *Five* concerns a post-bomb world and the attempts of a few survivors to create a new existence for themselves. After the film's explosive encapsulated beginning, we follow a girl, Roseanne (Susan Douglas) as she wanders in a deserted town. She stops at one point in front of a church whose sign has letters missing and she passes another sign which heavy-handedly reads "Repent ye sinners." On an excursion for supplies, Roseanne and another survivor Michael (who

Colossus: The Forbin Project **(Joseph Sargent, 1969). Recent SF films have generated wonder by refusing to separate the acts of reading and seeing. We are asked to consider print graphically and aesthetically as well as literally. (Universal)**

will finally play Adam to Roseanne's Eve) stop at a grocery store. A sign is posted on the door which poignantly and grimly reads "Back in 5 minutes," while in the window an arrangement of soap boxes labelled "Atomic Suds" vies for our attention. The kind of reading that *Five* has us do is quite ordinary to a cinematic context. Like those films which use signposts or billboards or newspaper headlines, *Five* automatically supposes a distinction between print and image. We read the words which supply us with information and then apply that information to the seen image. The process is, of course, incredibly rapid, but the distinction is still made; we do not *see* the print so much as *read* it, and we do not *read* the rest of the image so much as *see* it. Implicit here is the separation of reading and seeing, the separation of the processes of intellection and perception. Since this separation is consistent with how we ordinarily respond to print experience and viewed experience in actual life, the film does not cause us to wonder at either; instead, it quietly duplicates a usual and accepted dichotomy.

In contrast, more recent SF films have generated tension and wonder by their refusal (however conscious or unconscious) to separate reading and seeing, by their fusion of the two processes into one. What results is wondrously alien to our everyday experience. We are made self-conscious of our one-sided response to print as content and are asked by images to consider print graphically and aesthetically as well. Letters, words, numbers, diagrams and formuale create designs, move in screen space, convey color and light as well as content.

In *2001: A Space Odyssey,* when HAL murderously turns off the life support systems of the hibernating crew, red letters flash on a narrow rectangular black screen, which in turn is set against the white walls of the spaceship: "Computer malfunction," "Life functions critical," "Life functions terminal." The lines of a graph sympathetically trace themselves into a horrible and horizontal evocation of death. In both instances, we simultaneously read the content and see the content. The words and print themselves convey meaning, but so do their kinetic movements, mechanically calm yet flashing urgency, graphic configurations, colors, and the associations we have with them.

The Andromeda Strain is an instance of a film even more highly dependent on images in which print and diagrammatic material figure. (It would be of interest to compare the difference in function of such print and diagrammatic material in the film and in Michael Crichton's novel from which the film was adapted, the latter using such materials to break up the graphic complacency of the printed page so that the book seems constantly and immediately disrupted and the tale, therefore, seems more authentically present as well as more documentary because "documented.") Without the numerous images in which print and diagrams appear in the film and set

A Clockwork Orange (Stanley Kubrick, 1971). The word as image. Letters, words, numbers, diagrams, and formulae create designs, move in screen space, to mean their color and light as well as their content. (Warner Brothers)

up their own aesthetic suspense structure, it is highly likely that *The Andromeda Strain's* narrative would appear even more full of holes and a lack of satisfactory narrative resolution than Pauline Kael points to in her negative review of the film.[64] *Andromeda* is first a biological detective story which asks: Will a team of scientists unlock the secrets of a lethal alien growth and contain it before it infects the world? Yet, as Kael notes, at least a third of the film does not address itself to this question, focusing instead on the colorful process of decontamination. As well, there are no clues which function in effective detective-story terms. And what is even worse from a traditional narrative standpoint is the appalling fact that the scientist-detectives do not solve the problem at all; it anticlimatically solves itself (Andromeda mutates to a harmless state). Instead of the expected and promised narrative progression toward resolution, the initial narrative question is abandoned for another at the last possible moment: Can the scientists escape the underground laboratory before it self-destructs?

On paper, however, the film sounds more of a mess than it actually appears on the screen where it is made coherent and structurally unified by its visual emphases. With a plot fraying around its narrative edges, much of *The Andromeda Strain's* fascination and appeal for the viewer is aesthetic, visually rather than narratively based. In this visual construct, the numerous instances of visual print serve a multiple function. The first, of course, is to supply narrative information. The second is to authenticate "officially" (via reports, computer graphics and print-outs, signs, tags, teletype, etc.) the narrative events in the film. The film, for instance, begins and ends with an emphasis on documentation as such; there is a precredit print note to the viewer which confers on the film to come the cultural authenticity attendent to the printed word, and the closing sequence shows us magnifications of Andromeda which are followed by the print-out numbering and lettering: "601" (previously established as signalling a computer overload), "Disengage," "End Program," "Stop." During the film, there are numerous instances when seeing something printed or diagrammed *confirms* and *documents* our visual experience of it. (The documentation and the experience are sometimes even simultaneous as in one section of the scientists' descent into the underground laboratories of Project Wildfire when we see a split screen image of the event, the physical descent of the characters, and the document, a diagram of the project layout.) The third function of the transformation of the verbal and abstract into the visual is to graphically and kinetically create what might be called a visual onomatopoeia in which the print and formulae pictured evoke what they mean, and in some cases *look* something like what they mean (i.e., the computer print-outs of the results of the various cultures in which the Andromeda strain has been placed look, in their movement across the console and the theater screen, somewhat like the crystalline divisions of the strain itself or bacterial growth in a petri dish.) Numbers, formuale, and print are transformed in *Andromeda* by virtue of their graphic presentation. The lack of a coherent and sustained narrative suspense in the film is masked and replaced by the fourth function of print images: the creation of visual suspense. The succession of print images across the screen generates its own suspense, its own movement toward resolution, as we experience the disintegration of our relationship to the print's content. What we experience, if the print images continue long enough, can be considered a sort of centripetal decay; our attention wanders from the central content conveyed by the print to the graphic play of print within the screen rectangle. Our intellectual consideration of content decays as our emotional response to movement and color increases. This same kind of transformation of the verbal into the visual, the abstract into the experiential, occurs in the computer center of the resort in *Westworld,* as technicians work at consoles which wink numbers and colors at us. Viewing such films, we are fascinated by colorful and blinking lights which seem only accidentally to conform to letters and numbers. Like most people I have observed who play with electronic pocket calculators not to arrive at sums but, rather, to watch the changes of light and figure in the abstract design of the answer, we absorb the content of this visualized electronic print peripherally and respond most immediately and particularly to the look of the content, its color and shape and move-

Silent Running (Douglas Trumbull, 1972). The computer console. We are fascinated by colorful blinking lights, which seem only accidentally to conform to letters and numbers and yield abstract content. (Universal)

ment. We wonder at words written by no human hand, at the progression of numbers and letters across a screen in a manner unfamiliar enough to call our attention to the incredibly arbitrary shape of words and language.

This transmogrification of the word into an abstract, arbitrary, and wondrous visual design is, to date, best exemplified in a scene in *Zardoz,* a film whose extremely convoluted plot is summarized by Philip Strick:

> Pistol in hand, . . . he [Zed the Exterminator] stows away in the mouth of the flying sculpture [the manifestation of the Godhead] and is carried to the Vortex, a brilliant oasis of indolent intelligence where the Eternals live in immortal boredom and sterility, their petulant misdemeanours punished by senility, their occasional suicides by prompt resurrection. Fascinated by Zed, they argue over his fate; one group

... wants him destroyed, while another ... insists that he should be studied for a while. During the contest that follows, Zed acquires an encyclopaedic knowledge of the Vortex and its purpose, confronts the forces that enclose it, and restores to its delighted, centuries-old inhabitants the ability to remain dead when they die. The process of evolution is released once more, and the natural history of man can resume its course.[65]*

Zed's acquisition of an "encyclopaedic knowledge" of the Vortex occurs in a visually dazzling sequence which makes the abstract word visual, physical —and even infuses it with sexuality:

> Zed trades his sexual seed for all the knowledge stored within the crystal. Images of paintings, words, numbers, symbols are projected onto parts of the body (mainly close-ups of heads), creating a visual collage; words, songs, music construct an analagous effect in sound. As the camera moves across a chain of images ..., the pace accelerates until it reaches a sexual climax. As in the Bible, "knowing" has a sexual meaning. Zed is told, "Now you know all that we know." [66]

The "visual collage" of print in *Zardoz* makes language (and its components) concretely physical, colorful, and kinetic. It also simultaneously emphasizes the inherent abstractness of language by physicalizing it, by giving it visual substance in an abstract design. Becoming an integral part of the total screen image in *Zardoz,* language as image comes to have a concrete being and loses, therefore, much of its particularized meaning. Our response as viewers is to wonder at the transformation, to delight in letters and numbers and words sliding over the curves of a human body in a caress composed of color and light.

The way in which the SF film uniquely utilizes language as image certainly needs further exploration—as do our responses to these images. Literally "reading" the screen is a strange cinematic experience when, as viewers, our act of reading is made self-conscious. Obviously, we read all screen images in some fashion, but to read them as we would read print in a book and then be struck into a self-conscious awareness that we are *not* reading a book thrusts us into a new stance, gives us a new perception of letters and numbers as visual entities which exist independent of their meaning. (I am convinced that were I handed a book after watching a film full of print images I would newly respond to the staticness of the printed page, would separate letters in words or create kinetic chains of letters and spaces, notice a lack of color, find a graphic composition.) In conclusion, although the transformation of film language and dialogue into

---

* This same theme is treated far less interestingly and at much higher cost by the diffuse and more recent *Logan's Run* (Michael Anderson, 1976).

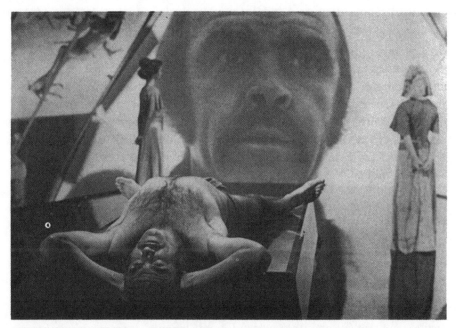

Zardoz (John Boorman, 1974). The word as image. Language's inherent abstraction is emphasized through its concrete visualization. (20th Century Fox)

print may have caused us to digress from a consideration of dialogue and language as film *sound*, that transformation is an attempt to realize an alien mode of communication through using a familiar means of communication; it is an attempt to simultaneously be alien *and* communicative. We really have come full circle back to the aesthetic resonance of "Gort, Klaatu barrada nicto." Both *Zardoz* and *The Day the Earth Stood Still* use verbal means to communicate nonverbally.

Nonverbal Sound

The Music of the Spheres

One might suppose that the SF film—because of its narrative and thematic preoccupation with the "future," with innovation, with "otherness'—would utilize music in a different way than do other film genres. Music in most other film genres, apart from the singular case of the screen musical, is not meant to be purposely noticeable or outstanding. Rather, it is conceived of as atmospherically supportive, conjunctional, and premonitory—that is, it evokes time and place and mood (and, as well, other past film music associated with the particular genre) and it supports the image rhythmically, tonally, atmospherically, rather than contrasting with or contradicting it; it acts as a conjunctive element which connects shots, scenes, and sequences together with some coherence external to image content, and which, by way of recurrent motifs and themes, links the viewer's experience of character or incident at a past moment of film time with his experience in the present moment; traditional film music also foreshadows events or changes of mood which will subsequently be revealed by a shift of image. Certainly, not one of these functions is in any way minor. Yet they all, at their most successful, tend to be fairly invisible.

One might expect, however, that in addition to functioning quietly in these crucial ways, music in the SF film would function more overtly, more flamboyantly, less traditionally. A speculative viewer/listener might, for example, see the possibilities of using music *as* an alien language, one indecipherable in its particular meanings yet emotionally communicative. Or, one could envision altering the shape and instrumentation of music so as to create a disorienting and dissonant physical and emotional response in the viewer. There are, certainly, other possibilities. Unfortunately, however, what is notable about most SF film music is its lack of notability, its absence of unique characteristics which separate it from music in other films.* Not only does most music from one SF film sound like the music from another SF film (a quality which could be explored positively as a function of the genre itself), but most of the music sounds like all of the music from most other narrative film. What this means, of course, is although SF music sounds the same from film to film, SF music has no characteristic sound. At least music in Westerns evokes the Western and derives from folk music and square dance music; and both jazz and the blues seem to maintain fairly close ties with the gangster film, often arising out of a documented temporal and spatial context. Even the horror film brings to some minds the sounds of an organ playing a Bach toccata and fugue. The SF film has had no such musical identity—although, perhaps, Stanley Kubrick has changed all that with his selection of Richard Strauss' *Also Sprach Zarathustra* as the theme music for *2001: A Space Odyssey*. (The music has since been used exploitatively to add "cosmic grandeur" to the images of a head of lettuce and a stomach remedy on two television

---

* Since this writing (and chronologically beyond the scope of this book), one film has definitely used music innovatively as both language and iconic sound—*Close Encounters of the Third Kind* (Steven Spielberg, 1977). Music plays a crucial and integral part in the narrative, emotional, and intellectual content of the film—as distinguished from the marvelously rousing but primarily atmospheric score of *Star Wars* (George Lucas, 1977). The music for both films was composed by John Williams.

2001: A Space Odyssey **(Stanley Kubrick, 1968). The SF film has had no generic musical identity—although Kubrick has created an iconic score meant to signify cosmic grandeur. (Metro-Goldwyn-Mayer)**

commercials and, thus, has become functionally further identified with spherical and rotating objects photographed emerging from eclipse.)

Certainly, few of the names of composers and musical directors connected with the original music in SF films would provoke recognition in anyone but their immediate families. Many studios used the same craftsmen again and again—certainly bargaining for more of the same rather than more but different. Thus, an Albert Glasser is responsible for the unmemorable but perfectly functional music in many Universal and American International films, consistently working with director Bert I. Gordon on such films as *The Amazing Colossal Man* (1957), *Attack of the Puppet People* (1958), *The Spider* (1958), and *War of the Colossal Beast* (1958). (Surely, the partnership of Glasser and Gordon will some day stir up *auteur* controversy when the Big Names have been written about exhaustively.) In the same anonymous ranks with Glasser are, among many others, Ronald Stein who wrote music for Allied Artists, and Raoul Kraushaar who did the same for Fox and Warner Brothers. My aim here is not to disparage these particular individuals but to point out the infrequency of musical "notables" composing, scoring, or directing for SF films.

Of course, on occasion, depending one can only suppose on a film's budget, commercial promise, and artistic intent, a big musical name has been seduced into the genre—very often, with atmospherically good, if not always innovative, results. Dmitri Tiomkin did the music for *The Thing* (Howard Hawks/Christian Nyby, 1950). Bernard Herrmann—famous for his musical contributions to *Citizen Kane* and other Orson Welles films, and as composer for many Alfred Hitchcock films—wrote for both *The Day the Earth Stood Still* and *Journey to the Center of the Earth* (Henry Levin,

209

1959), as well as for Francois Truffaut's British-French venture into science fiction, the 1966 screen adaptation of Ray Bradbury's *Fahrenheit 451*. Elmer Bernstein's talents redeemed much of the unintentional comedy of *Cat Women of the Moon* (Arthur Hilton, 1954). Ravi Shankar's music was used for *Charly* (Ralph Nelson, 1968), and Lalo Schifrin composed for a Jerry Lewis SF comedy *Way . . . Way Out* (Gordon Douglas, 1966), and *THX 1138*. And interestingly, although not significantly, the music for *Rocketship X-M* (Kurt Neumann, 1950), was composed by Ferde Grofé who wrote *The Grand Canyon Suite*.

Although this list may make lengthy reading, it is really pathetically short in comparison to the number of SF films made and released in the country since 1950. Most of the music written for SF films has not come from the ranks of critically acknowledged film composers. Rather, it has been primarily written by a handful of unrecognized composers who have been typecast to the genre, in perpetuity it seems. An example of this, as well as an exception because his name is known to the public, is Les Baxter, a composer for American International teenage-beach pictures (many of which had SF/fantasy elements) and SF films (a few of which had teen-age musical elements). A sampling of his credits for American International are: *Master of the World* (William Witney, 1961), *Panic in the Year Zero* (Ray Milland, 1962), *X, The Man With the X-Ray Eyes* (Roger Corman, 1963), *Bikini Beach* (William Asher, 1964), *Sergeant Deadhead, the Astronaut* (Norman Taurog, 1965), *Dr. Goldfoot and the Bikini Machine* (Norman Taurog, 1965), and *Wild in the Streets*.

This kind of musical typecasting is, of course, not only limited to the SF film where it has seemed particularly unconducive to musical innovation or experimentation. The process also works in reverse, keeping known composers typed also. Bernard Herrmann, when asked in an interview whether he deliberately sought out film assignments which called for "manic rhythms and moody, elegiac sequences, frequently in the minor key" answered:

> No. I don't seek it out—they seek me out. In California, they like to pigeonhole you. From the time I began working for Hitchcock, they decided I was a big suspense man. On other occasions, I've had fantasies or bittersweet romantic stories. I think I'd enjoy writing a good comedy score, but I've never had the luck to be offered such films. . . . Mancini gets the cheerful ones. So that's how it is.[67]

It is illuminating, however, that Herrmann, whose screen credits are extraordinarily impressive and who worked with some of the greatest and most innovative directors of this century, feels that the genre which allowed him the greatest opportunities for musical *experimentation* was science fiction:

The Day the Earth Stood Still (Robert Wise, 1951). Bernard Herrmann, composer for the film, was able to use experimental and avant-garde techniques in orchestrating and recording. (20th Century Fox)

The film with the most experimental, avant-garde techniques was the picture I did for Robert Wise, *The Day the Earth Stood Still* (1951). At that time, we had no electronic sound, but the score had many electronic features which haven't become antiquated at all: electric violin, electric bass, two high and low electric theremins, four pianos, four harps and a very strange section of about 30-odd brass. Alfred Newman said the only thing we needed was an electric hot water bottle, which he supplied.[68]

Had such musical giants as Herrmann been an available resource to the SF film, perhaps the incidence of inventive and experimental music might have been higher than it was. (There is, however, hope that the situation will change somewhat as the distinctions between low and high budget films disappear and SF films become mainstream entertainment as they now seem to be doing.*)

There are, of course, some SF films in which the music does stand out as dramatically and narratively effective and, as well, strange, innovative and "science fiction-y." Most of them have already been cited as the works of noted film composers. But one film not on that list which deserves mention for its original and experimental score is *Forbidden Planet*. In his enthusiastic review of the film, Bosley Crowther described the replacement of a traditional musical score by Louis and Bebe Barron's "accompaniment of interstellar gulps and burbles." [69] The Barrons, one-time collaborators with modern composer John Cage, [70] called their music for the film "Electronic Tonalities." Far from being merely strange and exotic, the score functioned narratively, developing motifs associated with characters (i.e., what John Baxter has described as Robby the Robot's "coffee-pot plopping theme" [71] as well as with events and mood. Unfortunately, few SF films have attempted to so experiment with original music. The two predominant musical sounds one remembers hearing in the wide spectrum of SF film are heavenly choirs and rock music, the first closely connected with the promise of a new Eden at the end of the postnuclear holocaust film, the second blared from car radios before a "thing" attacks the necking victims, or played before us by a "live" group on a beach or at a dance, again prior to an alien attack. What is memorable about these sounds is their recurrence and their musical insistence, their heavy-handedness. The bulk of other, and at least effectively supportive, kinds of SF music is invisible.

Invisible music, however, is definitely not a characteristic of the SF films of Stanley Kubrick. (No critic—at least not this critic—likes to keep bringing up the same examples; but in the case of Kubrick's imaginative use of sound it seems unavoidable, if not absolutely necessary.) Almost as if in recognition of the small ambitions of most film composers, Kubrick has found the major musical source for his films the classics. He uses classic popular song as well as great musical compositions. Kubrick, then, uses "unoriginal" film music originally, seeing music as not only supportive of his visuals but also as an active participant in the creation and/or destruc-

* As previously noted, this seems to be the case with John Williams' work in *Star Wars* and *Close Encounters of the Third Kind*. Prior to these SF films, his Academy Award, and public visibility, Williams, was well-known for his work on many prestigious films and considered a major film composer.

tion of image content. Thus, music in Kubrick films is used inventively and narratively and flamboyantly, causing the viewer to *listen* so that he can *see*. This last may seem merely a rhetorical statement. But it is really necessary, in order to determine meaning in a Kubrick SF film, to hear the soundtrack as well as see the visual content of the various images. *Dr. Strangelove, 2001: A Space Odyssey,* and *A Clockwork Orange* make a great deal less structural and narrative sense without their musical tracks. And even in a supportive role, music cannot be invisibly functional when it has been written by Beethoven or Strauss.

Dr. Strangelove, for example, is framed by two emphatic musical contradictions to the images which they "support." "The picture opens with two planes refueling in the sky in great metal coitus as the sound track croons *Try A Little Tenderness.* The film ends with the mushroom clouds of orgiastic world destruction as the track croons, *We'll Meet Again.*" [72] Thus F. Anthony Macklin describes the film in an article interpreting *Dr. Strangelove* as a "sex allegory: from foreplay to explosion in the mechanized world." [73] Either the image or the ballad alone would not justify his interpretation; together they cause even the most naive viewer to laugh with surprise at a new, alien, and sexual perception of image content. In *2001,* Kubrick finds that the only composers up to his cosmic schemes are Khatchaturian, Richard Strauss, Gyorgy Ligeti, and Johann Strauss. Apart from the all-pervasive and grandly persuasive *Also Sprach Zarathustra* previously mentioned and the "colossal sacred din of chanting" [74] associated with the black monoliths, one remembers as only one further example an orbiting space station in joyous dance with the universe, the emotional content of the image derived from the juxtaposition with it of *The Blue Danube Waltz.*

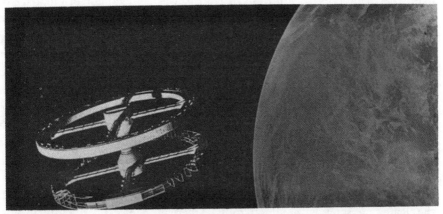

2001: A Space Odyssey (Stanley Kubrick, 1968). The orbiting space station in joyous dance with the universe to Strauss's Blue Danube Waltz. (Metro-Goldwyn-Mayer)

213

A Clockwork Orange (Stanley Kubrick, 1971). Music is an integral element of both the narrative and thematic development. (Warner Brothers)

Music is also used as an integral element of both the narrative development and the overall structure of *A Clockwork Orange*. Beethoven's work (particularly the Ninth Symphony) functions as both a narrative hinge upon which the plot swings and as a thematic device used to contrast artistic and ultimately violent individualism with unimaginative and benignly destructive mass mediocrity. Beethoven, of course, was a metaphor originated not by Kubrick but by Anthony Burgess in his novel. But Kubrick does more than add a few musical flourishes to his realization of the Burgess novel. He selects other classical (and in some instances popular) pieces of music to not only emotionally heighten particular scenes, but also to provide an artistic superstructure which results in a film form congruent with film theme. Pauline Kael, who disliked the film intensely, nevertheless recognizes the structural use of music as she puts it down as "self-important": "each sequence is scored to Purcell (synthesized on a Moog), Rossini, or Beethoven, while Elgar and others are used for brief satiric effects." [75] One of these effects is surely one of the most discomfiting in all modern film. Kubrick shows us a brutal beating and rape choreographed to "Singin' in the Rain," a song with which most American viewers are familiar and which iconically evokes the fresh innocent faces of Gene Kelly, Debbie Reynolds, and Donald O'Connor. The scene, therefore, functions horrifically, not just as a pandering and self-conscious exercise in sadism and violence (as some critics believe), but as a densely anarchic sequence in which virtue and freshness and, just possibly worst of all, old movie memories are almost insupportably mocked. The violence and rape is done to the song and what it stands for as much as to the human victims in Kubrick's film; and while we are protected from actual participation and empathy with the victims on the screen, we *are* victims of the violence done our memories and associations in the present moment of viewing. Other incongruous juxtapositions of image and music in the film also make the viewer reexamine his preconceptions about music (and more widely, art) or his preconceptions about the content of an image. When Rossini's "William Tell Overture" supports a hyped-up fast-motion series of images of Alex sexually wearing out two teeny-boppers, how do we respond? Surely, at the very least, those of us who grew up with the altruistic and very asexual Lone Ranger will find our memories of the "masked man" and that old radio show's theme music subtly altered. More complexly and more generally, such a scene also calls into question the relationship between life and art that some of us humanists would like to believe exists. In the conditioning process of the Ludovico Technique used to change young thug Alex into a good clockwork citizen, Dr. Brodsky "inadvertently" plays Beethoven's Ninth Symphony behind images in which "Hitler stomps and sieg-heils to classical music." [76] We cannot help but be made aware of the fact that humanism and a love of the arts don't necessarily go together; the Nazis were great music and art lovers. So is Alex. Music and art, perhaps, have no relevance to our behavior at all. Robert Hughes, in an article which focused on the film's use of cultural artifacts,[77] comes to a similar conclusion. Thus, "when romantic and classical music is used as the background for rape, Hughes feels Kubrick is saying that the old idea that Art is Good for You, Art Gives Moral Uplift, is a lie. Beethoven to Alex means sex and slaughter." [78]

In this film, as in all his SF films, Kubrick uses music structurally as well as narratively to illuminate his central themes. Music is not merely an invisible supportive cinematic element as it is in most other SF films. It speaks to us in ways which are far more aggressive and conceptually based than traditionally employed film music. Obviously, Kubrick's use of music is not the only way music should or could be used in the genre. But this discussion of film music for science fiction, and its emphasis on Kubrick, points to a lack of presently practiced alternatives. Unfortunately, at this moment when there seems to be a resurgence of audience interest in the SF film, and when big money is involved in SF productions, the general lack of musical experimentation continues.

Interestingly, in contrast to the lack of musical adventureousness in the SF film, the use of innovative and dramatically expressive sound effects has been widespread from science fiction's beginnings in the fifties as a film genre. It is almost as if SF filmmakers unconsciously decided to *replace* dramatic music with dramatic sound effects, to replace an emotionally derived (and therefore subjective) soundtrack with an externally based (and therefore objective) one. The "music" of machinery, in contrast to twelve-tone or electronic music, is "found" rather than created music; it therefore seems inherently objective although it can be used emotively. The strange tonalities of the wind and surf are also "found" in the external world and although they, too, can be used emotively and dramatically, they do not appear *imposed from without,* they do not call attention to a film's fictional structure. This innate desire for authenticity, this necessary obsession with documenting the incredible which informs the SF film is, I believe, one of the primary reasons music in the SF films has suffered from a lack of attention—and sound effects have been more important to the genre. In a constant search for ways in which to create credibility, the SF filmmaker has naturally gravitated toward a soundtrack built primarily from elements within the image, and not imposed on it from without. The SF film uses such sound dramatically and emotively, but the origin of that sound derives from the objectively posited and photographed narrative world of the film.

Examples are more than plentiful, but a chronological sampling of SF films from the fifties on should be sufficiently illustrative of how contextual and, thus, "found" sound effects can be used emotively. *The Thing*—a seminal 1950 SF-monster film in which an "intellectual carrot" from another world terrorizes an American military base in the Arctic—wrings the last loud and buzzing zap of drama out of the narratively plausible electric trap in which the sentient vegetable is finally caught and cooked. The geiger counter's "found" sound by which the creature's presence is detected becomes a recurrent and sinister aural motif; besides flashing (in black and white), its accelerating static is grating, irritating, and discomfiting to the listener who, therefore, may physically respond to the sound in a way which is analagous to the discomfort and edginess of the characters. Thus, the "objective" and narratively "found" sound of the geiger counter or of a tap dripping water creates a bridge into the emotional world of the film.

In another 1951 film, *Five,* a different kind of "found" sound is exploited for emotive purposes; here—in what later becomes typical postnuclear-holocaust-film fashion—the sound of some unholy, but wholly

The Thing (**Christian Nyby/Howard Hawks, 1951). Sound effects: the last loud "zap" of drama is wrung out of the electric trap that kills the Thing. (R.K.O./Winchester)**

natural atomic wind predominates. (And, if it's not an atomic wind in later films, it will be a desert wind or a seacoast wind; they all sound mournfully identical.) After an opening image of an atomic explosion, a narrator tells us "This is a story about the day after tomorrow" and he refers to "the deadly wind." While the viewer watches good high-contrast cinematography of smoke and flames superimposed over landmarks of the world's major cities, he hears a distanced amalgam of screams, sirens, music, and wind on the soundtrack, the latter a recurrent motif used throughout the film to aurally make the empty city a ghost town.

In these two films, the major "sounds" of science fiction appear, sounds which recur throughout the genre. The one is the sound of machinery, alien

War of the Worlds (Byron Haskin, 1953). The sound of the alien: biology
and technology are combined for incongruence and contradiction.
(Paramount)

in its buzzing and zapping, its mechanical ticking or clicking, inhuman
in its effortless humming or in its metronomic mockery of human heart-
beats; the other is the sound of natural forces which are usually out-shouted
in modern life by man-made noise, natural forces like the wind and the
sea made alien and threatening by the amplification and isolation of their
sound on the track—crashing surf, screaming wind, both become aural
icons, metaphors for extreme desolation.

There is, as well, a third recurrent sound in the SF film which combines
attributes of both the mechanical and the natural—and, thereby, accrues
an incongruence appropriate to its function. This is the sound of the alien:
the Martian or the giant ant or the "Monster from the Id." In *War of the
Worlds* (1953), while the mechanical Martian warships emit whining rays
which sound like the product of angry rotors (the shape of the ships beg
for biological analogy and animalize the machine), the Martian probes
sound (and look) like electronic snakes mechanically hissing. The giant
ants in *Them!* (1954) are biological monsters (mutations caused by atomic
testing) yet their attacks are heralded by "the accompaniment of a shrill,
ear-splitting whine curiously reminscent of air-raid warnings"[79] and they

Them! (Gordon Douglas, 1954). The sound of the alien: the giant ants emit whines like sirens and signal their presence with a noise like a geiger counter. (Warner Brothers)

reveal their presence in the desert with a sound fairly similar to that of a geiger counter. Nonhumanoid aliens and terrestrial monsters in almost every SF film combine biology and technology in various ways so as to become living contradictions. A machine may emit what seems like biological sound (the hiss of a snake); an animal may sound like a machine (the geiger counter). As well, both machine and animal may combine biological and mechanical qualities in the sounds they make (as when we speak of the "screeching of tires" or the "squealing of the brakes" in a car). This third kind of sound effect functions as a crucial element in the creation of the alien or monstrous by its ability to evoke in the viewer/listener a chain of conflicting and incongruous associations.

These three basic "sounds" are used in nearly all SF cinema and are generically resonant. In a broad sense they are akin to the sound of a horse snuffling or a railroad straining in the Western, the sounds of squealing tires and gun shots in the gangster film. Unlike the sound effects in these genres, however, with the possible exception of the wind the sounds of the SF film are iconically functional only on a general level (i.e., the sounds of machinery) and become much more particular and differentiated from

219

each other in film to film. The variety can be illustrated by endless example. In *This Island Earth* (Joseph Newman, 1955), for instance, the sounds of interplanetary war may evoke the memory of the interplanetary war in *War of the Worlds*—but the sounds themselves are not at all the same; *This Island Earth* envisions different weapons and, consequently, different sound effects, zapping rather than shrill whining. *Forbidden Planet* (1956), loosely fashioned as it is from Shakespeare's *The Tempest*, is (as John Baxter notes) an isle "full of voices" from the "whopping shriek of the invisible monster as it attacks" [80] to the still active underground power stations of the long dead Krel which exists as "a buzzing, howling, throbbing world like the blown-up belly of a computer." [81] In a less prestigious potboiler *Beginning of the End* (Bert I. Gordon, 1957), the giant locusts make their initial entrance by sound alone: "The scene opens on a pair of adolescents necking in their car off a desert road. Their attention is caught by a weird clicking sound, the boy looks up in horror, the girl screams, the music stings and the scene fades." [82] (Again an insect sounds mechanical.) In the fairly novel *The Monolith Monsters* (John Sherwood, 1957), the sound effects of rocks shattering and splintering are made almost pain-

This Island Earth (**Joseph Newman, 1955**). **The sounds of the SF film are iconically functional but vary in particularity from film to film. Zapping war machines in this film are quite different from the whining war machines in** *War of the Worlds*. **(Universal)**

ful to the viewer so that combined with the image of "a bizarre procession of lurching crystals of silica"[83] toppling and growing upwards again only to fall, the viewer is inclined to hear the shattering as anthropomorphized screams of pain. And, as do other Jack Arnold films, *The Space Children* (1958), creates uneasiness with natural forces; the drumming presence of the sounds of the landscape act like a headache: "the muffled boom of the surf audible in almost every shot" and the "grey windy world of the sea shore"[84] blowing constantly at the base of one's consciousness. In the often-maligned SF-horror film *The Fly* (Kurt Neumann, 1958), a not often employed dislocation of sound is used to good effect in what Ivan Butler describes as "a nice moment when a deatomised cat yowls from all over the room at once."[85] And the atomic wind reappears, along with emotionally effective and disproportionate echoes, in the postholocaust *The World, the Flesh and the Devil* (Ranald MacDougall, 1959), a film whose selective sound track emphasizes the wind sighing through an empty New York City, blowing newspapers, whining around corners, and uses it as an aural metaphor for the folly and death of man. Dislocated sound appears in *THX 1138* (1971), the dislocation appropriate to a film which posits a computerized, homogenized, overpopulated, and spied-upon society. Philip Strick finds an "enduring interest" in the film's soundtrack, "a multi-layered stir of electronic echoes, in which individual voices are often lost among the simultaneous transmissions."[86] In contrast, in the only occasionally adventurous *Soylent Green* (Richard Fleischer, 1973), a film which also posits a world populated beyond its food supply, the soundtrack of echoes and whispers is not electronic and certainly not dislocated. The script describes the look and sound of the apartment building in which Detective Thorn (Charlton Heston) lives:

> The building is illuminated by a single red bulb high in the ceiling on top of the stairwell. But there is life on the entry and on the stairs. Nearly every foot of space is occupied by a man or woman or child. Thorn has to pick his way through the mass of humanity to get up the stairs. Some are sleeping, others are aware of Thorn and his packages. There are hollow eyes, gaunt faces, the sick, the old, the young, the dying. There are the *sounds:* whispers, murmurs, sobs.[87]

What is interesting about both *THX 1138* and *Soylent Green* is that they achieve a certain similarity of effect although the sounds of the "overpopulous masses" are manifested through different means in each film. Both the electronically transmitted whisperings and overlaid sounds of *THX 1138* and the directly human whisperings and overlapping cries and coughs and sobs of *Soylent Green* are so modulated and thinned and distanced that they both acquire the qualities of SF wind, its sighing desolation, its thin moaning, its intimations of mortality and its hollow evocation of T. S. Eliot's wasteland.

Finally, athough less emphasized here in its particular instances because of its ubiquitous presence, the sound of science fiction is the sound of machinery—or more appropriately, the sound of technology. (The distinction has to do with delicacy and "cool"; machinery clunks while technology—even in malfunction—never sounds so stocky and primitive.) From the fifties to the present, from *The Thing* and *Destination Moon* onward, the sounds of technology have created their own music for the genre. The sounds of electricity (the residue from *Frankenstein,* and a bit too literally, emotionally, and aurally "hot" for SF to absorb comfortably) quickly gave way to various beepings, tappings, tickings, hummings, and thrummings, songs sung by rocketship gauges, levers, and engines, by cyclatrons and atomic reactors, by computer consoles. And more recently, the singing itself has given way to a less celebratory, less optimistic treatment of the same sounds. Humming machinery sounds less cheerful and smugly content in today's SF films (i.e., *Westworld,* 1973). If instruments or computers or engines hum or sing, they remind one of autistic children, curled inward to a world which allows no living thing to share its consciousness.

The Leaden Echo and the Golden Echo

This chapter has not been meant as either an apologia or a justification for the aural elements of the American SF film: dialogue, music, sound effects. Obviously, for every one instance of convincing and effective dialogue (however achieved in context), there are surely more than ten instances of dialogue which is inadequate to its purpose. The same is true, merely less so, of SF music and sound effects. No amount of critical discussion should nor can change a lousy film into a good one—or alchemically turn a leaden soundtrack into a golden one. On the other hand, a critical analysis can serve to illuminate and describe prevalent aural patterns and tendencies in the genre and point out particular aesthetic problems unique to that genre. Such has been the intent here with this exploration of the soundtrack of the SF film, a soundtrack which has often failed to meet the challenge of its accompanying visuals and which has been the butt of ridicule because of its generally reductive qualities, its inability to live up to the expectations set by the visual imagery it accompanies. If anything, the purpose of this chapter has been to suggest that this negative overview of SF dialogue is too simple, too stereotyped, and too clichéd to be illuminating. Hopefully, it has become apparent that conflicting impulses govern SF dialogue and its resultant effectiveness in a given context, and that this conflict can be treated or resolved by adopting various modes of aural communication.

4

Postfuturism

This chapter was written nearly a decade after the previous ones. It seems quite appropriate, however, that there be such a gap, such a rupture, between previous chapters and this last one—for in the time and space between, both our lived experience and our cultural representations of time and space have visibly changed. Ten years ago the digital watch, the personal computer, the video game, and the video recorder were elite objects rather than popular commodities. Now they are an integral part of our everyday lives—consuming us as much as we consume them. In the most pervasive and personal way, these electronic artifacts (whose function is representation) both constitute and symbolize the radical alteration of our culture's temporal and spatial consciousness. Such a change in our contemporary "sense" of time and space cannot be considered less than a change in our technology, but it also must be considered something more—for, as Heidegger says, "the essence of technology is nothing technological."[1] Technology never comes to its particular specificity in a neutral context for neutral purpose. Rather, it is always "lived"—always historically informed by political, economic, and social content, and always an expression of aesthetic value.

Altered States

Any understanding of the aesthetics of the contemporary SF film depends upon our understanding the ways in which the experience of time and space have changed for us and the cinema in this last and most popularly electronic decade of American culture. As a major capitalist industry and

223

The Last Starfighter (Nick Castle, 1984). Video Game Consciousness: a new mode of "being-in-the-world." This video game serves as an Earthly "recruiting station" for Starfighters in the Star League of Planets. (Universal)

institution, American cinema has increasingly incorporated the new electronic technology into its very modes of production, distribution, and exhibition. And, as a symbolic medium whose function is representation, the American cinema has also increasingly articulated the new "sense" and "sensibility" generated by this technology and its spatial and temporal transformation of contemporary experience. As might be expected, this articulation is nowhere more evident or given more emphasis than in the SF film — for SF has always taken as its distinctive generic task the cognitive

Wargames (John Badham, 1983). Terminal Identity: a "new subjectivity constituted at the computer station or television screen." This expert player is also a teenage computer genius and "hacker." (United Artists)

mapping and poetic figuration of social relations as they are constituted and changed by new technological modes of "being-in-the-world."

In sum, the SF films of the late '70s and '80s differ from their predecessors — the culture's technological transformations radically altering their technical and aesthetic character and, more importantly, their conception and representation of the lived world. These differences go much further than a simple transformation of the nature and manner of the genre's special effects or of its representation of visible technology. Whether "mainstream" and big-budget or "marginal" and low-budget, the existential attitude of the contemporary SF film is different — even if its basic material remained the same. Cinematic space travel of the 1950s had an aggressive and three-dimensional thrust — whether it was narrativized as optimistic, colonial, and phallic penetration and conquest or as pessimistic and paranoid earthly and bodily invasion. Space in these films was semantically inscribed as "deep" and time as accelerating and "urgent."[2] In the SF films released between 1968 and 1977 (during a period of great social upheaval and after the vast spatial and temporal Moebius strip of *2001: A Space Odyssey* had cinematically transformed progress into regress), space became semantically inscribed as inescapably domestic and crowded. Time lost its urgency — statically stretching forward toward an impoverished and unwelcome future worse than a bad present. Pointing to the dystopian despair of a country negatively involved in both domestic and international contestation and unable to avoid its representation in constant and pervasive media imagery, Joan Dean tells us:

> The science fiction films of the early seventies mirror a developing neo-isolationism (perhaps a result of a costly involvement in Southeast Asia); a diminishing fear of nuclear apocalypse (partially a result of the thaw in the Cold War); and a growing concern with domestic, terrestrial issues — most of which are related to totalitarian government control of people's lives or to over-population, food shortages, pollution and ecology. Consequently space travel appeared only infrequently. . . . Likewise, extraterrestrial visitors to this planet diminished in number.
>
> The single theme . . . that dominated the science fiction imagination between 1970 and 1977 was overpopulation and its concomitant problems of food shortage and old age.[3]

Not successful box office, the films of this period are overtly despairing in their evocation of a future with no future. Traditional space has no further frontiers and appears as constraining and destructive of human existence as a concentration camp. Traditional time no longer comfortably or thrillingly promises progress as anything other than decay and entropy. The films dramatize, as well, disenchantment with a "new" technology whose hope has been exhausted, which has become "old" — no longer hyperbolized in particularly flamboyant or celebratory special effects or fearful displays.

Then, in 1977, George Lucas's *Star Wars* and Steven Spielberg's *Close Encounters of the Third Kind* were released, initiating what seemed a sudden and radical shift in generic attitude and a popular renaissance of the SF film. Both films could hardly be described as "cool" and "detached" in their vision, or "cautionary" and "pessimistic" in their tone. Through some strange new transformation, technological wonder had become synonymous with domestic hope; space and time seemed to expand again, their experience and representation becoming what can only be called "youth-

Close Encounters of the Third Kind (Steven Spielberg, 1977). **The popular renaissance of SF: technological wonder becomes synonymous with domestic hope; space and time are seen as promising and "youthful." (Columbia)**

ful." Mechanical and biological aliens were realized as cuddly, if powerful, innocents. These seminal films and the ones that followed shared little attitudinal similarity with their generic predecessors. Even the low-budget and marginal SF films that emerged in the mid-80s as a kind of "counter-cultural" response to the spatial simplicity and suburban cleanliness initiated by Lucas and Spielberg were hardly pessimistic or paranoid, representing instead a peculiar form of born-again "heart." Celebrating all existence as wondrously e-stranged and alien-ated, films like 1983's *Liquid Sky* (Slava Tsukerman) and *Strange Invaders* (Michael Laughlin), or 1984's *Repo Man* (Alex Cox), *The Brother from Another Planet* (John Sayles), and *Night of the Comet* (Thom Eberhardt) accept or embrace trashed-out, crowded, and complex urban space, and appreciate the temporal closure of the future for all the surprising juxtapositions such closure allows and contains.

Although there are exceptions, unlike their predecessors most of today's SF films (mainstream or marginal) construct a generic field in which space is semantically described as a surface for play and dispersal, a surface across which existence and objects kinetically dis-place and dis-play their materiality. As well, the urgent or hopeless temporality of the earlier films has given way to a new and erotic leisureliness — even in "action-packed" films. Time has decelerated, but is not represented as static. It is filled with curious things and dynamized as a series of concatenated events rather than linearly pressured to stream forward by the teleology of plot. Today's SF film evidences a structural and visual willingness to linger on "random" details, takes a certain pleasure (or, as the French put it, "jouissance") in holding the moment to sensually engage its surfaces, to embrace its material collections as "happenings" and collage. Indeed, both playfulness and pleasure are cinematic qualities new to SF in the late '70s and the '80s, replacing the cool, detached, and scientific vision authenticating the fictions of its generic predecessors.

The changed sense of space and time experienced in the last decade has also transformed SF's representation of the "alien," the cultural "Other." (Ridley Scott's 1979 *Alien*, John Carpenter's 1982 remake of *The Thing*, and Tobe Hooper's unpopular 1985 *Life Force* stand as the few contemporary echoes of the earlier period in which space was inscribed as deep, and invasion still possible.) The title of *Enemy Mine* (Wolfgang Petersen, 1985) only emphasizes this major shift in attitude toward the cultural (and biological/mechanical) Other. In part, of course, this shift owes much to the last decade's "recovery" from the upheavals of the late '60s. During the last decade, the representations of both American politics and popular culture have attempted to recuperate and re-vision the past (and televised) failure of bourgeois patriarchy — both in relation to its challenge by the Civil Rights, youth, and feminist movements of the late '60s, and by its loss of face and imperialist power in Southeast Asia. Most recently (and coincident with SF's most loving treatment of the alien), this "recovery" has been celebrated in self-congratulatory and electronically represented acts of "redemption" — among them the "Live Aid" concert and the media blitz surrounding the recording of "We are the world, we are the children."[4] It is no accident that two related cinematic coincidences serve to mark both the mid-'70s renaissance of SF and its mid-'80s popularity as somehow entailed with the revisioning of America's history of failure and guilt in Vietnam. It is just after the 1977 release of *Star Wars* and *Close Encounters* (the first with its inverted tale of an evil imperialism fought by "underdog" rebel heroes, the second with its scrawny, little, and powerful aliens and childlike human males) that the first films to directly address American involvement in Southeast Asia are released to wide popularity: *Coming Home, The Deer Hunter,* and *Apocalypse Now*. All represent American men as the naive and innocent victims of an incomprehensible and criminal war. It is just as telling to note that in 1984 (at the height of SF's new popularity), Academy Award consideration is given to two performers who represented two different but similarly sympathetic, sweet, forgiving, and loving "aliens" — the one from "outer space" in *Starman* (John Carpenter) and the other from Cambodia in *The Killing Fields*. In effect (and counter to the further revisions of *Rambo*), recent SF has figured the alien as a heartrendingly, emotionally empowered "innocent" — and its human protagonists as striving less toward an assumption of power (with all its negative responsibility and potential for failure) than toward an assumption of Heideggerean "care" (in the mainstream films) or a peculiar transformation of Heideggerean "dread" (in the marginal films).[5]

In part, however, this shift in sensibility toward the alien and Other seems also a function of that new technology which has transformed the spatial and temporal shape of our world and our world view. The popularization and pervasiveness of electronic technology in the last decade has reformulated the experience of space and time as expansive and inclusive. It has recast human being into a myriad of visible and active simulacra, and has generated a semantic equivalency among various formulations and representations of space, time, and being. A space perceived and represented as superficial and shallow, as all surface, does not conceal things: it displays them. When space is no longer lived and represented as "deep" and three-dimensional, the '50s concept of "invasion" loses much of its meaning and force. The new electronic space we live and figure cannot be invaded. It is open only to "pervasion" — a condition of kinetic accommodation and dispersal associated with the experience and representations of television, video games, and computer terminals. Furthermore, in a culture where nearly everyone is regularly alien-ated from a direct sense of self (lived experience commonly mediated by an electronic technology that dominates both the domestic sphere and the "private" or "personal" realm of the Unconscious), when everyone is less conscious of existence than of its image, the once threatening SF "alien" and Other become our familiars — our close relations, if not ourselves.

As in the 1950s, the contemporary SF film seems to divide into two groupings related, in great measure, to the conditions of their production. But the two groups are no longer divided as a function of their big-budget optimism or low-budget pessimism. Rather, "mainstream" and "marginal" films differ in the way they both celebrate a thoroughly domestic space and domesticated technology, embrace the alien Other, and realize a temporal reformulation of the genre's traditional "futurism."[6] The dominant attitude of most mainstream SF has been *nostalgia* — an attitude clearly evidenced by *Star Wars*' shiny evocation of the future as "Long, long ago . . . ," by *Close Encounters*' yearning for childhood rather than for its end, and by the blatant pronouncement of the very title of *Back to the Future* (Robert Zemeckis, 1985). More complimentary than contradictory, the dominant attitude of most marginal SF toward the genre's traditional "futurism" has been a literal (rather than ideological) conservatism: an embrace of *pastiche*—a nonhierarchical collection of heterogeneous forms and styles from a variety of heretofore distinguishable spaces and times. Indeed, the marginal nature of these independent SF films goes far beyond their production budgets and distribution problems, for their playful erasure of the boundaries marked between past, present, and future, between outer space and domestic space, between alien and human, locates them liminally—both "within" and "without" the genre. Their presence and claim upon SF questions the very temporal and spatial premises upon which the genre has traditionally based its identity.

Whatever their apparent differences, then, the generally sanguine attitudes and spatial and temporal realizations of both mainstream and marginal SF are surprisingly coincident. However significantly opposed in mise-en-scène, *Starman* and *The Brother from Another Planet* offer us the same protagonists—the same male human being born again in a state of wonderful and innocent "alien-nation." *D.A.R.Y.L.* (Simon Wincer, 1985) and *Android* (Aaron Lipstadt, 1982) are made of the same innocent and sweet machinery. And, although their modes of sublimity resonate quite differently, the transcendent endings of both *Cocoon* (Ron Howard, 1985) and *Repo Man* have much in common with each other. In sum, whether mainstream or marginal, the majority of contemporary (and popular) SF films celebrate rather than decry an existence and world so utterly familiar and yet so technologically transformed that traditional categories of space, time, being, and "science fiction" no longer quite apply.

At this point, we might look more specifically at how the last decade of "popular electronics" has altered the spatial and temporal state of our lived and represented experience, how the decade's technological "essence" is more than technological.[7] The pervasive experience of electronic technology in the last ten years has caused traditional orientational systems to lose much of their constancy and relevance for us. New spatial and temporal forms of "being-in-the-world" have emerged (to find their most poetic figuration, if not their proper names, in the SF film). For example, previous mention was made of '50s space perceived and represented as three-dimensional and "deep." Today, however, the traditional perception of "depth" as a structure of possible bodily movement in a materially habitable space has been challenged by our current and very real kinetic responses to —but immaterial habitation of—various forms of "simulated" space (from flight training to video games). As a function of this new "sense" of space, our depth perception has become less dominant as a mode of representing and dealing with the world. To a great degree, it has become flattened by the superficial electronic "dimensionality" of movement experienced as occurring on—not in—the screens of computer terminals, video games,

Tron (Steven Lisberger, 1982). "Simulated" Space: Depth is electronically schematized rather than re-presented. Here the electronic high priest presides over the Input/Output Tower of a video game/computer culture. (Disney)

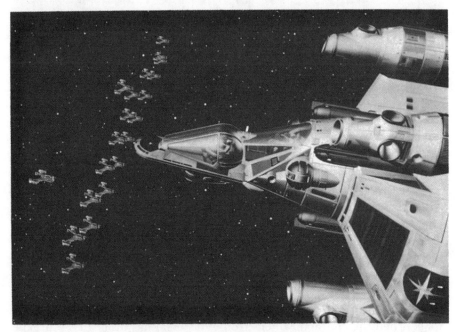

The Last Starfighter (Nick Castle, 1984). "Simulated" Space: Terminal battles still effect kinetic response, but take place across—rather than in—a space that cannot be humanly in-habited. (Universal)

music videos, and movies like *Tron* (Steven Lisberger, 1982) and *The Last Starfighter* (Nick Castle, 1984).

Our experience of spatial contiguity has also been radically altered by digital representation. Fragmented into discrete and contained units by both microchips and strobe lights, space has lost much of its contextual

Blade Runner (Ridley Scott, 1982). Space as Text rather than Context: self-contained, convulsive, discontiguous. Excessive scenography and decentered mise-en-scène become more figure than ground. (Ladd/Warner Brothers)

function as the ground for the continuities of time, movement, and event. Space is now more often a "text" than a context. Absorbing time, incorporating movement, figuring as its own discrete event, contemporary space has become experienced as self-contained, convulsive, and discontiguous —a phenomenon most visibly articulated through the mise-en-scène and editorial practices of *Blade Runner* (Ridley Scott, 1982) and *Repo Man*, and most audibly announced in *The Adventures of Buckaroo Banzai: Across the 8th Dimension* (W.D. Richter, 1984) when the king-of-all-trades hero philosophizes on this new sense of spatial fragmentation and equivalence to his rock concert audience: "Remember, wherever you go, there you are."[8]

If the digital "bit" has fragmented our experience and representation of space, then the character of electronic dispersal has dislocated our experience and sense of "place." We are culturally producing and electronically disseminating a new world geography that politically and economically defies traditional notions of spatial "location." As a system of orientation, conventional geography has served to represent relative spatial boundaries predicated by differences not only of latitude and longitude and "natural" geophysical punctuation, but also of national real estate. Conventional geography, however, cannot adequately describe where contemporary Palestine is located. Nor was it able to circumscribe the boundaries of a

Vietnam that "placed" itself both "inside" and "outside" the American living room. Our new electronic technology has also spatially dispersed capital while consolidating and expanding its power to an "everywhere" that seems like "nowhere." Again, traditional orientational systems fail to describe our new economic and political experience. Rather, it is the "political unconscious" of the new American SF film that most powerfully symbolizes and brings to visibility this apparent paradox of the simultaneous spatial dispersal and yet "nuclear" concentration of economic and political power (although, as the unconscious is wont to do, it elaborates and projects its negative self-imagery onto an evil "Other").[9] The "Empire" of the *Star Wars* trilogy literalizes both the "cosmic" technological expansion and dispersal of economic and political power and the most intense and implosive technological concentration of that power—in the "black star" that is figured as the Death Star. It is *Tron*, however, that most visibly casts its similar narrative in electronic form—the evil "Master Control Program" both concentrating and dispersing corporate electronic power and militarism across a video game culture in which even the "good guys" are electronic simulacra, occupying a new sort of space that defies traditional geographical description.

Return of the Jedi (Richard Marquand, 1983). Spatial dispersal and concentrated power are figured as the evil Empire, led by an anonymously embodied and technologically extended Darth Vader. (20th Century Fox)

Tron (Steven Lisberger, 1982). The evil Master Control Program as omnipotent and pervasive—concentrating and dispersing corporate electronic power and militarism across a totalized electronic culture. (Disney)

In this respect, *Rollerball* (Norman Jewison, 1975) seems a somewhat prescient attempt to figure the conjunction of electronic and corporate power—although, as with other SF films between 1968 and 1977, its vision is bleak and hopeless rather than celebratory. Tyrannical corporations have replaced national identity and individual difference with a global and electronic consumer culture—one ambiguously "located" in relation to the concentrated and dispersed display space of the television screen. The electronic and "nuclear" proliferation of multinational capitalism has increasingly concentrated and centralized control over the world as marketplace, but that center now appears decentered—occupying no one location, no easily discernible place. Where is OPEC? IBM? AT&T? In 1975 their power and pervasive presence both "everywhere" and "nowhere" was perceived and represented as threatening and disturbing, but ten years later that concentrated power and its decentered nature are seen as merely normal. One of the teenage Valley Girl heroines of 1984's *Night of the Comet* whines to comic effect: "You're not going to blame me because the phone went dead. I'm not the phone company. Nobody's the phone company any more." How, in fact, can traditional orientational systems help us to conceptualize, comprehend, describe, or locate a corporation called National General? The "multinationals" (as we have come to familiarly call them) seem to determine our lives from some sort of ethereal "other" or "outer" space. This is a space that finds its most explicit figuration in the impossible towering beauty of *Blade Runner's* Tyrell Corporation Building—an awesome megastructure whose intricate facade also resembles a microchip. It is a space that finds its most alienated and inhuman articulation as the "Corporation" in *Alien*, and its most outlandish

Blade Runner (Ridley Scott, 1982). Megastructure as Micro-chip: The figuration of multinational space in the intricate façade of the Tyrell Corporation Building. (Ladd/Warner Brothers)

expansion in the mining complex on Jupiter's moon, Io, in *Outland* (Peter Hyams, 1981).

Our traditional orientation toward ourselves as singular and private "individuals" has also been severely challenged by recent technological change. So has our certainty about what it means to shape time humanly through images supposedly generated in the privacy of subjective memory and desire. Today, privately experienced "interiority" appears less and less a necessary condition of human being. Intrasubjective "personal" vision once invisible to others has become publicly visible and commodified through media imagery. Our private "memory" has been increasingly constituted from previously mediated "spectacle" rather than from "direct" experience. Indeed, both *Brainstorm* (Douglas Trumbull, 1983) and *Dreamscape* (Joe Rubin, 1984) merely figure what is, in fact, the ground of contemporary culture's production of subjective visual activity as objective and/or intersubjective visible activity. Similarly, our temporal sense also has been electronically transformed and made visible. Challenging our conventional orientation toward social and personal history as a linear and progressive movement, the nonchronological Moebius strip of television allows us to see and re-cognize the complexity and thickness of temporal experience.

Brainstorm (Douglas Trumbull, 1983). Private Experience as Public Spectacle: Subjectivity is objectified through technology. (MGM)

Retension and protension are personal structures suddenly made publicly visible in "instant replays," "previews," and "rerun" narratives that subvert the temporally linear notion of "series" in their display of familiar actors, characters, and events in nonchronological representations of their youth and age, of past, present, and future. Pervasive and invasive, immediately mediating our spatial and temporal experience of the world, and then analyzing, replaying, dramatizing, rerunning, and exhausting it in insatiable acts of consumption, television has produced a historically novel form and model of cultural visibility and reflexive consciousness—heightened in the last decade by the video recorder and the personal computer. Now, more than ever before, different strata in our society have converged in their passionate interest in the image, in representation, in the very processes of mediation and simulation.

In "Postmodernism, or The Cultural Logic of Late Capitalism" (the essay that critically informs both the structure and emphasis of this present chapter), Fredric Jameson tells us that we are in the midst of

> a prodigious expansion of culture throughout the social realm, to the point at which everything in our social life—from economic value and state power to practices and to the very structure of the psyche itself—can be said to have become "cultural" in some original and as yet untheorized sense.[10]

Immersed in media experience, conscious of mediated experience, we no longer experience any realm of human existence as unmediated, immediate, "natural."[11] We can only imagine such an experience (now aware that imagination, too, is an "imaging," a mode of mediated representation). This new sense we have that everything in our lives is mediated and cultural explains, perhaps, why Deckard and Rachel's escape into the "natural" landscape at the end of *Blade Runner* seems so implausible and artificial. The landscape seems completely imaginary—unnatural in its "naturalness," its lack of the "real" social density we have previously experienced. Thus, the "nature" cinematography strikes us an inauthentic "special effect" compared to the technical special effects we have seen and accepted as authentically "natural"—and we become reluctantly aware of both cinema and narrative straining in their work to produce a traditionally "happy" ending.

Throughout the last decade, even our bodies have become pervasively re-cognized as cultural, commodified, and technologized objects. This is a phenomenon women and advertising agencies have long been aware of, but it now more globally informs a society obsessed with physical fitness. In the last decade we have come to idealize the human organism as a "lean machine"—sometimes murderously "mean," sometimes aerobically "perfect," and nearly (and yet never) impervious to that temporal bodily "terminator": death. Re-cognizing the body as machine transforms '60s narcissism. A cultural sensuality emerges based on bodily production as the production of bodies, and an androgynous erotics is figured in sweat, work, and the notion of the "routine" rather than in sexual difference. Indeed, in a decade when organ transplants and remarkable prosthetic devices are commonplaces, we are (for better and worse) theorizing our bodies, ourselves, as cyborgs.[12] We have become increasingly aware of ourselves as "constructed" and "replicated"—not only through our abstract knowledge of recombinant DNA, but also through our heightened reflexive experience of using an always acculturated (and, therefore, "artificial") intelligence, and of being a "self" always (re)produced and projected as an image available to others. As Jameson puts it, we have become "a society of the image or the simulacrum," a society that transforms "the 'real' into so many pseudoevents."[13] In Walter Benjamin's "age of mechanical reproduction," the unique status of the work of art was challenged by the technological transformation of the social world.[14] In an age of electronic reproduction and replication, however, it is the unique status of the human being that is challenged by technological transformation.

In the context of our newly exteriorized self-consciousness, the contemporary SF film has emphatically figured reflexive robots, computers, androids, and replicants seeking emotional as well as functional fulfillment. They evidence doubt and desire, a sense of negation and loss, a self-con-

The Terminator (James Cameron, 1984). Theorizing Ourselves as Cyborgs: The human organism as "lean" machine—sometimes (as here) murderously "mean," and nearly impervious to that *temporal* bodily "terminator," Death. (Orion)

sciousness and sentimentality new to the genre. They are (as *Blade Runner* suggests) "more human than human." However prideful, Robby—a distinctly 1950s robot—displays none of the comical anxiety and continual

The Empire Strikes Back (Irvin Kershner, 1980). More Human than Human: The comical anxiety and continual self-interrogation of CP30—who usually needs shutting up. (20th Century Fox)

self-interrogation of CP30, or the tenderness of "Val" and "Alta" in the robotic family romance of *Heartbeeps* (Allan Arkush, 1981). However intellectually powerful, the computer of *Colossus: The Forbin Project* (Joseph Sargent, 1970) feels no need to seek the origins of its own existence and meaning as does V(oya)ger in *Star Trek: The Movie* (Robert Wise, 1979), nor "watching" displays of human affection and sexuality does it experience the love and jealousy "felt" by the small "PC" of *Electric Dreams* (Steve Barron, 1984). There are no previous SF film counterparts to the prurient sexual curiosity and image-consciousness of Max in *Android*— who, completely aware of his own existential status as an imitation, still strives to further model himself after images of images: the personae of Jimmy Stewart and Humphrey Bogart he has seen in old movies. And nowhere before in the SF film (if in Mary Shelley) has such a fully self-conscious longing for life and eloquently ferocious challenge to humanity been articulated as in *Blade Runner*. Its "replicants" not only have human "memories"—given to them (as to ourselves) in "imaginary" constructions documented and conserved as the referential "reality" of photographic im-

Return of the Jedi (Richard Marquand, 1983). More Human than Human: Leia and Chewbacca warn CP30 to be quiet during a rebel raid on Endor. (20th Century Fox)

ages. Supremely self-conscious and reflexive, "more human than human," they are also capable of irony and poetry.

In the ten years that separate the first three chapters of this book from this last, our traditional systems for representing ourselves to ourselves have become no longer fully adequate to our experience. Hierarchical distinctions between surface/depth, here/there, center/margin, organic/ inorganic, and self/other are now commonly challenged in our daily lives.

Heartbeeps (Allan Arkush, 1981). More Human than Human: Val and Aqua are just a couple of robots in love, who eventually go off and literally "make" a baby in what is less a comedy than a poignant family romance. (Universal)

Thus, in the last decade, new symbolic descriptions of contemporary experience have begun to emerge and dominate older ones. One such new description has been the theorization of "the cultural logic of late capitalism" (and its radical entailment of new technological modes of production) as "postmodernism." Another new description has been the practice of this cultural logic as figured in the transformed poetics of the contemporary American SF film.

Postmodernism and Aesthetic Production

It is of critical importance that "postmodernism" be understood not merely as a cultural "style," but rather as a "new systemic cultural norm."[15]

241

Android (Aaron Lipstadt, 1984). Reflexive Robots: A newly exteriorized self-consciousness is figured as android Max contemplates not only the difference between man and machine, but also the difference between the sexes. (Island Alive/New Cinema)

Fredric Jameson bases his description of this new dominant logic and its aesthetic representation on Ernest Mandel's periodization of capitalist expansion into three historical "moments," each crucially marked by a "technological revolution within capital itself."[16] Market capitalism flourished in the 1840s aided by the technological innovations of steam-powered mechanization, and gave rise to "realism" as the dominant cultural logic — aesthetically represented not only by the bourgeois novel, but also by the testimonial verisimilitude of the photograph. In the 1890s the combustion engine and electric power literally reenergize market capitalism into the

242

new and more expansive structure of monopoly capitalism. Correlatively, a new cultural logic of "modernism" emerges and begins to restructure and dominate "realism," representing the new perceptual experience of an age marked by the strange autonomy and energetic fluidity of, among other mechanical phenomena, the motion picture (which, while photographically verisimilar, cinematically fragments and reorders time and space in no necessary accordance with the logic of "realism").

With the 1940s, however, and coincident with the technological development of nuclear and electronic power marked progressively by the atom bomb, the television set, and the computer, comes a new moment of capitalist expansion. So total that it is often transparently (and negatively) articulated as "postindustrial," this new and present moment, as Mandel points out, is a "period in which all branches of the economy are fully industrialized for the first time."[17] Indeed, "late or multinational or consumer capitalism" emerges as the unprecedented and "prodigious expansion of

Blade Runner (Ridley Scott, 1982). Reflexive Replicants: Priss, contemplating another human female simulacra, another pleasure model, is capable of irony and poetry. (Ladd/Warner Brothers)

capital into hitherto uncommodified areas," including "a new and his-torically original penetration and colonization of Nature and the Uncon-scious."[18] The totalizing incorporation of Nature by industrialized culture, and the commodification of the Unconscious into a visible and marketable "desire" produced as media spectacle have now expanded capital to its "purest form," and with that expansion we have seen the emergence of a new cultural logic: "postmodernism."[19]

Born in the USA and with the nuclear age, extended by the mass pro-liferation of electronic culture, the expansive logic of multinational cap-italism has altered the previous "sense" we lived and made of time, space, and world. And, although this logic coexists with other and different ways of structuring and representing social experience (for example, realism and modernism), in the last decade it has come to dominate them. The changes marked in our representations now run deep — their postmodern characteristics not merely fashionable or "stylish" adornments to older forms. Thus, as Jameson employs the term, "postmodernism" describes a deeply lived structure of social relations and representations. Indeed, inso-far as "aesthetic production today has become integrated into commodity production generally,"[20] the logic of late capitalism has radically trans-formed both the structure of our social lives and the aesthetic character of our cultural representations — from the modern architecture Jameson finds so telling to the science fiction films discussed here.

In this regard, it can be argued that, at least to some degree, the cultural logic of postmodernism contextualizes or informs not only the most radical of contemporary cultural productions, but also the most traditional and conservative. As Jameson puts it, "The postmodern is . . . the force field in which very different kinds of cultural impulses — what Raymond Williams has usefully termed 'residual' and 'emergent' forms of cultural production — make their way."[21] Thus, any understanding of the socially symbolic meanings attached to aesthetic changes in the SF film over the past decade must derive from an understanding of the changed cultural sphere in which the films were produced. It is also true, however, that such an un-derstanding of the logic that informs this cultural sphere must be reached indirectly — through a consideration of the aesthetics and structure of con-crete cultural production. Through both its conservative and radical works, then, the new SF film brings postmodern logic to visibility — symbolically representing the new structures of experience in both the spatially material form of its figures and the temporally material form of its narratives.

Previous discussion, for example, has described the increasing dom-inance of postmodern logic as both a function and effect of social existence in a culture that has become increasingly mediated, decentered, and dis-persed — at the same time it has become increasingly homogenized, repli-cated, and unified in the proliferation of electronic technology and commercial franchise. The global scope and paradoxical nature of this culture make its logical structure difficult to envision or comprehend. And yet this is precisely what is achieved by a spatially materialized figure in the clearly postmodern *Repo Man*. The mediated, decentered, and dispersed "homogenization" of American culture becomes visible and comprehensible as the metageneric commodities casually dispersed across the film's decentered mise-en-scène. Pervasively present and as completely undifferentiated and equivalent as all of Otto's experience, the white cans and boxes marked merely "FOOD" visibly represent a culture whose identical and homogenized nourishment belies its cosmetic diversification and fragmentation.

Similarly, if less obviously, films that are not properly postmodern also figure the new cultural logic and visibly comprehend it—even as they predominantly function according to the more traditional and "residual" cultural logics of realism and modernism.[22] Nostalgic and conservative films such as *Close Encounters, E. T.: The Extra-Terrestrial* (Steven Spielberg, 1982), and *Starman*, for example, identify and celebrate their landscape as American precisely by symbolically figuring our political franchise in the warm neon and comforting logos of the powerfully concentrated and yet spatially dispersed ubiquity of commercial franchise. When the familiar lights of the McDonalds "golden arches" suddenly go out in *Close Encounters*, we know something truly strange is about to happen to our world —and later, when the military secretly and easily transports itself across country under the cover of Baskin-Robbins ice cream trucks, et. al., our laughter arises more from recognition than from surprise.

The "clutter" experienced by a thoroughly commodified culture, the "new" turned into instant junk, the "pastiche" constructed by unrelated material accumulations which merely share the same space—these visible manifestations of the logic of late capitalism find their figuration in contemporary SF whether the films are "politically conscious" or not. Certainly, they constitute the very mise-en-scène and aesthetic value of recent marginal SF—"new wave" and postmodern films such as *Liquid Sky, Repo Man*, and *Buckaroo Banzai*. But this material clutter, this representation of novelty as exhausted, this manifestation of accumulation as pastiche are also frequently figured in mainstream and conservative films. However condensed and quarantined, they are nonetheless emphasized and given positive value —usually in the cluttered space and material litter of the bourgeois child's bedroom. In such mainstream films as *Close Encounters, E. T., Wargames* (John Badham, 1983), and *The Last Starfighter*, for example, the suburban bedroom stuffed with toys and emblazoned with commercial logos figures as a microcosm of contemporary consumer culture in its "purest form." Thus, although in different ways and to different degrees, the littered and trashed urban culture celebrated in marginal SF

The Incredible Shrinking Woman (Joel Schumacher, 1981). The "clutter" of a thoroughly commodified culture: here, microcosmically figured in the suburban child's bedroom. (Universal)

and the material excess of the littered and trashed suburban bedroom celebrated in mainstream SF both emerge as related representations of the new cultural logic of late capitalism. In this sense, "postmodernism" pervades the contemporary SF film — its deep structural logic symbolized by the genre's new figures and aesthetic values, and dramatized by its new attitudes and thematics.

According to Jameson, the two major themes that inform and dominate postmodern representation are an "inverted millennarianism" and an "aesthetic populism." The former replaces "premonitions of the future, catastrophic or redemptive" with the sense of "the end of this or that."[23] The latter effaces the distinction between "high culture and so-called mass or commercial culture," embracing and incorporating the

> whole 'degraded' landscape of schlock and kitsch, of TV series and Readers' Digest culture, of advertising and motels, of the late show and the grade-B Hollywood film, of so-called paraliterature with its airport paperback categories. . . .[24]

Both these themes are nowhere so blatantly addressed as in the contemporary SF film. "Inverted millennarianism" is consistently figured in, among other things, the visual "trashing" and yet operative functioning of what used to be shiny "futurist" technology. It is also evident in the decorative

Blade Runner (Ridley Scott, 1982). The Future as Past: The mise-en-scène visually "trashes" what used to be shiny futurist technology in a narrative enunciating the future through the conventions of 1940s film noir. (Ladd/Warner Brothers)

The Terminator (James Cameron, 1984). The Future as Past: "Tech noir" in design, the narrative's time-travel plot is regressive and circular, signaling the end of a belief in the future. (Orion)

and/or narrative conflation of the past and present with the future. Certainly *Blade Runner* serves as a powerful exemplar—not only in its set design and mise-en-scène (which reveals the future as a recycled pastiche of the present), but also in its enunciation of the future through the mediation of a 1940s "film noir" narrative structure. Also exemplary is *The Terminator* (James Cameron, 1984). Not only does it literally and reflexively spell out in disco lights the "Tech Noir" that visibly informs the aesthetic of much recent SF, but its regressive and circular time-travel plot also narrativizes the genre's symbolic comprehension of the "end" of modernism, of "futurism," of the belief in "progress".[25] This inverted millennarianism is figured and dramatized in those cheerful and comic mainstream films that narrate the "future" as "past." Producing the future as already "over" is the explicit work, for example, of both the earliest and latest of contemporary SF blockbusters. *Star Wars* locates itself "long ago in a galaxy, far, far away. . . ," softening the future's end by displacing it in a mythical past — and now promising us a strange inverted future of "prequels" rather than sequels. And *Back to the Future* (Robert Zemeckis, 1985), the most popular of recent "time travel" films, tells all in its regressive title, but softens the blatance of its postmodernist disbelief in the future with a comic nostalgia born of consumer reflexivity and commercial hindsight. Not only is the film's "time travel" marked in terms of brand-name identification, but its "time machine" also takes the form of a DeLorean, that defunct "futurist" car which itself signifies the instantaneous transformation of the "new" into the "classic," the future into the past.

Back to the Future (Robert Zemeckis, 1985). The Future as Past: The DeLorean time machine as the instant transformation of the "new" into the "classic." (Universal)

Strange Invaders (Michael Laughlin, 1983). Aesthetic Populism: The low-budget production announcing and celebrating itself as a simulacra of old grade-B "schlock" movies. (Orion).

Both marginal and mainstream SF also articulate the theme of "aesthetic populism" which Jameson sees informing the cultural productions of late capitalism. In one sense, this is hardly surprising—for the cinema as mass medium and commodity has generally effaced the boundaries between elite and mass culture its early existence emphasized.[26] In another sense, however, it is only recently that the SF film (long thought to be among the most "degraded" of genres) has been embraced by the mainstream industry —and by cineastes. It also is only recently that the SF film has so reflexively embraced its own former status as "schlock" and "kitsch," and/or embraced the "whole 'degraded' landscape of schlock and kitsch" that represents contemporary American popular culture. In this latter regard, the flawed comedy *Americathon* (Neil Israel, 1979) was a bit ahead of its time with its cheerful vision of the President of the United States functioning as "telethon host" and introducing a parade of questionable celebrities so as to raise money and save America from bankruptcy. Again, the clearest articulation of this "aesthetic populism" is currently found in the reflexive double articulation of marginal SF cinema. Predominantly independent productions, locating themselves self-consciously and precariously on the boundaries of the genre (and thus suspect as SF), films like *Buckaroo Banzai, Strange Invaders, Night of the Comet*, and *Uforia* (John Binder, 1986) not only announce and celebrate their own existence as the simulacra of grade-B "schlock" movies, which, of economic necessity, had visibly cheap sets and/or cheesy special effects.[27] They also foreground and locate themselves in a culture that is "schlock" — its artifacts and happenings as strange as those generically constructed in science fiction, but as normal as the "Hawaiian Days" and "Mexican Fiesta Days" promotionals and costumes found under the flourescent lighting of your homogenized supermarket chain (*Uforia*), or in the pages of the National Enquirer (*Strange Invaders*), or in the windows of suburban shopping malls (*Night of the Comet*).

Recent mainstream and big-budget SF is no less fascinated by the landscape of contemporary popular culture. These more conservative films either wholeheartedly and transparently absorb and displace it, or explicitly foreground and wonder at it. *Star Wars*, of course, has been frequently noted as "a compendium of American pop and pulp culture, carefully crafted out of many and unabashed borrowings" from comic strips, paraliterature, and old movies that are displaced and reconstructed as a coherent mythology.[28] Other contemporary big-budget films (quite unlike their '50s counterparts) often interrupt their narrative momentum and technological displays to perform a little cultural ethnography. *Close Encounters*, *Time after Time* (Nicholas Meyer, 1979), *E.T.*, *Starman*, *Cocoon*, and *Back to the Future* all show off American popular and "schlock" culture: old movies and TV series, material artifacts, peculiar cultural habits and institutions. While Jameson sees the postmodern theme of aesthetic populism theorized in the title of a contemporary architectural manifesto called *Learning from Las Vegas*,[29] both theme and title are made materially concrete and visible in *Starman* — which presents us, in one episode, with an alien who literally "learns from Las Vegas" (the capital of "schlock" culture) what it is to be an American in the "schlock" culture of late capital. The last half of the schizophrenically structured *Explorers* (Joe Dante, 1985) is even more overt. The film suspends its initial Spielbergian sentimentality and *Boy's Life* nostalgia to become a hyperstimulating and hysterically funny postmodern pastiche of "schlock" culture. Using its big budget to construct purposely tacky "B-movie" aliens, *Explorers* bombards us with a noisy, static-ridden, and snowy media blitz of random pieces and juxtapositions of old cartoons and movies (including old '50s SF), TV news, game shows, variety shows, and series, which its aliens have used as a primer and model of American language and culture. (They talk in the voices and modes of the likes of Marilyn Monroe, Henny Youngman, Groucho Marx, Ed Sullivan, and various game show hosts.) Indeed, in a moment extraordinary for its explicit articulation of the postmodern "problematic," one of the young protagonists gets all mixed up trying to explain to the aliens (and to us) how this pastiche of images is to be differentiated, and why some

Close Encounters of the Third Kind (Steven Spielberg, 1977). Aesthetic Populism: Big-budget ethnography displaying American popular culture. Note not only the television soap opera, but also the beer can and the piece of Corning Ware. (Columbia)

of these images are more "real" than others in their depiction of American life and culture.

The dominant themes of "inverted millennarianism" and "aesthetic populism" find both their figuration and narration articulated and valued in what can be identified as a postmodern aesthetic. Symptom and symbol of the lived reality of social existence and practice during this most expansive moment in the history of American capitalism, such an aesthetic constitutes and marks its cultural productions with certain discernable features. As Jameson describes them, they are:

a new depthlessness, which finds its prolongation both in contemporary "theory" and in a whole new culture of the image or the simulacrum; a consequent weakening of historicity, both in our relationship to public History and in the new forms of our private temporality, whose "schizophrenic" structure (following Lacan) will determine new types of syntax or syntagmatic relationships in the more temporal arts; a whole new type of emotional ground tone—what I will call "intensities"—which can best be grasped by a return to older theories of the sublime; the deep constitutive relationships of all this to a whole new technology, which is itself a figure for a whole new economic world system . . . the bewildering new world space of late multinational capital.[30]

The "new depthlessness," the "weakening of historicity," the "new type of emotional ground tone," and the "deep constitutive relationships of all this to a whole new technology" are remarkably evident and variously foregrounded in the SF films of the last decade. Indeed, this evidence attests to a marked change in the aesthetics of the genre laid out in the previous three chapters, allowing us to periodize their discussion of the "classic" American SF film as occurring within the context of a newly emergent, but not yet dominant, cultural logic. That is, the first wave of the genre's popularity (in fact, its first mass articulation as a film genre) begins in the 1950s and emerges, we now might argue, as the first socially symbolic cinematic representation of late American capitalism's new expansion toward its "purest" state. Following Jameson, we could say that in its figuration and narration of American culture's "deep constitutive relationships" to the new nuclear and electronic technology, the genre was constituted as an attempted mapping of "the bewildering new world space of late multinational capital." In this first "Golden Age" of the SF film, the emphasis of such mapping, however, was predominantly on the fearsome and wondrous *novelty* and *strangeness* of this new technology — and on the new forms of cultural *alien-ation* generated by this technology and its entailment with "a whole new economic world system." The vision of these '50s films, whether celebratory or paranoid, was markedly "cool" — either bearing documentary "witness" to the new world space and technology, or manifesting visual response in a removed and e-stranged state of "undecidability" as to what sort of affective behavior might be appropriate to such suddenly original situations. The first "Golden Age"of the SF film, then, emerges coincidentally with the emergent cultural logic of late capitalism, and the genre's valuation of wariness and wonder articulate that logic as a new groundbreaking aesthetics.

It is the second "Golden Age" of the SF film, however, that actively assumes and articulates those features which aesthetically represent postmodern logic. Emerging coincidentally with late capitalism's most electronically expansive and prolific decade, the genre's altered aesthetics articulate not a wariness and wonder at the emergence of a new cultural logic, but rather an acceptance of and wonder at that logic's current pervasiveness, its now common grounding of social existence, its very *lack of novelty*. Indeed, unlike its '50s predecessors, the contemporary SF film's predominant emphasis is on mapping not the fearsome and wondrous "newness" of the new technology, but rather its awesome and wondrous *familiarity*. The films no longer symbolically figure the alien-ation generated by a "whole new economic world system," but rather our *incorporation* of that new system and our *absorption* by it. Thus, the cinematic vision of the contemporary SF film has changed. No longer attitudinally and visually "cool," it is neither wary and removed from the new world space and technology, nor does it seem to evidence the need to bear documentary witness to them, thus "authenticating" their existence by means of a pronounced "objective" gaze. The new SF also does not seem affectively "undecided." Rather, the genre evidences "a whole new emotional ground tone" — one that seems moved to celebrate the consumable artifacts and specular productions of late capitalism. The new SF film seems unprecedentedly sanguine about the conservation and conversion of human existence — genially altering the spatial and temporal boundaries that limit the meaning of both "human" and "existence," and now joyfully embracing what used to be the threatening alien Other as friend, playmate, brother, and lover. The genre's mainstream films also have become a showcase, not so much for the wonders of science and technology as for the effective display of an affect made visible and material by means of "Industrial(ized) Light and Magic." Again, it is fully telling that a recent SF film title makes this shift to a "new emotional ground tone" utterly explicit. The affective state of "euphoria" (once perceived as subjective and personal) has been located in UFOs and objectified as a public, religious, mass-mediated, commodified, and self-reflexive state of *Uforia*.

The new depthlessness, the weakened historicity, the new emotional tone, and the new relationship to the "new" (whether technological or biological) thus constitute the features of a new SF aesthetics, one representative of the changed values and logic of late capitalism. In those SF films previously referred to as marginal, these features are easily recognized and celebrated as an aesthetic ideal. Not merely informed by new perceptions of spatial, temporal, emotional, and technological existence, marginal SF also consciously reformulates old SF "formulas." The films overtly overthrow the aesthetics of "residual" logics: their temporal linearity and progressive narrative movement, the limiting boundaries and composition of their generic space, their idealization of formal harmony, and, indeed, their generic integrity. Marginal SF also reflexively takes the context of its own cultural positioning and aesthetic production as its narrative content. Initially marginalized in a conservative mass medium, these low-budget and "off-beat" films have become popular nonetheless — for, as marginal representations, not only have they been co-opted and commodified as "cult" fetishes, they also represent the increasing dominance of a cultural aesthetic of marginality. It is revealing that the aforementioned *Uforia* was initially and briefly released in 1981 (under the title *Hold on to Your Dreams*) and then shelved. Now, after the success of *Repo Man* (also delayed in reaching theatrical distribution) and a general MTV-induced willingness to embrace nonlinearity, visual decentering and dispersal, and generic pastiche, *Uforia* has been re-released and recognized by major and mainstream critics.

In most of the contemporary mainstream SF films, however, the new cultural logic of nonlinearity, visual decentering and dispersal, generic pastiche, and the general transformation of cultural difference into an equi-valent and nonhierarchical heterogeneity, is consciously rejected as an aesthetic ideal. Nonetheless, that new logic is represented implicitly—unconsciously informing and subverting the "traditional" representations of coexistent and residual cultural logics and their aesthetic values. *Star Wars*, for example, does not embrace itself as a "pastiche" in the same manner as does *Buckaroo Banzai*. The former attempts to erase the traces of its cultural scavenging to construct a unifying and harmonious "mono-myth",[31] while the latter foregrounds the heterogeneity of its cultural ac-cumulations. Born of an American mother and Japanese father, Buckaroo is an accomplished race-car driver, neurosurgeon, inventor, rock star, and adventurer, who lacks "personhood" in any psychological or coherent de-velopmental sense; he is all "image and action," "made up of pieces of the pop cultural landscape, and . . . defined moment by moment—each one erasing any smudges of history from the last—by aggressive actions."[32] Buckaroo is a far cry from either Luke Skywalker or Han Solo, for *Star Wars* strives to unify its spatial, temporal, and psychological fragmenta-tion and heterogeneity into the coherence of an intergenerational and in-terplanetary history. Nonetheless, the de-historicized postmodern logic of cultural "recycling" explicit in *Buckaroo Banzai* also informs the deep structure of *Star Wars*—from its construction of spaceship models (built with all sorts of historically incongruent parts from a collection of model kits) to its immense consumption of prior literary and cinematic genres and texts.

Given its current cultural pervasiveness, the logic of postmodernism will out—finding its expression and aesthetic representation in the "political unconscious" of even the most conservative of contemporary SF, and its most explicit and self-reflexive articulation in the genre's marginalized films. Whether mainstream or marginal, however, contemporary SF makes concrete and visible the features Jameson identifies as characterizing post-modern representation. In contemporary SF, we can see the "new depth-lessness" literalized as a *deflation and inflation of space*. The "weakening of historicity" is made concrete in the genre's recent and pervasive *confla-tion of time*. The "new emotional ground tone" aesthetically transforms the representation of deep and private *special affect* into the representa-tion of superficial and visible "*special effect*." And our new familiar rela-tionship to otherness (to the new and strange, to difference and heteroge-neity) finds its socially symbolic representation in the genre's *embrace of the "alien,"* and its *erasure of alien-ation*. The remainder of this chapter, then, will trace these constituent features of postmodern logic as they are given privileged and quite literal representation in this current and second "Golden Age" of the American SF film.

254

Remarking on the "originality of postmodernist space," Jameson tells us that the last decades have seen "a mutation in built space itself," the constitution of a "hyperspace" that challenges our older perceptual apparatus and functions as "an imperative to grow new organs, to expand our sensorium and our body to some new, as yet unimaginable, perhaps ultimately impossible, dimensions."[33] For Jameson, this originality emerges most clearly in postmodern architecture, which constructs and represents space as total and absolute and yet also as decentered and disorienting. On the one hand, postmodern space "aspires to being a total space, a complete world." It has "curiously unmarked ways-in" that "seem to have been imposed by some new category of closure," and, indeed, ideally "ought not to have entrances at all."[34] Thus, postmodern space is "hyper-real": a representation determined to totalize, stand for, and replace all other space. As Jean Baudrillard identifies it, this "absolute space" is also the space of "simulation."[35] On the other hand, no matter how totalizing and hermetic, postmodern space is not easily maneuvered; it has no orientational center, no gravitational pull. One is easily lost in it. Furthermore, one is likely to "lose sight" of the fact one is lost, or of where one was spatially "bound" — for plural and random trajectories are suggested by postmodern space's accommodation and containment of an excess of everything. The new architectural tenets underlying the postmodern construction of space "celebrate hybrid expression, complexity, eclecticism, and 'variable space with surprises'."[36]

Recent mutations in SF screen space also figure and make visible the new aesthetic and social values concretized in the spatial representations of contemporary architecture. "Hyped up" to an unprecedented degree, the genre's spatial reformulations are symbolized by three new "mappings" of spatial existence in postmodern culture. The first responds to a perceived *deflation of space*, and emphasizes a new and highly privileged surface topography. The second responds to a perceived *inflation of space*, and attempts to schematize visibly the ways in which space has come to dominate our consciousness and our hold on experience. The third mapping responds to the way in which living space both superficially (as deflated in nature) and excessively (as inflated in function) conflates into a heightened spatial experience perceived as autonomous, *absolute*. Synthesizing the perceptions of the first two maps, this third map visualizes most clearly those features that characterize and symbolically represent the postmodern aesthetic.

The new value afforded the *deflation of space* in the SF film is in precise accord with Jameson's suggestion that "the supreme formal feature" of mutated, postmodern hyperspace is "a new kind of flatness or depthlessness, a new kind of superficiality in the most literal sense."[37] This "suppression of depth" finds representation in the obvious pictorial flatness mapped and dramatized by films like *Tron* and *The Last Starfighter*, both of which use and privilege computer graphics and electronic image generation. In these films and others, the "deep" and indexical space of cinematographic representation is deflated—punctured and punctuated by the superficial and iconic space of electronic simulation. This deflation of deep space, however, is presented not as a loss of dimension, but rather as an excess of surface. The hyperspace of these films is proudly two-dimensional—even in its depiction of three-dimensionality. Like "superrealism" in contemporary painting, it hyperbolizes material and surface detail while it schematizes (rather than represents) texture. It thus presents itself as "more visible" than the cinematographic image, less clouded by atmosphere. More real than real, this hyperspace signifies a replication and clarification of the cinematographic image, an objectification of its vision accomplished from a space with no atmosphere, no respiration, no experience of depth or gravity. Indeed, this particular SF mapping of spatial existence in postmodern culture constructs a privileged equivalence between electronic space and "outer" space.[38] Both are spaces we regularly experience

Star Trek II: The Wrath of Khan (Nicholas Meyer, 1982). The Deflation of Space: Not a loss of dimension, but a clarification of detail. More real than real, this hyperspace constructs a privileged equivalence between "outer" space and electronic space. (Paramount)

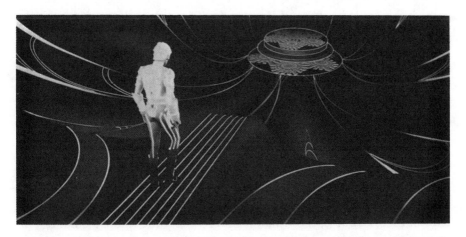

Tron (Steven Lisberger, 1982). The Deflation of Space: Human subjectivity as terminal identity, a mutation in human embodiment. (Disney)

and yet cannot "inhabit" without technological mediation, without some transformation or mutation of our bodies, without (as Jameson suggests) the growth of "new organs"—be they a "joy stick," a "mouse," or a spacesuit.

Tron provides us with both the most explicit map of this new deflated space of electronic culture and its consequent demand on human being. Computer generation has flattened and schematized three-dimensional space into the two-dimensional, conceptual space of video games and computer programs. A responsive flattening of human body and character occurs, digitalizing both human motive and movement into discrete and serial pixels, so that *analogic physical progress* is reformulated as *binary information process*. Indeed, only superficial beings without "psyche," without depth, can successfully maneuver a space that exists solely to display. What Scott Bukatman has called *terminal identity* is literalized by the new human embodiment figured in *Tron*. Those pixelated beings make visible that "unmistakably doubled articulation" marking both the end of the traditional subject and a "new subjectivity constructed at the computer station or television screen."[39] *Tron* also presents this new electronic subjectivity and terminal space as nearly "absolute." For most of the film, almost everything and everyone have mutated into a simulation, and the category of the "real" (that narrative "real world" mainframing the computer program world) is short-circuited and loses power. Simulation seems the *only* mode and space of being. Thus, what Baudrillard says of the electronic pervasiveness of television can also be said of the electronic world visualized by *Tron*: "There is no longer any medium in the literal sense: it is now intangible, diffuse and diffracted in the real, and it no longer can even be said that the latter is distorted by it."[40]

Tron is exceptional in its formally sustained mapping of the deflated existential space produced by the narrative drama of electronically (em)powered, multinational capitalism. Most of the new SF films that use electronic graphics, image enhancement, and simulation are more conservative — figuring the depthless space and digital movement of postmodernism against the ground of that traditionally "deep" cinematographic space associated with bourgeois realism (and, occasionally, modernism).[41] The "weakest" of these productions tend, as Jameson suggests, "to slip back more comfortably into a thematic representation of content — into narratives which are more *about* the processes of reproduction" than they are the formal result of them. That is, they include and feature "the whole technology of the production and reproduction of the simulacrum" (video games, huge computers, personal computers, and the like) — but they only minimally "tap the networks" of this new "reproductive process" and only occasionally "afford us some glimpse into a postmodern or technological sublime," or that "whole new postmodern space in emergence around us."[42] *Wargames*, for example, is among those films still dominated by residual cul-

Wargames (John Badham, 1983). Screen Space: The mere "outer shell" of the computer and other electronic technology has little emblematic or visual power. (United Artists)

Wargames (John Badham, 1983). Terminal Space: Screen space electronically reformulated in a sublime display of computer consciousness (here, of a surprise nuclear attack that is only represented, but will be "really" responded to). (United Artists)

tural logic—but even it generates moments of postmodern space, aware that the mere "outer shell" of the computer and other electronic technology has, as Jameson puts it, "no emblematic or visual power."[43] To generate this new technology's active "sublimity" (even in the midst of a cautionary drama warning us of the terminal consequences of our new terminal lives), screen space is reformulated as "terminal space" and is clearly privileged.

Certainly, this privilege has always been afforded the "special effects" of SF—their value a combined function of their overall "scarcity" in the film's economy, the anticipatory desire this scarcity constitutes in the spectator/consumer, and the cinema's fulfillment of that desire in a self-celebratory and bravura technological display.[44] Nonetheless, the privileged punctuation of *cinematic* effects (taken as "normal" and therefore transparent) by clearly marked *electronic* effects is not an instance of cinema celebrating itself and its "own" technology. Jameson tells us that "machines of reproduction rather than of production . . . make very different demands" on both the "capacity for aesthetic representation" and the "aesthetic embodiment" of their flattened and imploded processes.[45] The extra-special "specialness" and isolation granted the electronic deflation of traditionally deep cinematic (and social) space can be seen as a conservative attempt to *contain* this new technology—to keep it, as Michael Stern suggests, an "abstract category" simultaneously fetishized and quarantined so that it seems "magical, socially ungrounded" and its threat of total diffusion is de-fused.[46] Thus, these "privileged moments" of electronic effects attest not to a cinema displaying and celebrating its *own* technological capacity for representation (a function of special effects in the big-budget films of the genre's first "Golden Age"). Rather, these moments attest to a cinema attempting to protect its representational function against domination by a radically *other* mode of representation. What formally and thematically conservative SF films like *Star Wars*, the *Star Trek* series, and *Wargames* assert through their foregrounded but limited use of electronic representation is not a mere difference in degree of "specialness", but a major difference in kind.

The discrete — if flamboyantly marked — use of electronic representation to puncture and deflate the deep space of cinematographic representation also serves another function in these films — one that inverts the earlier relation between SF's "special effects" and its more transparent representations. A previous chapter suggested how this latter transparency and "realism" functioned to authenticate the SF "special effect" as also "real." The *direction* of this authenticating function, however, seems highly dependent upon the similar cinematographic nature of previous "transparent" and "special" effects. When the electronic punctuates the cinematic, the direction of that authenticating function tends to reverse itself. Here Baudrillard is particularly illuminating. In a discussion of the simulated, "imaginary stations" of American amusement parks like Disneyland, which

Tron (Steven Lisberger, 1982). "Imaginary Stations": Flattened, electronically simulated space conservatively affirms the cinema image as "real" by contrast. (Disney)

260

punctuate the supposedly "real" lived space that surrounds them, he tells us:

> Disneyland is presented as imaginary in order to make us believe that the rest is real, when in fact all of Los Angeles and the America surrounding it are no longer real, but of the order of the hyperreal and of simulation. It is no longer a question of a false representation of reality (ideology), but of concealing the fact that the real is no longer real, and thus of saving the reality principle.[47]

In this sense, the privileged isolation of hyperreal, flattened, electronically simulated space and imagery is again articulated as a conservative and nostalgic move — one affirming the dimensional representation of the cinematographic image as "real" by contrast. Nonetheless, this strategy also simultaneously and dialectically affirms the inescapably mediated nature of postmodern existence in a culture where "everything that was lived directly has moved away into a representation."[48]

The hyperreality of electronic simulation, then, authenticates and conserves the "reality" of cinematic representation, where it is used to punctuate and contrast with the older model of "deep" space, affirming the latter's contours, texture, and thickness as the primary ground for human movement and existence. The privileging of electronic depiction here depends upon its *marked difference* from cinematographic representation rather than upon its *integration* with it (however much integration may be "promoted" by the narrative). Electronic simulation's hyperreality is valued precisely because it is an abstraction of cinematic representation. Where the latter re-presents three-dimensional space and the analogic variations of light and atmosphere that constitute the sensual experience of texture and contour, the former computes and simulates represented space — analyzing, schematizing, and digitally coordinating it so that three dimensions, texture, and contour are diagrammed rather than pictured. Thus, this different kind of representation and degree of abstraction not only points to the less schematized "realism" of cinematographic representation, but also concretely figures — and displays — the kind and degree of power and pervasion "effected" by multinational capital's entailment with electronic technology, and its constitution of video game consciousness. All the electronic battles figured against the ground of cinematic realism, humanism, and sentiment in *Star Wars* and *The Last Starfighter* are easy to watch. Nonphotographic and thus not existentially indexical, they don't count. They just compute, become the source of "high scores" that elevate mortality into the astronomical abstraction of a truly new metaphysics. Such displays signify both the end of "realism" and the "death" of the cinematographic image — and thus account, perhaps, for the conservative and nostalgic humanism of the narratives in which they appear, narratives

Blade Runner (Ridley Scott, 1982). Excess Scenography: Space valued for its acquisitive power. The eroticization and fetishization of material culture as multidimensional and sensuous "clutter." (Ladd/Warner Brothers)

quite different in tone from earlier examples of the genre.

The second SF mapping of space in postmodern culture describes the sense in which its categorical and existential values have been *inflated*. This inflation is symbolically marked in two quite different representations. One visualizes an "excess scenography" so rich, intricate, and complex that it tends to diffuse the film's temporal force, and occasionally—as in *Dune* (David Lynch, 1984)—its narrative coherence.[49] The other emphasizes a particular kind of "emptied" terrestrial space, one free of the familiar material clutter that generally obscures the sight and site of a potential cultural "opening."

The "excess scenography" of *Blade Runner*, for example, is more than mere background. As Bart Mills says: "The setting *is* the film."[50] An abundance of things to look at serves to inflate the value of the space that contains them, and emphasizes a particular kind of density and texture. This visualization of contemporary spatial experience eroticizes and fetishizes material culture, spatializing it as multidimensional and sensuous "clutter." Indeed, the space mapped here is valued for its acquisitive power, its expansive capacity to accumulate, consume, and hold on to "things." The space of films like *Escape from New York* (John Carpenter, 1981), *Blade Runner, Blue Thunder* (John Badham, 1983), and *Dune* "collects" material culture as a value "in itself." It rescues cultural artifacts from their overdetermination by time and function through its power to accumulate, save, transform, recycle. Thus, *Blade Runner's* production designer speaks of the film's "additive architecture."[51] And, according to Mills,

> [Ridley] Scott says his method is to 'build layers of texture,' so that visual information is imparted in every square inch of screen. Details proliferate. The umbrellas carried by extras have lighted tips because the streets are so murky. The television monitors that have replaced traffic signals provide deliberately poor pictures. Skyscrapers are built on top of existing structures — and are shown on the screen in their hundreds of stories. . . . *Blade Runner* is a movie that's not so much filmed as designed.[52]

The "designed" space of these films is both a de-signed and re-signed space. The visual demands made on the spectator by an abundance and accumulation of things, by excess scenography, de-sign "texture" as a sign-function of depth and possible movement and re-sign it as a sign-function of quantity and stasis. No-thing is lost in these films; every-thing remains. And "remaindered," things begin to look both shabby and newly strange, begin to serve new functions, to adhere together in new combinations and take on a new "style." Syd Mead, *Blade Runner's* visual consultant, speaks of "retrofitted utilization."[53] And David Lynch realizes *Dune* as a place where "everything looks old, like its been around for a while."[54] This new designed and resigned SF space collects and contains the temporal flow of narrative and history as if it were both museum and city dump. Which, indeed, it is in many of these films. *Dune* stands as the costume museum, its spatial collection of 16th- and 19th- century dress a sign of the narrative's temporal weakness, fragmentation, and paralysis. Densely textured and visually sensual, *Dune's* space becomes absolute and overwhelming with its "four different planet environments and more than four thousand costumes."[55] Hence the peculiar hysteria of its insistent narration and dislocated interior monologues, their temporal information desperate of ever achieving momentum and dramatic visibility amid the eye-stopping excess of the film's mise-en-scène. *Dune's* perversely sensual appeal seems generated by its hermetic and temporally paralyzing materiality. As Hal Hinson aptly says of Lynch, "Decay is built into his images. His special talent is that he has found beauty in entropy."[56]

Dune notwithstanding, this entropic aesthetic most commonly finds its realization in those SF films that concretize and privilege the material aggregations of the city dump — the most literal among them *The Terminator*.[57] Trash and waste, pollution and decay, are visualized as curious and beautiful, postmodern sensibility finding aesthetic pleasure and sublimity

Blade Runner (Ridley Scott, 1982). Space as City Dump: "Remaindered," things begin to look both shabby and newly strange, to adhere together in new combinations, to take on a new "style." (Ladd/Warner Brothers)

Dune (David Lynch, 1984). Space as Museum: Collecting and containing the temporal flow of narrative and history, the film's paralyzing materiality is articulated, in part, by its "more than 4,000 costumes." (Universal)

in the accumulations and transformative decay of the cityscape where, as Jameson points out, "even the automobile wrecks gleam with some new hallucinatory splendour." He continues:

The exhilaration of these new surfaces is all the more paradoxical in that their essential content — the city itself — has deteriorated or disintegrated to a degree surely still inconceivable in the early years of the 20th century. . . . How urban squalor can be a delight to the eyes, when expressed in commodification, and how an unparalleled quantum leap in the alienation of daily life in the city can now be experienced in the form of a strange new hallucinatory exhilaration — these are some of the questions that confront us.[58]

These questions confront us concretely in SF films that inflate space by accumulating in it an excess of things. In them, those values of dimension and texture, density and complexity associated with the older "depth models" of realism and modernism have been preserved but reformulated. That is, they have been brought literally to the surface and made concretely visible. They have, in the most superficial — if paradoxically profound — way been completely *materialized*. Indeed, the sensuous visualizations of SF "urban noir" stand as monuments to the culture of late capitalism — even as the plots lament it. The crowded, aggregate, and polyglot megapopolis is a sign of the success of neocolonial and multinational "incorporation." The omnipresence of waste is a sign that the digestive system of advanced capital's body politic is not only working, but working "overtime" and at full capacity. And the darkness of these SF films is visually celebratory, representing (as Jameson suggests) the grand "moment of a radical eclipse of Nature itself."[59]

It is to this "eclipse of Nature itself" that SF's other and opposite mode of spatial inflation responds. Generally conservative and regressive, films like *Close Encounters* and *Starman* increase the value of space by "emptying" it of the familiar material clutter that so commonly fills it up and eclipses Nature. Nostalgic for wide open space, these films leave urban clutter and literally "go west" (or, at least, midwest) — looking for an open and dark terrestrial sky that can serve as an empty screen, a clean slate, for some new and marvelous and somehow "natural" (if still "technological") display. What is most fascinating about these films is the way they differ from their '50s and '60s counterparts, which sought new frontiers in "outer" space or found the open, uncultivated, and "natural" spaces of the desert or the Arctic dangerous.

With a few exceptions like the *Star Trek* films, the "empty" and "open" space most highly valued by contemporary SF is terrestrial and domestic. Within the context of a culture that seems to have totally eclipsed Nature, these films desire no new intergalactic frontier, but merely the "opening" provided by an expanse of earthly sky. Indeed, the blackness of outer space now holds less iconic power for us than the gathering and roiling clouds and unlit night sky privileged in *Close Encounters, E.T., Starman,* and to a lesser degree in *Cocoon.* As well, instead of fearing "natural" and un-

Close Encounters of the Third Kind (Steven Spielberg, 1977). Emptied Space: Responding to the "total eclipse of Nature itself" by a totally colonized and commodified planet, nostalgic SF spatially inflates the value of a dark and open terrestrial sky. (Columbia)

cultivated space, these nostalgic films seek it—knowing full well that it no longer exists. One need not feel overly threatened by the possibility of "absolute" emptiness when one knows a McDonalds, Pizza Hut, Baskin Robbins, and Holiday Inn are just out of frame. Thus, the landscape of "empty" space is gentled from the hostile desert and Arctic to the merely less cluttered space of midwest farmland, western rangeland, suburbia. Here one can look for an "opening" impossible to perceive in that "absolute" and oppressive space constituted by excess scenography. Indeed, in this regard it is interesting to return to *Dune*, which, among its many failures, counts a contradictory but telling "double articulation" of the current inflated value of space in a culture that has eclipsed Nature. On the one hand, *Dune* celebrates this eclipse through both its excess scenography and its narrative problematic, and so the "natural" open space of the desert is meant to be threatening. On the other hand, although the desert is narratively projected as a hostile space, it visually functions like a breath of fresh air— releasing us from the dark, hermetic, hot-house interiors and demanding clutter of the film's insistent and material erotics. In sum, within the cultural logic of late capitalism, a vast space that has, as yet, had no-thing in it is inconceivable. Unlike the '50s films, today's SF can only imagine and

The Incredible Shrinking Woman (Joel Schumacher, 1981). Emptied Space: Pat—unlike Scott Carey—cannot escape into some cosmically empty and uncommodified universe. (Universal)

mirror a reverse spatial inflation—nostalgically valuing a space emptied of every-thing.

This reversal of '50s consciousness in regard to the difference between "empty" and "emptied" space is wonderfully marked by *The Incredible Shrinking Woman* (Joel Schumacher, 1982), which reformulates 1957's *The Incredible Shrinking Man* (Jack Arnold) not only in terms of gender, but also in terms of the diminished dimensions of human being in the now totally commodified consumer culture of advanced capitalism. A reverse visualization of Scott Carey's ascetic and primal basement universe in which he proved "things" were not literally the measure of man, the new film satirically emphasizes that things are. Scott's "mutation" places him ultimately in philosophical confrontation with the vast "empty" space of the atom and the universe. Pat's "mutation" is quite different; space for her is not philosophically enlarged, but merely "emptied" by her own increasing lack of material presence. Her confrontation is with a frying pan and the kid's toys. She is literally overwhelmed by the affluent clutter of her suburban existence. As she shrinks in bodily response to the "excess scenography" of her life-world, her home becomes "emptier," but only literally so—for the phenomenological size and importance of "things" even more emphatically appropriate and dominate her space and consciousness. A figure of the 1980s, Pat—unlike Scott—cannot escape into some cosmically empty and uncommodified universe.

The third SF map of spatial existence in postmodern culture conflates spatial deflation and inflation, emphasizing both the value of a surface detail that lacks dimension and text-ure and the value of an excess scenography that substitutes quantity for depth and accumulation for movement. This mapping concentrates spatial value as autonomous, or *absolute*, and is characterized by the discontiguity of a busy, eclectic, and decentered mise-en-scène that not only undermines, but also playfully mocks the temporal and causal relations that supposedly give narrative its coherence. All meaning is generated by spatial relations. Indeed, narrative coherence is deconstructed as co-Here-nce and celebrated as a purely spatial value. This "wherever you go, there you are" sense of spatial autonomy is most clearly represented and privileged not only in *Buckaroo Banzai*, but also in *Liquid Sky, Strange Invaders, The Brother from Another Planet, Repo Man, Real Genius* (Martha Coolidge, 1985), *Uforia*, and even in the mainstream *Explorers*. Because they tend to synthesize the paradoxical sense in which we now live space as both deflated and superficial and inflated and complex, these cinematic articulations constitute the most recent, sophisticated, and formally postmodern of the three mappings discussed here.

The above films use few electronic effects and, in fact, tend to mock both the technological origins of special effects and their privileged appearances and function in the narrative. Nonetheless, without weakly displaying electronic technology or more forcefully punctuating cinematographic space with electronic space, these films still constitute space as shallow and deflated. Rather than merely borrow upon electronic space, they radically reformulate cinematographic space according to the new electronic coordinates and experiential values of postmodern culture. Their superfici-

The Adventures of Buckaroo Banzai: Across the 8th Dimension (W.D. Richter, 1984). Absolute Space: A "bewildering immersion in constant busyness" articulates space as both superficial and complex. (20th Century Fox)

ality and depthlessness are the cinematic effect of what Jameson describes as a "bewildering immersion" in "constant busyness." Speaking of the distracting space and "suppression of depth" that characterize the Bonaventure Hotel in Los Angeles, Jameson might well be speaking of the continually dispersed and decentered mise-en-scène of *Liquid Sky* or *Repo Man* in which "a constant busyness gives the feeling that emptiness is here absolutely packed . . . without any of that distance that formally enabled the perception of perspective or volume."[60] In this newest group of SF films, constant busyness and motion are enhanced by the material clutter of excess scenography to distract the eye from locating itself in the fixed position from which the conception of personal movement, depth, and interiority (or subjectivity) becomes possible.

Confronting all this visual excess and its competing demands, the spectator's attention skims over and across the surface of space and things. Being itself is decentered and dispersed, and the identity of both spectators and characters again becomes constituted as "terminal"—flattening residual psychic depth into the visibility of convulsive activity displayed on complex space. Elements of the mise-en-scène once arranged in space to represent depth now arrange themselves shallowly on and across space, and the dispersal of both the spectators' and characters' intention and attention disperse the films' narrative focus. The effect is a material overload that exceeds visual grasp and gives everything, everyone, and every activity a certain non-hierarchical equivalence. Indeed, most of these films are "marginal" in a profound way. Not only generally low-budget and made independently or on the margins of the Hollywood mainstream, they also visually embrace and dramatize marginality. That is, they are not merely marginal productions, but they also produce marginality—decentering and dispersing the convulsively motivated activity of their marginal characters toward the margins of the screen's "outer" space. It is no wonder that aliens look at home in the mise-en-scène, or that the films' marginal terrestrials find nothing particularly strange or estranging about their close encounters of the third kind.

Often, the visual excess of activity and scenography makes us want to see films like *Liquid Sky, Repo Man,* and *Uforia* again. But our perceived sense of "lack" has nothing whatever to do with concealment, with cinematic or narrative "depth," with "hidden" meanings that must be teased out. Rather, it has to do with the sense of having "missed" something. In these films, spectatorial desire is constituted from excess rather than from deprivation.[61] There is more than meets the eye here, but the "more" is always available to vision, not hidden from it. What we see is precisely what we get—and so we want to exhaust our curiosity in the surfeit of this new surface space, to see everything that is displayed and dispersed there, to generate meaning from the absolutely visible flux of material and action in complex but superficial relation.[62]

All three of the SF maps discussed here represent postmodern "hyperspace" as a screen space lived on the surface. Either it lacks the "third" dimension (and merely computes or conceptualizes it)—as in *Tron.* Or it substitutes the aggregations of excessive quantity or an opposite nostalgic "emptied-ness" for depth—as in *Blade Runner* and *Starman.* Or it constructs a bewildering and excessive conjunction of material and movement that decenters and disperses older forms of intention, attention, and subjectivity—as in *The Adventures of Buckaroo Banzai,* significantly subtitled *Across the 8th Dimension.* Thus, in some contemporary SF films, the "new depthlessness" described by Jameson is figured as a representation through and of electronic technology's visible and visual flattening of spatial experience. In others (particularly the "new wave" and most postmodern of recent SF), the "new depthlessness" and its aesthetic valuation are much more pervasive—transparently informing the mise-en-scène, constituting the new "hyperspace" not only as a figure of contemporary experience, but also as its ground. Despite their differences, however, nearly all contemporary SF film to some degree constructs and maps the special semiotic power and aesthetic value that "depthlessness" now has for the visual consumer in postmodern culture.

The Collapse and Conflation of Time

Our contemporary cultural inflation of the value of space and surface has several existential and aesthetic consequences, which, again, find symbolic dramatization in the formal structures and narrative thematics of the contemporary SF film. Jameson identifies one of these consequences as the "weakening of historicity," and he goes on to explore "the question of temporal organization . . . in the postmodern force field," and "the problem of the form that time, temporality and the syntagmatic will be able to take in a culture increasingly dominated by space and spatial logic."[63] The inflated value of space and surface has led to a deflation of temporal value, to a collapse of those temporal relationships that formulated time as a continuous and unifying flow — constituting the coherence of personal identity, history, and narrative. Indeed, the insistent detail and homogenous representations of electronic culture entailed with the acquisitive eclecticism and "normless" heterogeneity of material culture have transformed temporal coherence into spatial co-Here-nce. This transformation, with its consequent transformation of identity, history, and narrative, marks what Jameson sees "as the waning of the great high-modernist thematics of time and temporality, the elegiac mysteries of *durée* and memory."[64]

In this regard, *Blade Runner* stands as a particularly instructive film, one elegantly poised at the precise point where the high-modern and the postmodern meet to diverge. While its thematics explicitly elegize the "mysteries" of *durée* and memory, its mise-en-scène explicitly celebrates space as a "field of stylistic and discursive heterogeneity" able to "transform the stream of time and action into so many finished, complete, and isolated punctual event-objects."[65] Indeed, the film's double transformation of the *temporal field* that constitutes human memory and narrative coherence (each a "stream of time and action") into the *spatial field* that constitutes photographs and excessive scenography (each "finished, complete, and isolated punctual event-objects") both symbolizes and enacts not only the problematic subject/object nature of the "more human than human" replicants, but also *Blade Runner's* own thematic and aesthetic ambivalence about the traditional privilege the category of time has had over space in Western culture. On the one hand, its mise-en-scène valorizes space for its capacity to accumulate and conserve past experience as a future present of tangible "things."[66] On the other, the narrative elegizes temporal memory, its invisible flow, its ephemerality, its lack of tangibility. Dying, the more grandly human than human replicant Roy Baty says to Deckard, "I've seen

Blade Runner (Ridley Scott, 1982). The "mysteries" of *durée* and memory: Roy Baty's high-modernist elegy in a postmodern mise-en-scène: "All these things will be lost in time . . . like tears . . . in rain." (Ladd/Warner Brothers)

things you people wouldn't believe . . . Attack ships on fire off the shoulders of Orion . . . All these things will be lost in time . . . like tears . . . in rain."

Most of the new SF films, however, are not so truly ambivalent about the transformation of temporal experience into spatial experience as is *Blade Runner*. They are either conservatively nostalgic about the weakening of historicity—unconsciously revealing that weakness in their very attempts to historicize both the past and future. Or they are primarily celebratory about the conservative value of space—reveling in its material present-ness, its capacity to "overtake" time by "saving" the past as a collection of styles and artifacts and "containing" the future as the latter's "neohistory" (which is more spatial spectacle than temporal drama or narrative). Nonetheless, despite their explicit aesthetic and ideological differences, both generic modes emerge as equally symptomatic of the postmodern breakdown of temporal values and both express that breakdown through a mise-en-scène and/or narrative structure that denies the temporal relationship of past, present, and future as relational. The new SF film tends to conflate past, present, and future—in decor constructed as temporal pastiche and/or in narratives that either temporally turn back on themselves to conflate past, present, and future, or are schizophrenically constituted as a "series of pure and unrelated presents in time."[67]

Back to the Future is perhaps the most explicit representation of SF's new conservative nostalgia and its conflation and homogenization of temporal distinctions. It is literally "backward" looking, its time travel movement regressive. Thus, when Marty wants to get "back—to the future" from the past, his goal is merely the present. (Despite its title, there is no imagined future at all in this film.) As well, the peculiar mise-en-scène conflates and homogenizes temporal distinctions to a spatial "nowhere" in time, to a charming and mildly satirized "erewhon" that has no connection with 1955 as a "real" historical past. In both the 1980s and the 1950s, Marty inhabits a nostalgically imagined, romantically generalized American small town. Stripped of historical referents and significant temporal specificity, it appears abstract and highly stylized. Clothing, popular music, and brand names provide the only historical markers here—in what Jameson sees as postmodern culture's "desperate attempt to appropriate a missing past . . . now refracted through the iron law of fashion change and the emergent ideology of the 'generation'."[68]

This refraction, this softening of the film's vision of a "real" historical past, is an effect of the postmodern spatialization of time into something(s) visible. It is also an effect of living in an almost totally mediated society in which existence is most significantly experienced indirectly—in the pseudo-events/objects of images, simulations, and spectacles. The mise-en-scène of *Back to the Future* spatializes neither 1955 nor 1985, but the television time of "Leave It to Beaver" and "Father Knows Best." Marty's home town thus has only a pseudo-historical existence, as an earlier representation in a previous *text*. (Indeed, '50s television small towns and suburban neighborhoods are the home base for nearly all the films of Steven Spielberg and associates, functioning as the overdetermined sign of "nostalgia-in-itself"—that is, a nostalgia with an always already nostalgized referent.)

"Intertextuality," then, functions "as a deliberate, built-in feature of the aesthetic effect" of postmodernism's weakened historicity. The new nostalgic SF film's explicit or implicit reference to other and previous texts acts to constitute "pseudo-historical depth, in which the history of aesthetic styles displaces 'real' history"—and with it not only a sense of the "real" past, but also a sense of a "real" future.[69] *Back to the Future* is a generic symptom of our collapsed sense of time and history, both no longer regularly experienced in any radical, direct, or active way. As Jameson sees it, we are immersed in

> a new and original historical situation in which we are condemned to seek History by way of our own pop images and simulacra of that history, which itself remains forever out of reach.[70]

Back to the Future (Robert Zemeckis, 1985). The Collapse of Time and History: Time and history are running out for inventor Doc Brown at the film's climax —but not to worry. They are television time and "sit com" history. (Universal)

This perhaps explains why *Back to the Future* could not have been other than a comedy. Its historical investment doesn't "really" count—and its textual referent is pre-Archie Bunker family situation comedy. What makes the film interesting is that its nostalgia for the televised past is tinged with the ironic self-consciousness of a computerized and Yuppie present. Hence its final transformation of Marty's family into one like that in the sitcom "Family Ties" (another intertextual reference further enhanced by the intertextual presence of Michael J. Fox playing Marty).[71]

Back to the Future is not the only new SF film in the "nostalgia mode," nor is it the only one "condemned to seek History" (both past and future) "by way of pop images." More generally, I have pointed to the nostalgically "remembered" childhood transparently articulated by Spielberg's films as a childhood remembered (and lived) indirectly—"in" the movies and "on" television. This same use of pop images as constitutive of childhood memory and experience takes on a markedly hysterical cast in Joe Dante's films. Whether in his contribution to *Twilight Zone—The Movie* (1983), or in *Gremlins* (1984), or in his quasi-SF *Explorers*, Dante's recognition that "pop images" have universally pervaded, transformed, and homogenized human and alien consciousness is nearly always divided between a transparent and conservative nostalgia for those images (as the only ones we've got) and an explicit and hysterical criticism of them (because they're the only ones we've got).

The nostalgia mode tends, however, to conserve its mediated "past" and "remember" pop images transparently—in a politically "unconscious" and uncritical way. The *Star Wars* trilogy, of course, stands as most representative (and popular) of the appropriation of pop imagery to nostalgically constitute the pseudo-history of "long, long ago . . . in a galaxy far, far away." But there are other examples. Both *The Final Countdown* (Don Taylor, 1980) and *The Philadelphia Experiment* (Stewart Raffill, 1984) are time-travel films that fantasize about being World War II war movies. And all three of the *Star Trek* films constitute a particularly poignant and intertextually grounded pseudo-history of their own. (Indeed, the pre-quels and sequels slated for both the *Star Wars* and *Star Trek* films ensure both intertextuality and the literal "generation" of a pseudo-history.) The "futurism" of the *Star Trek* films is nostalgically backward-looking to earlier visions of the future—perhaps best dramatized in *Star Trek: The Motion Picture* when Kirk (and the film) nostalgically gazes at the refitted but still familiar (and now technologically old-fashioned) starship Enterprise for what seemed to some less nostalgic spectators an interminable length of overreverent screen time. As well, the television series characters (persistently youthful over years of reruns) have been embodied in the much older, if refitted, bodies of their previous performers, and thus have acquired a spatially marked history of an experience they do not narratively possess—

Star Trek II: The Wrath of Khan (Nicholas Meyer, 1982). **Pseudo-History:**
The older but refitted crew of the Starship Enterprise poses for a publicity
still. The resurrected "futurism" of the film series is nostalgically backward-
looking to the TV series' earlier vision of the future. (Paramount)

necessitating and made up for by the explicit and lengthy meditations on
aging, regret, loss, and death found in all three films. Finally, the three
films together narratively reenact the nostalgic drama of the television series'
own death and resurrection—most explicitly figured in *Star Trek III: The
Search for Spock* (Leonard Nimoy, 1984), which begins with mourning the
loss of the series' most poetic figure, then mounts what seems a hopeless
search for the dead, and ends with a resurrection, the function of a project
called Genesis and the function of the film series itself. Despite all their
"futurist" gadgetry and special effects, then, the *Star Trek* films are conservative and nostalgic, imaging the future by looking backward to the
imagination of a textual past.

    Dune, however, illuminates a conservatism and nostalgia more gravely
affected by the spatial paradigm that dominates postmodern culture. The
film desperately aspires to the status of transparent historical epic, but
does not achieve even the primitive temporal continuity and coherence of
historical chronicle. Exemplary of Jameson's observations about the "nostalgia mode," *Dune's* lavish but temporally abstracted pastiche of costume
and architecture utterly displaces any illusion of "real" planetary history
with, instead, a "history of aesthetic styles." It is fitting that *Dune's* "time

Dune (David Lynch, 1984). The Failure to Temporalize: The giant "time traveler" is literally sluggish—and hermetically sealed in what appears to be an old museum display case. (Universal)

traveler" is literally, gigantically "sluggish"—and hermetically sealed in the controlled atmosphere of what appears an old museum display case. *Dune's* narrative failure is a failure of its attempt to temporalize, to historicize, to escape its absorption in its own space. Commenting on the contemporary "crisis of historicity," Jameson tells us:

> If, indeed, the subject has lost its capacity actively to extend its pro-tensions and re-tensions across the temporal manifold, and to organize its past and future into coherent experience, it becomes difficult . . . to see how the cultural productions of such a subject could result in anything but 'heaps of fragments' and in a practice of the randomly heterogeneous and fragmentary and the aleatory.[72]

While *Blade Runner* successfully balances itself narratively and visually between the high-modern and the postmodern, the high-modernist narrative impulse of *Dune* plunges fatally into the absolute space of the postmodern and breaks down into a heap of fragments.

Pointing out that "the randomly heterogeneous and fragmentary and the aleatory" are "very precisely some of the privileged terms in which postmodernist cultural production has been analysed," Jameson goes on to emphasize that these terms also describe "schizophrenic writing"—a manifestation of a breakdown in the "active temporal unification" of language into a "signifying chain" whose links forge the coherent movement and continuity of both language and personal identity.[73] At its most basic, this breakdown of active temporal unification occurs at the level of the single sentence, but it further manifests itself textually as a breakdown of the active temporal unification that constitutes the movement of narrativity and the coherence of narrative. In this sense, *Dune* can be regarded as a schizophrenic text, and symptomatic of the breakdown of high-modernism in the context of postmodern culture's weakened temporal logic.

Thus, the new spatial logic that informs and/or dominates cultural production in the postmodern period has important temporal consequences for the contemporary SF film and its narrative structure. Whatever its mode of articulation, the genre's inflation of spatial value tends (in varying degrees) to overcome the temporal curiosity that has traditionally provided an impetus for the movement, momentum, and continuity of action and event into the "next" and contiguous space. The films' vision and ours tend to become fascinated, transfixed, and absorbed by the *present* space — with the new and abstract electronic depthlessness of its display, with the sensual overload of its excessive scenographic materiality, with the random and heterogeneous dispersal of busyness that has no particularly pressing purpose. Jameson's description of the "schizophrenic" consequences of the breakdown of temporal logic reads almost like a literal description of both the mise-en-scène and editorial discontinuities of SF films like *Liquid Sky, Repo Man, Night of the Comet, The Adventures of Buckaroo Banzai,* and *Uforia.* He speaks, for instance, of "the *rubble* of distinct and unrelated signifiers," and of schizophrenic communication as "reduced to an experience of pure *material* Signifiers, . . . of a series of pure and *unrelated presents* in time."[74] While music video is, perhaps, the most exemplary cultural representation (and celebration) of this materialist/consumerist subordination of temporal logic to spatial logic, we can also see its effects in recent SF. Although maintaining a certain minimal level of narrative and temporal "coherence," the films just mentioned really only co-Here and "make sense" spatially. They are "picaresque" tales — episodic, fragmented, serial rather than sequential, and little concerned with the temporal consequences of "cause and effect."

Indeed, as both a "strung out" and concatenated series of episodes, the "plots" of these films are difficult to summarize. Trying to respond to *Repo Man,* for example, one reviewer strategically reverts to a rhetorical question:

What do a car repossession company, a smarmy TV evangelist, a handful of zoned-out L.A. punks, a lobotomized nuclear physicist, a notorious pair of Hispanic car thieves and a Chevy Malibu with a trunk full of extraterrestrial aliens have in common? Not a whole hell of a lot, except that they're all key elements in *Repo Man*, a new comedy of staggering weirdness and originality.[75]

After an elaborated description, another reviewer says:

> You'll get a headache if you try to make sense of all this. *Repo Man's* plot deliberately ping-pongs between Otto's adventures as a repossessor and the increasingly wigged-out activities of the alien-busters. The characters don't stop to worry about the wild improbability of it all; why should you? In *Repo Man*, everyone is wired into his own version of reality, and all the wires are crossed.[76]

In *Repo Man* and the other films mentioned above, traditional narrative/temporal logic has yielded to an episodic/spatial logic crammed full of "punctual event-objects" connected less by narrative causality than by literally material signifiers. Editing derives its primary structure not from plot motivation, but from the motivation of things. A dangling dashboard ornament, for example, provides the noncausal and material "connection" between two of *Repo Man's* discontinuous episodes. And, in a mockery of plot and narrative causality, *Buckaroo Banzai* explicitly directs our attention to a watermelon placed in a drill press in the midst of an extraordinarily cluttered mise-en-scène and busy chase. "Why is there a watermelon there?" asks "New Jersey" of Buckaroo as they race through the industrial bowels of YoYoDyne. "Tell you later," says Buckaroo but, of course, he doesn't. (And, as spectators, we laugh—knowing full well he won't, and that we don't really care if he does.) This bit of structural reflexivity makes explicit the film's overall rejection of narrative/temporal logic and its embrace of episodic/spatial logic.

The "excessive" plots of these most postmodern of SF films are, indeed, a subversion of plot, sequence, and consequence (the temporal relations of cause and effect). "Too much" plot is akin to "eight" dimensions—impossible to make sense of, eluding one's grasp, intangible. But not to worry. In the staggeringly material culture of late multinational capitalism, a new kind of sense and knowledge emerge from a literally superficial empiricism. This new postmodern "positivism" articulates its observations as nonsense, and its causal logic as non sequiter. Thus, prone to explaining the nature of his "LA LA" (or Los Angelean) world on the basis of direct and superficial observation, Miller in *Repo Man* concludes: "The more you drive, the less intelligent you are." He also

> gives a disjointed but oddly logical speech about flying saucers and South America that ends up explaining where all the people on earth came from and where they're going. The "cosmic unconsciousness" and "the lattice of coincidence" account for the fact . . . "that you'll be thinking about a plate of shrimp and suddenly someone will say plate or shrimp or plate of shrimp."[77]

In *Night of the Comet*, Reggie's boyfriend convinces her to spend the night with him in a projection booth through the following logical argument:

Reggie
If we spend the night here, we're going to miss the comet.

Larry
It's not like you can't see it on TV.

Reggie
Yeah, well maybe I want to see it for real. Okay?

Larry
Hey, television's real. Television's very real.

Indeed, Sheldon in *Uforia* sums up this new empiricism (and its ultimate result) when he warns UFO believer Arlene, "If you don't stop believing in things that can't be proved in black-and-white, you're going to crack up."

This "cracking up," however, is hardly enacted or dramatized negatively, as schizophrenic failure. There is no dis-ease here with the "breakdown" in the temporal relations that forge (and are forged by) a "signifying chain." Rather than a breakdown, what we have is a transformation of representational function from time to space. Indeed, a wild humor and exhilarating liberation from temporal logic transforms the schizophrenic fragmentation and incoherence of a film like *Dune* (which held high-modernist temporal values) into the explicit, happily re-signed, "mad-cap" spatial logic of postmodern *comedy*. "Cracking up" doesn't cause dis-ease here. As Jameson suggests, when "schizophrenic disjunction . . . becomes generalized as a cultural style," it "ceases to entertain a necessary relationship to the morbid content we associate with terms like schizophrenia."[78] Brought to consciousness, made explicit and embraced, the new spatial logic is, indeed, logical—Co-Here/nt. This novel spatial formulation of meaning is positively characterized by Jameson in "a paradoxical slogan; namely, the proposition that 'difference relates'."[79] Thus, the deemphasis on temporal unification can no longer be seen negatively as desperate, schizophrenic, or diseased. Indeed, even at its most re-signed and nihilistic (as in *Liquid Sky*), the new postmodern SF film celebrates the ease (not the disease) of its ability to make temporal nonsense into spatial new sense.

The Transformation of Special "Affect" into Special "Effect"

As we have seen, the new dominance of spatial logic over temporal logic leads to an original form of literalism, one completely in harmony with the materialist/consumer culture of late capitalism. A heightened sense of space and its capacity for generating meaning compensates for a weakened sense of time. Thus, the temporal disease of "schizophrenic disjunction" is literally "cured" by materially and spatially "getting our shit together." The heterogeneous gathering of our material culture (the visible manifestation of "difference relating") serves as an explicit and spatialized sign of an alternative relational capacity, a newly realized and superficial form of cultural and mental "health." When "heaps of fragments" are no longer regarded with (and as signs of) dis-ease, they become, as Jameson points out, "available for more joyous intensities," for a "euphoria" that displaces "the older effects of anxiety and alienation."[80] Yet these joyous intensities and euphoria emerge in a particularly "detached" form:

> the liberation, in contemporary society, from the older *anomie* of the centered subject may also mean, not merely a liberation from anxiety, but a liberation from every other kind of feeling as well, since there is no longer a self present to do the feeling. This is not to say that the cultural products of the postmodern era are utterly devoid of feeling, but rather that such feelings — which it may be better and more accurate to call 'intensities' — are now free-floating and impersonal, and tend to be dominated by a peculiar kind of euphoria....[81]

The peculiarity of this postmodern euphoria is that it is structured and represented not as the intense feeling and expression of a *centered subject constructed in time*, but rather as the intense feeling and expression of a *decentered subjectivity objectified in space*. This is *extroversion* in its most extreme and literal formulation.

In the contemporary SF film, we can see this extroversion of feeling materialized in the genre's transformation of the centered subjectivity of *special affect* (joyous intensities and euphoria) into the decentered subjectification of *special effects* (grand displays of "industrial light and magic"). Thus, although special effects have always been a central feature of the SF film, they now carry a particularly new affective charge and value. In the genre's earlier period, special effects generally functioned to symbolize the "rational coolness" (and fearsome "coldness") associated with high technology and scientific objectivity, and were "authenticated" and made credible by the genre's "documentary" visual attitude. In contrast, today's special effects generally function to symbolize the "irrational warmth" of intense (and usually positive) emotions, and their credibility is not the issue. The genre has transformed its "objective" representation of a "high" technology into the "subjective" symbolization of a technologized "high."

This displacement and objectification of affect into an emotionalized technological effect is blatantly apparent in conservative mainstream SF, where big budgets allow for the most grandiose celebrations and displays.

The "rationally" sleek rocketships, mathematically "ascetic" flying saucers, and "functionally" complex beauty of spaceships like "Discovery" or "Valley Forge"—all previous celebrations of the wonder of some perceived scientific and technological "objectivity"—have been replaced by a subjectified, if still industrial, light and magic. Contemporary mainstream SF effects no longer function as signs of a *wonderfully functional* science, technology, or alien-ated culture (either "theirs" or ours). Rather, they function as signs of a science, technology, and alien-ated culture celebrated as *functionally wonderful*. Indeed, now the primary sign-function of SF special effects seems to be precisely to connote "joyful intensities," "euphoria," and the "sublime."

In this regard, I first want to reconsider briefly those SF films that deflate cinematographic space into electronic video game and computer space. Here, the "new depthlessness" leads to an intense experience of surface, to euphorically explosive displays. It is hardly a coincidence that the controls on video games are called "joy sticks." The punctual special effects of films like *Star Wars, Tron,* and *The Last Starfighter* are perhaps the purest SF manifestation of what Jameson sees as decentered affect—feelings or "intensities" that are "free-floating and impersonal." His comment that the "privileged space of the newer art is radically anti-anthropomorphic" is demonstrated in the dizzying roller-coaster speed and artful dodging sche-

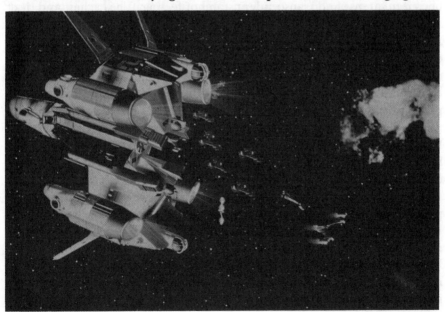

The Last Starfighter (Nick Castle, 1984). The Intense Experience of Surface: Free-floating and impersonal "affect" becomes electronic special effect. The spectator is liberated from the temporal and gravitational pull of a human "space of praxis." (Universal)

matically (not humanly) accomplished in screen flights and battles. This is a maneuvering "incompatible with the representation of the human body."[82] And, perhaps precisely because of this incompatibility, its spectacular superficiality and kinetic energy are synaesthetically "felt" by the viewer as an exhilarating liberation. Merely schematizing depth and yet realizing movement, the timeless space constituted by marked electronic effects isolates the humanly embodied spectator from the temporal and gravitational pull of a human "space of praxis" and allows "free" play in an inconsequential present. As Jameson puts it:

> isolated, that present suddenly engulfs the subject with undescribable vividness, a materiality of perception properly overwhelming, which effectively dramatizes the power of the material — or better still, the literal — Signifier in isolation. This present of the world or material signifier comes before the subject with heightened intensity, bearing a mysterious charge of affect . . . which one could . . . imagine in the positive terms of euphoria, the high, the intoxicatory or hallucinogenic intensity.[83]

Concurrent with (and perhaps now superseding) these purest and most literal displays of "free-floating and impersonal" affect are those mainstream special effects that are not just literally but also thematically connected to intense and transcendent states of feeling. The earliest and most arguably representative of these occur in *Close Encounters of the Third Kind* (1977). It initiates a new iconography of beatific human wonder, editorially linking affect to effect. Heads tilted, eyes gazing upward with childish openness and unfearful expectancy—this is the human face of transcendence whose emotion is enacted by what it sees. What it sees are playful little "ice cream cones" and "tinkerbells" of kinetic light, an annunciation of the sublimely affective extraterrestrial "merry-go-round" of light, color, and music to follow. This alien carousel of a spaceship is not built on principles of economy and rationality, but as a material apotheosis of good feeling, and its presence euphorically fulfills and objectively resolves Roy Neary's intense and incompatible desire both to regain his lost patriarchal power and become a born-again child.[84] Following *Close Encounters*, this narrative and thematic signification of special effect as special affect becomes a major formulation of the genre's mainstream. In the 1979 *Star Trek: The Motion Picture*, the dazzling finale of effects is a literal display of biotechnical affection as human and machine merge in a blazing orgasm of cosmic lovemaking. *E. T.* (1982) uses special effects to fantasize kids on flying bicycles — certainly less a celebration of rational science and hard technology than an affective reflexivity meant to evoke Peter Pan, and Dorothy Gale attempting to save Toto from Miss Gulch. It also gives its little alien a "faith healing" finger matched only in special affect

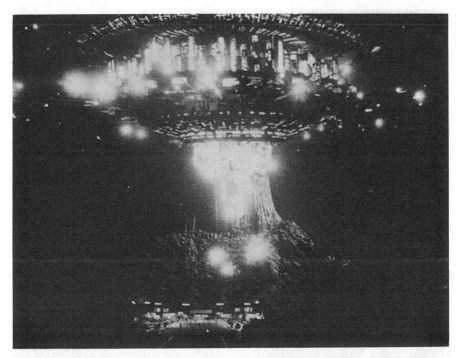

Close Encounters of the Third Kind (Steven Spielberg, 1977). The Sublimely Affective "Effect": The alien spaceship not as wonderfully functional, but as functionally wonderful—a merry-go-round of light, color, and music. (Columbia)

by his "heartlight" (even further sentimentalized in an immensely popular Neil Diamond song).

In what might seem a major contrast, the narrative of the 1983 *Brainstorm* emphasizes the empirical scientific research and hard technology traditionally associated with earlier examples of the genre. Its special effects, however, function not to celebrate the object-ivity of science and technology, but rather to objectify subjective experience literally and thematically. The screen image itself affectively expands to hold the intense effects of a technology narrativized as capable of transferring the subjective and emotionalized experience of one person directly to another—giving us the machinery and its effects "inside out" in intense 70mm displays of high sentiment, sexual overkill, and even death (seen as a sublime light show).[85] Also first seeming "scientific" and "technological" in its major premises, the 1984 *Dreamscape* parallels *Brainstorm's* "objective" transformation of affect into "subjective" effect. Figuring a technological process whereby dreams can be literally inhabited by active "others," *Dreamscape* saves its biggest effects for the affective expression of the irrational intensities of "dreamwork."

E.T.: The Extra-Terrestrial (Steven Spielberg, 1982). Special Effect as Special Affect: E.T.'s literally visible "heartlight" materially demonstrates his feeling for Eliot. (Universal)

Starman appears in the same year, sharing few of these residual aspirations to "rationalize" either its narrative or its special effects. The various "joyous intensities" of *Starman* have little to do with science and hardware, much to do with love and sex—and are objectively effected by Starman's (dare I pun here?) clearly magical, luminescently blue, and extraterrestrially potent "balls." Starman functions (like E.T. before him) as a sentimental (and now sexualized) "faith healer"—literally regenerating not only a dead deer, but also a grieving and childless widow (and through her, himself). Again, the film's closing special effects sublimate rather than celebrate their technological origin, functioning instead to represent the intensity of loss and the transcendence of love. *Starman's* final affective effect encloses the parting couple in a hermetically contained snowfall romantically suffused with a localized and literally rose-colored glow. The year 1984 also gives us *2010* (Peter Hyams), the utterly disappointing sequel

Starman (John Carpenter, 1984). Romantic Effects: Starman and Jenny say goodbye in a hermetically contained snowfall romantically suffused with a literally rose-colored glow. (Columbia)

to Kubrick's *2001: A Space Odyssey* (1968). Dave Bowman's "image" reappears in the midst of multinational crisis to announce that "Something wonderful is going to happen." That "something" has nothing whatever to do with reason, or with the science and technology the film would seem to foreground. Rather, *2010* attempts to effect this transcendent and affective "something wonderful" in the unimaginative appearance of a second "sun" up in the sky, which looks more like the star of Bethlehem than the star of Bethlehem, and in the Genesis of a new Garden of Eden. The quasireligious intensities explicit in *2010* (and implicit in many of the other films mentioned) also appear in 1985's *Cocoon*. The film's effects are affectively connected to intensities of love and sex, and to the sublimity of a faith materially rewarded with the material transcendence of age and death. A particularly original narrative transformation of affect into effect occurs when the film's young protagonist sensually experiences the "joyous intensities" of being immersed in and penetrated by the sexually and emotionally probing light that is the "authentic being" of his alien lover.

From *Close Encounters* on, then, special effects in mainstream SF have been transformed from signs of a rational and objective science and technology to representations of a joyous, and "sublime," intensity—themati-

Cocoon (Ron Howard, 1985). Romantic Effects: Alien and human prior to the "joyous intensities" of their emotional and sexual merger in affective special effects. (20th Century Fox)

cally linking postmodern culture's new "detached," "free-floating," and "liberated" sense of emotional transcendence with the transcendental. Alien-ated emotional transcendence becomes objectified in the transcendental and loving alien, and the alien-ated experience of "rapture" or "religious transport" is narrativized literally—as human beings are ecstatically "carried away" in body and spirit, as "religious transport" is effected by "alien transportation." Indeed, many critics have pointed (in a less than appreciative way) to the religious motifs associated with so many of the mainstream SF films: the arrival of various alien Messiahs, the transcendental nature of special effects that manifest miracle rather than science, the emphasis on faith and love as cure-all, and the many allusions to "virgin" birth. Given the particular confused state of political affairs in contemporary American culture, these religious motifs are often interpreted as symbolizing a cultural predisposition toward fascism.[86] They are, in fact, quite reminiscent of similar motifs in a few SF films of the Cold War period. The narratives of *E. T.* and *Starman* both bear a certain relation to *The Day the Earth Stood Still* (Robert Wise, 1951), and the explicit and politically linked religiosity of *2010* surely resembles *The Next Voice You*

Hear (William Wellman, 1950) and *Red Planet Mars* (Harry Horner, 1952).

Nonetheless, there are distinct tonal differences between these earlier cautionary SF films and their contemporary mainstream counterparts. While I am not in disagreement with those political readings that identify mainstream and conservative SF as valorizing authoritarianism and offering it as the solution to multinational strife, I would suggest that the desperate search for a messianic leader or dictator is not the whole thrust of these contemporary narratives. In a postmodern world perceived as totally colonized and capitalized, these close encounters are more celebratory than desperate, and erstwhile messiahs and dictators are also figured as childlike, little, cute, friendly, and often as open to victimization by us as we are to them. Indeed, as both the "sublime" proof of the now "pure" and totalized "universe" of late capitalism and the objectified figures of our own alien-ated postmodern "joyous intensities" and "affect-ion," we might say (as a colleague of mine has) that the "aliens R U.S."[87]

In this regard, it must be stressed that the "joyous intensities" and "euphoria" of which Jameson speaks find their affective expression not only in the special effects of the conservative mainstream, but also in the progressive marginalia of contemporary SF. In both modes, decentered feelings of joyous intensity, euphoria, and sublimity are visually and narratively objectified in the literal "transcendence" and "transports" of love, sex, religious fervor, and extraterrestrialism. Thus, the difference between the representations and narratives of contemporary mainstream and marginal SF lies not in their decentering and objectification of affect, but rather in their degree of reflexivity and playful awareness of that decentering and objectification. At its most aware, we get the articulation of subjective affect as objective effect in the title *Uforia*. Indeed, there is a sometimes perverse and nearly always comic playfulness in those marginalized, low-budget, and most postmodern SF films, which both "mock" big-budget special effects and yet further elaborate and explicitly acknowledge their affective function.

On the one hand, marginal SF films like *Liquid Sky, Strange Invaders, Repo Man, The Brother from Another Planet,* and *Uforia* re-solve their budgetary incapacity to deliver extravagantly sublime and joyfully intense special effects by generally foregrounding many of their own as deliberately un-sublime and joyfully tacky. The alien spaceship of *Liquid Sky* is extraordinarily tiny and looks like a dinner plate. The various effects in *Strange Invaders* harken back to old "B" SF movies. A radioactive luminescence "soups up" a Chevy Malibu to provide the major "special" effects in *Repo Man*, while *The Brother from Another Planet* crashlands on Earth in a totally unprepossessing spaceship with an instrument panel that looks like a '40s radio. And the UFO that finally comes to "transport" Arlene and Sheldon in *Uforia* is a purposefully low-wattage send-up of the Mothership

Strange Invaders (Michael Laughlin, 1983). Joyfully "Tacky": Marginal SF finds sublimity in the cheap, common, and cheesy—and in an explicit celebration of its own cheapness. (Orion)

in *Close Encounters*. Indeed, what constitutes this playful mockery is precisely a characteristic postmodern feature of the "society of the spectacle": an explicit celebration of "quotation" and the foregrounding of intertextuality. Not only does *The Brother from Another Planet*, for example, play upon E.T.'s people-healing finger by giving its alien protagonist a video-game healing hand, but it also cannot resist the sustained esoteric play upon French silent cinema's intersection with SF—both René Clair's *The Crazy Ray* (1923) and Jean Renoir's *Charleston* (1927), the latter offering first images of a "map-screen" and a set of tacky instruments, with a narrative concerning a black and civilized alien landing his bubble of a spaceship in a primitive Paris, where he is taught the Charleston by a lascivious "native" girl. These low-budget films are hardly like their '50s counterparts, which created earthly paranoia from their dearth of special effects. Instead, they celebrate their "lack" as an opportunity to scavenge and recycle. These SF films refer to previous SF films—and thus their marginality as SF (or quasi-SF) emerges, in great part, from their self-aware and explicitly articulated metageneric position.

On the other hand, this position in no way denies the objectification of affect represented by the spectacular effects of the big-budget films. Special effects in these marginal films serve not only as metageneric play and commentary on previous SF texts, but also as representations of objectified affect in their own textual systems. In *Liquid Sky*, the alien is supposedly attracted to a chemical released in the human brain by heroin or orgasm, and video effects mark the "G-spot" where annihilation is solarized

—a negative positively colored and euphorically transformed. The radiation-powered Malibu that takes off over the skies of Los Angeles at the end of *Repo Man* is a positive and utterly literal figuration of a "free-floating" affect. That car flight is an object-ification of the affective sense of both a penultimate "tripping out" and the exhilarating feeling of some final self re-possession. And both *The Brother from Another Planet* and *Uforia* valorize and believe in the "joyous intensities" and "faith-healing" powers of their protagonists—even as they mock and expose their own belief as either a belief in other texts (*E. T.* in the case of *Brother*), or a free-floating belief in belief (a meta-belief in *Uforia* that finds belief in religion, UFO's, and money laughable, but belief itself absolutely necessary).

Indeed, marginal SF serves not only to elaborate and make explicit mainstream SF's transformation of special affect to special effect, but it also suggests that this transformation is much more pervasive than the isolate and punctual instances of affective special effects in the mainstream films would allow. If marginal SF "mocks" the big-budget films, its mockery is directed at a conservative vision that still sees special effects as "special" cases and "free-floating affect" as localized in only certain kinds of objective display. The vision of marginal SF does not reject the mainstream formulation, but radically extends it to represent what is perceived as an all-

E.T.: The Extra Terrestrial (Steven Spielberg, 1982). Affective Wonder: E.T. and Eliot in Spielberg's iconography of wonder, transparently used editorially to link affect to effect. (Universal)

Night of the Comet (Thom Eberhardt, 1984). **Reflexive Wonder: Marginal SF explicitly plays with intertextual reference (here, Spielbergian iconography). (Atlantic)**

pervasive condition of postmodern existence. Thus, there's little difference emphasized between the alien-ated and object-ified interior of a spaceship, a '50s living room, an all-night convenience store, a new-wave night club. The "heaps of fragments" that constitute the intense and spatialized present tense of postmodern culture, the exhilaration of heterogeneous collections and collage, the sense that "difference relates" in the object-ivity of *outer* space—all constitute a euphoric and (according to Jameson) a "hysterically sublime" encounter with materiality and surface.[88] This is a euphoria and sublimity objectified, as in the case of the hysteric, on the body. But that body, in the case of contemporary SF, is itself object-ified, alien-ated. Thus, the double "negative" of objectification and alienation serves to objectify and alienate hysteria—and becomes the "positive" comedy of postmodern SF. Whether in mainstream or marginal SF films, the objectification and alienation of affect results in the embracement of alien-ation—or its very erasure.

Embracing the Alien, Erasing Alienation

The extroversion, objectification, and alien-ation of subjectivity and affect discussed above have certain consequences for social relations in the American culture of multinational capitalism. Both the praxis of a new material "literalism" (dominated by spatial logic) and the comfortable familiarity with which the "society of the spectacle" now regards signs of its own alienation have served to transform previously negative perceptions and representations of the "alien" into positive ones. Indeed, in a culture in which nearly everyone engages images more intensely than personal experience, in which subjectivity and affect are regularly decentered, dispersed, spatialized, and objectified, and in which even alienation is alienated and literalized, it is hardly surprising that the figure of the "alien" no longer poses the political and social threat it did in the SF of the 1950s. In that decade, alienation of the postmodern kind was still new and shiny, and aliens were definitely and identifiably "Other." Today's SF films either posit that "aliens are like us" or that "aliens R U.S." Alien Others have become less other — be they extraterrestrial teddy bears, starmen, brothers from another planet, robots, androids, or replicants. They have become our familiars, our simulacra, embodied as literally alienated images of our alienated selves. Thus, contemporary SF generally embraces alien Others as "more human than human" or finds it can barely mark their "otherness" as other than our own.

Whatever their ontology, the majority of aliens in the new SF film are represented as our friends, playmates, brothers, and lovers. The mindlessly destructive BEM's of the '50s have found popular contemporary counterparts only in the 1979 *Alien*, and two remakes of '50s films: *Invasion of the Body Snatchers* (Philip Kaufman, 1978) and *The Thing* (John Carpenter, 1982). And the coldly rational, nearly unstoppable alien Other once prevalent in the early genre has found contemporary popularity only in *The Terminator*. This is not to say that alien Others are never represented as threatening and villainous in contemporary SF, but rather to emphasize that if and when they are, it is generally within a narrative context in which other aliens are shown as friendly and "humane." In quite a transformation of earlier generic representations, most of the new SF films do not represent alien-ness as inherently hostile and Other. (Here, of course, the *Star Wars* trilogy provides the most obvious and wide-ranging example.)

This new and quite sanguine attitude toward postmodern alien-ation and its literalization in a positive figure of the alien Other is shared by both mainstream and marginal SF. Nonetheless, both articulate that figure and its positive meaning in a significantly different manner. In the more conservative mainstream films like *Close Encounters, E.T., Starman, Cocoon,* and *Enemy Mine*, the "difference" of the alien Other becomes absorbed in the homogeneity of a new universal "humanism." More postmodern and marginal films like *Repo Man, The Brother from Another Planet*, and *Uforia* suggest that the "difference" of the alien Other is not so much absorbed as diffused and even erased by postmodern culture's paradoxically totalized heterogeneity. Thus, in conservative SF, the alien Other is valued by virtue of being marked as more "positively" human than we humans presently are — that is, for being just like us, only identifiably and differentially *more* so. In postmodern SF, however, the alien Other is valued for being un-marked as alien or other, for being different just like us, only *no more* so than an/other alien-ated and spaced-out being. The narratives of the conservative mainstream SF film maintain "difference" and "otherness" in the name of homogeneity and embrace the alien as an other who is like us. More radically, the narratives of the postmodern marginal SF film maintain "difference" and "otherness" in the name of heterogeneity and erase alienation by articulating it as a universal condition in which we are aliens and aliens are us. The implications of this distinction are symbolically and culturally quite significant.

Michel Foucault provides some assistance in helping us understand the two quite different logics that inform mainstream SF's "embrace of the alien" on the one hand, and marginal SF's "erasure of alienation" on the other. In one of his essays he makes an important distinction between relations of *resemblance* and relations of *similitude*. Relations of resemblance, he tells us, may assert sameness, but they "demonstrate and speak across difference," and are hierarchical, requiring the "subordination" of one term to the other that provides the original model.[89] Relations of similitude, however, assert difference, but speak across sameness and are non-hierarchical and reversible. He explains:

> Resemblance has a "model," an original element that orders and hierarchizes the increasingly less faithful copies that can be struck from it. Resemblance presupposes a primary reference that prescribes and classes. The similar develops in series that have neither beginning nor end, that can be followed in one direction as easily as in another, that obey no hierarchy, but propagate themselves from small differences among small differences. Resemblance serves representation, which rules over it; similitude serves repetition, which ranges across it. Resemblance predicates itself upon a model it must return to and reveal; similitude circulates the simulacrum as an indefinite and reversible relation of the similar to the similar.[90]

To maintain — as conservative mainstream SF does — that "aliens are just *like* us" is to assert and dramatize a resemblance — with human being as the "model," the "original element" that "orders and hierarchizes" the "copies that can be struck from it." *E. T., Starman, Blade Runner's* replicants, *Heartbeeps'* robots, and the like are predicated upon and subordinated to a human model, and their "faithlessness" as copies is ironically and conservatively an idealization of that model. Conservative SF's embrace of the alien as "the same" maintains alien-ness as the difference that makes a difference, that enables the representation of a new "humanism,"

Blade Runner (Ridley Scott, 1982). More Human than Human: Relations of resemblance constitute a "new humanism." Here, Baty and Deckard "demonstrate and speak across difference" to assert their sameness. (Ladd/Warner Brothers)

The Empire Strikes Back (Irvin Kershner, 1980). More Human than Human: Relations of resemblance are constituted as Yoda proves "aliens are just like us"—only wiser and better. (20th Century Fox)

Iceman (Fred Schepesi, 1984). More Human than Human: Relations of resemblance are constituted as Iceman and contemporary human "speak across differences" and communicate in SF's new humanism. (Universal)

E.T.: The Extra Terrestrial (Steven Spielberg, 1982). More Human than Human: Relations of resemblance as E.T. proves that "aliens are just like us" —only littler and cuter. (Universal)

and it constitutes those hierarchical relations based on homo-geneity into a myth of universal and nonhierarchical homogeneity. To narrativize aliens as "just like us" across their differences is to conserve the primacy of human being. Thus, replicants are advertised as "more human than human" and Starman tells Jenny after they make love, "I think I am becoming a planet Earth person." Mainstream SF's articulation of resemblance between aliens and humans preserves the subordination of "other worlds, other cultures, other species" to the world, culture, and "speciality" of white American culture. We can see this new American "humanism" literally expand into and colonize outer space, making it safe for democracy, multinational capitalism, and the Rolling Stones. Sent into outer space to look for extraterrestrial life in *Starman*, Voyager II "exports" a recording of "I Can't Get No Satisfaction"—its (re)production of desire a fitting anthem for consumer culture (later sung by Starman).

Marginal and postmodern SF, however, articulates the relations between aliens and humans in quite another way. To maintain not that "aliens are like us", but rather that "aliens *are* us" is to assert and dramatize a relation of similitude—one that can be reversibly articulated as "We are aliens." Human being does not serve as an original model here. Indeed, true to postmodern logic, films like *Liquid Sky, Repo Man,* and *The Brother from Another Planet* suggest there is no original model for being, and that (as Foucault notes) the similarity we see across difference "develops in series that have neither beginning nor end," representing the circulation of "the simulacrum as an indefinite and reversible relation of the similar to the similar" propagated nonhierarchically from "small differences among small differences." Margaret, the androgynous new-wave model of *Liquid Sky*, and her spaced-out friends, or Otto and his myriad bizarre acquaintances in *Repo Man* are as slightly different from each other as they are different from the marked "aliens" and yet they are as similarly alien-ated as are any of the aliens. Similarly the same and different, the Brother from another planet is as human and alien as any alien-ated human extraterrestrialized in New York's Harlem.

In sum, the most postmodern SF does not "embrace the alien" in a celebration of resemblance, but "erases alienation" in a celebration of similitude. Thus, it is not critical of alienation. Indeed, the postmodern SF film maintains only enough signs of "alien-ness" to dramatize it not as "the difference that makes a difference" but as the "difference that makes a sameness." The "alien" posited by marginal and postmodern SF enables the representation of alienation as "human" and constitutes the reversible and nonhierarchical relations of similitude into a myth of homogenized heterogeneity. That is, nationalism no longer exists as a difference in the culture of multinational capital. Sexual difference is eradicated in *andr(oid)-ogyny*. Identity is ephemeral, and superficially realized by "style." A

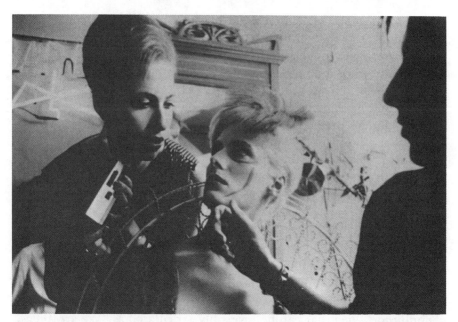

Liquid Sky (Slava Tsukerman, 1983). Aliens R U.S.: Relations of similitude are reversible. Margaret and her spaced-out and androgynous friends constitute a series of differences that make a sameness. (Cinevista)

Repo Man (Alex Cox, 1984). Aliens R U.S.: Relations of similitude as reversible. Identity as "style" in a "series which has neither beginning nor end" and emerges nonhierarchically from "small differences among small differences." (Universal)

The Brother from Another Planet (John Sayles, 1984). Aliens R U.S.: Relations of similitude as reversible. The Brother is as human and as alien as any alien-ated human extraterrestrialized in Harlem. (Cinecom)

spaceship is no less strange and no less familiar in its material presence than the local Safeway. Indeed, narrativizing "aliens R U.S." is not so progressive as it might seem. Rather, such narratives represent and dramatize the cultural logic of late capitalism whereby the very conditions of cultural alienation are not only found acceptable, but also euphorically celebrated as liberating. In this regard, Foucault's emotionalized description of similitude is particularly apt. "Similitude," he tells us, "multiplies different affirmations, which dance together, tilting and tumbling over one another."[91]

Postfuturism and the "End" of Science Fiction

This chapter has periodized the American SF film from its first major emergence in the 1950s through its current period of popularity within the context of postmodernism, or "the logic of late capitalism." Looking backward, we can see the genre first flourishing as a symbolic representation of the new intersections of science, technology, and multinational capitalism, whose most visible signposts were the atomic and hydrogen bomb and the electronics of television. The films of the 1950s dramatize the *novelty* of multinational capitalism, and represent both its expansive promise and its threatening unfamiliarity in visualizations that emphasize shiny and "futuristic" technology and cosmic expansion or evidence technological dread and xenophobia. From the late 1970s to the present, the films of the genre's second "Golden Age" are quite different. That is, they dramatize the *familiarity* of multinational capitalism, and represent its totalized domestication, commodification, and pervasion of worldly space in visualizations that valorize the cluttered abundance of consumer culture, nostalgize brand names and childhood, and evidence pleasure in waste and "heaps of fragments." Gone are dread and xenophobia. Gone also is a sense of the possible future. In their place are euphoria and a totalized "pluralism" — both of which are realized in space and do not logically admit the temporalizing of a future.

Indeed, if "science fiction" was once a generic category predicated on speculating and imagining a probable or possible future, the genre seems endangered — its work now producing regressive fantasies on the one hand, and "delirious" comedies totally absorbed in the material present on the other. Today's SF either nostalgically locates the future in an imagined past and thus articulates it as "over," or it complacently locates the future in the present, celebrating it as "here" and "now." It seems as if the SF film — coincidentally born with the culture of late capitalism and the genre most symbolic of it — has total(iz)ed itself in a historical movement logically isomorphic with the totalizing incorporation of Nature by industrialized and consumer culture, with the expansion of capitalism to its "purest form."

This generic development, however, should not be viewed merely as an opportunity for condemnation, and, perhaps, for another postmodern manifestation — that of nostalgia for the genre's past. As Jameson points out, both the cultural critic and the moralist are themselves now

> deeply immersed in postmodernist space, so deeply suffused and infected by its new cultural categories, that the luxury of the old-fashioned ideological critique, the indignant moral denunciation of the other, becomes unavailable.[92]

Since we are not "outside" the postmodern paradigm and its cultural logic, since it is not merely one stylistic option among others but rather our "cultural dominant," we need to consider the SF genre dialectically. That is, as Jameson goes on to urge, we need to think

> this development positively *and* negatively all at once; to achieve, in other words, a type of thinking that would be capable of grasping the

demonstrably baleful features of capitalism along with its extraordinary and liberating dynamism simultaneously, within a single thought, and without attenuating any of the force of either judgement. We are, somehow, to lift our minds to a point at which it is possible to understand that capitalism is at one and the same time the best thing that has ever happened to the human race, and the worst. The lapse from this austere dialectical imperative into the more comfortable stance of the taking of moral positions is inveterate and all too human: still, the urgency of the subject demands that we make at least some effort to think the cultural evolution of late capitalism dialectically, as catastrophe and progress all together.[93]

If we want to think of the generic development of SF as a catastrophic one, certainly we can point to its "baleful" features. The early films can be generally characterized by their celebration of and consequent paranoia about imperialism and colonial expansion; their fetishization of technology; their arrogant xenophobia grounded on the perpetuation of difference and the need for an alien Other. And, in the films of the "Second Golden Age" we can point an accusative finger at their regressive infantilism; their nostalgia for an impossible and trivialized past, and their incapacity to imagine a future; their fetishization of consumer culture, both its images and its trash; their complacent pluralism, which ascribes equal value to every "thing" and every "position." We can, in fact, think of the genre in its entirety as the ideological production of poetic displacements: "so many attempts to distract and to divert us from . . . reality or to disguise its contradictions and resolve them in the guise of various formal mystifications."[94]

However, accurate as such negative readings of the genre may be, we are also charged with thinking the development of the SF film as progressive, and with pointing to its "extraordinary and liberating dynamism." As a symbolic representation of the cultural logic of late capitalism (both in its early and late phases of dominance over residual logics), the genre has visibly and literally articulated what can be read as a new form of "realism" — one responsive to and complexly mimetic of a "genuine historical (and socio-economic) reality." Contemporary SF has attempted to map the new world space we inhabit, to imagine other forms of being, to give us a picture of multinationalism, to represent narratively the altered significance of difference, sameness, boundaries, marginality. The films have become increasingly explicit and less displaced in relation to their "real" terrain — that is, in a new and peculiarly literal (if still symbolic) way, they are more "down-to-earth" in their spatial and social location of narrative problems. Furthermore, their current celebration of alienation and/or complacence about alienation has positive as well as negative consequences. Not only do these articulations negate the genre's earlier xenophobia, but they also can be seen as an attempt at what Jameson calls "disalienation":

301

the practical reconquest of a sense of place, and the construction or re-construction of an articulated ensemble which can be retained in memory and which the individual subject can map and remap along the moments of mobile, alternative trajectories.[95]

This is a progressive move. It at least allows for the possibility of some new form of empowerment, if not that empowerment itself.

Right now, at this writing, the most simultaneously catastrophic and progressive SF films are those I have identified as marginal. Their visual and narrative logic is at once the most informed by the logic of late capitalism *and* the most liberated by it. On the one hand, their lack of temporal imagination (and interest) is paralytic in regards to envisioning a future, but, on the other, it is dynamic in the intense attention it pays to the spatialized present. While everyone is alien-ated and every "thing" is e-stranged in these marginal films, everyone and every thing is also given a liberating equivalence to play out "differences" without hierarchical structures of domination, to newly synthesize "difference relates." The political, social, and economic value of the other as Other has little currency in these films — a devaluation that unfortunately erases real political, sexual, and class differences, and yet also fortunately dissolves their limiting boundary conditions. Indeed, marginal SF films tend to be generically "dissolute" as well as culturally "deconstructive." That is, while their subversion of the boundaries between inner city/outer space, estranged/alien, male/female, familiar/novel, real/imaginary, ordinary/extraordinary "deconstructs" the hierarchical relations that ground capitalist notions of power, desire, and value, this subversion also "dissolves" the very structure and notion of the film genre as a bounded category of texts valuing the marked and hierarchical difference between signs of "science" and signs of "fiction." When "science" and "fiction" are no longer visualized and narrativized as oppositional, the genre becomes dissolute — dissolves. In one sense, this is a liberating move. In another, it is catastrophic. Given that the SF genre is the only cinematic category to imagine and image our possible futures, its dissolution leaves a symbolic chasm.

We have seen that the SF film is always historicized, grounded in its (and our) own earthly American culture — in the economic, technological, political, social, and linguistic present of its production, in the ideological structures that shape its visual and visible conceptions of time, space, affect, and social relations. Certainly, this is an ontological characteristic of *any* cultural artifact. It assumes particular significance, however, in relation to a genre whose expressed imagination would transcend its historical limitations, whose very identity and difference from other genres are figurally marked by this attempt at transcendence. SF's own historical limitations provide, at once, both the boundary conditions that the genre would imaginatively escape and the ground absolutely necessary to its sig-nification of that escape. Thus, the necessary and sufficient symbolic con-ditions that determine the genre's existence and identity are at odds with each other, even as they are completely dependent upon each other. While this tension between "invention" and "convention" informs any symbolic activity that is not merely replicative, it is most consciously privileged and doubly articulated in SF—heightened and stressed as constituting both the genre's mode of discourse and its discursive object. Indeed, this tension is what forms the basic aesthetic structure of the American SF film. It is what has seemed to unite all the films as a genre, no matter how divergent they are in plot, theme, and specific iconography.

More mundanely but just as importantly, this generic tension between "invention" and "convention," between imaginative flights of figural work and comfortably familiar symbolic activity, is also economically determined. In its major function as a commodity, a genre whose discursive mode and object both privilege and figure "invention" against the ground of "con-vention" must continually strive to make its previous technological and narrative articulations seem obsolete. Thus, the most popular SF films keep appropriating the culture's newest technology—on the one hand, literally "incorporating" it as part of the film medium (e.g., computer-generated imagery), and on the other, symbolically "displaying" it as "in-vention," as a more special "special" effect. This literal and symbolic appro-priation and commodification of new technology obviously entails larger and larger sums of money, which must be recuperated at a profit, and the possibilities for radical invention, or for invention not based in the techno-logical, become more and more limited and marginalized. Although the SF film ostensibly strives to transcend the conventional and, perhaps, reach toward the avant-garde "and beyond" to the radical, the demands of the genre's commodification also compel it to inscribe itself as familiar, un-threatening, unrevolutionary, and easily understood. True in the 1950s, and truer yet today, an axiom emerges: the more a film costs, the fewer risks it is likely to take. Thus, culturally located in the margins of main-stream American cinema, it is the low-budget SF movie—whether of the '50s or '80s—which tends to embrace its inadequacies as a defensive ma-neuver, and is often aesthetically and narratively energized toward inven-tion precisely by the low budgets constraining it. The big-budget main-stream SF film, however, is not so driven.

Given the relatively recent major changes in the economy, structure, and quantity of American film production, this seems especially true of to-day's most popular, most "mainstream" SF films. (Behind the figuration of enormously expensive and inventive technological displays, the ideological conservatism and conventionality of most of last decade's SF "blockbusters" are as much a function of the conditions of their economic production as they are a function of the political climate of Reagan's postmodern and Disneyesque America.) Indeed, today more than ever before, the genre has become extremely self-conscious in its will to be high-cost effective. Its contemporary and seemingly playful reflexivity, in the big-budget super-productions, is not only a characteristic feature of postmodern textuality, but also a form of both cautious and celebratory self-regulation. Thus, despite the SF film's visible and blatant articulations of its own inventiveness, the genre's most popular films work visually to produce not the novel, but its illusion, its replication, its simulacra.

This chapter is being written at a time when the American SF film is still at peak popularity, but (as previously mentioned) is also most threatened in its particular existence as a genre. Indeed, the aesthetic premises for the cinematic existence of the American SF film that this book attempts to describe in its first three chapters have become increasingly unstable in this postmodern age. First, it is getting more and more difficult to determine precisely what constitutes an "American" film these days. The multi-national rather than monopolistic character of late capitalism informs and models today's film industry in all of its aspects: financing, production, distribution, and exhibition. Second, as previously noted, the aesthetics of postmodernism would deny the existence of both the generic boundaries marking SF as a discrete structure of poetic representation and the hierarchical relation of difference that structure poses between the extraordinary and the mundane. Whether "unconsciously" informed by a postmodern aesthetic or "consciously" articulating it, recent SF films have been in the process of celebrating their own generic destruction. Thus, we might do well to consider the implications of this self-destruction and what sort of reformulation might effectively maintain the genre's identity and its particular representational function.

Not content to embrace the aesthetics of postmodernism, although certainly appreciating its value and significance, Jameson ends his consideration of representation in the culture of late capitalism with a call for the invention of "radically new forms" capable of doing justice to the complexity of our historical moment. He sees in these new forms the possible emergence of a new "political art" that will neither long for the past nor merely re-present the present "world space of multinational capital." While taking this last as "its fundamental object," the new political art would achieve

a breakthrough to some as yet unimaginable new mode of representing this last, in which we may again begin to grasp our positioning as individual and collective subjects and regain a capacity to act and struggle which is at present neutralized by our spatial as well as our social confusion. The political form of postmodernism, if there is any, will have as its vocation the invention and projection of a global cognitive mapping, on a social as well as a spatial scale.[96]

This call for the invention of "new modes" able to represent our "real" position as individuals and collective subjects in late capitalism and yet empower us to act and struggle against its constraints may, in fact, have already been answered—and by a quite singular film that reformulates "science fiction" so that it is not "neutralized" by the postmodern visualization of spatial and social confusion. Expectedly, this "post-postmodern" SF film is more marginal than marginal—and, unexpectedly to some (although not to others), it is articulated within the context of feminism. I refer to *Born in Flames* (Lizzie Borden, 1982).[97] This is a new mode of representation for the SF film: one that does not regress to the past, does not nostalgize, and does not complacently accept the present as the only place to live. It does indeed imagine a future—but one contiguous with the present, and in temporal and spatial relation to it. It is political and empowering and has a momentum not "transfixed" by excess scenography or caught up in an overwhelming and paralyzing material heterogeneity. It is also not visually pleasurable in ways we have been led to expect and desire, but its very grittiness reacts against the hallucinatory splendor and euphoria generated by the postmodern fascination with surface. This is a film in which trash looks like trash, and objects regain their functional value in a social context. This is SF that is definitely not dissolute.

Perhaps, then, the science fiction film still has a future—and in its representations we can still locate the image and imagination of ours. *Born in Flames* is a singular instance of this imagination. Nonetheless, its existence suggests that we look for further responses to mainstream SF "regression" and marginal SF "postfuturism" from a feminist SF cinema. In literature, the intersection of feminism and SF has proved not only generically deconstructive, but also generically reconstructive. I should like to end this book by looking toward the aesthetics of wonder and future possibilities that such an intersection might constitute for SF cinema.

Notes

Chapter 1 Notes_____

1. Lawrence Alloway, *Violent America: The Movies 1946-1964* (New York: Museum of Modern Art, 1971), p. 53.

2. Judith Merril, "What Do You Mean: Science? Fiction?" *SF: The Other Side of Realism,* ed. Thomas D. Clareson (Bowling Green, Ohio: Bowling Green Popular Press, 1971), p. 53.

3. Ibid., p. 60.

4. Ibid.

5. This extremely broad definition of the science in SF can be attributed to the efforts of John W. Campbell, Jr., who took over the editorship of *Astounding* in 1937, and who was fascinated with scientific theory and engineering in fields as diverse as anthropology, communications, social psychology, sociology, cybernetics, and education. The stories he selected for publication in the magazine broadened the traditional SF definition of science considerably.

6. Sam Moskowitz, *Explorers of the Infinite: Shapers of Science Fiction* (New York: World Books, 1957), p. 11.

7. James Blish, "On Science Fiction Criticism," *SF: The Other Side of Realism,* p. 167.

8. Kingsley Amis, *New Maps of Hell* (New York: Harcourt, Brace & Co., 1960), p. 18.

9. Richard Hodgens, "A Brief Tragical History of the Science Fiction Film," *Film Quarterly* 13 (Winter 1959): 30.

10. Michael Butor, "Science Fiction: The Crisis of its Growth," *SF: The Other Side of Realism,* p. 157.

11. Carlos Clarens, *An Illustrated History of the Horror Film* (New York: Capricorn Books, 1967), p. 118.

12. John Baxter, *Science Fiction in the Cinema* (New York: Paperback Library, 1970), p. 8.

13. Ibid., p. 7.

14. Ibid., p. 11.

15. Ibid., p. 10.

16. Ibid.

17. Thomas Clareson, "The Other Side of Realism," *SF: The Other Side of Realism,* p. 22.

18. Jacques Siclier and André S. Labarthe, *Images de la Science-Fiction* (Paris: Les Editions du Cerf, 1958), p. 59.

19. Denis Gifford, *Science Fiction Film* (London: Studio Vista/Dutton Pictureback, 1971), pp. 112-14.

20. Baxter, *Science Fiction in the Cinema,* p. 102.

21. Later, many SF films used Campbell's device which has been linked by many critics to the paronoia of the McCarthy era and the Red Scare. See, for example: *Invaders from Mars* (William Cameron Menzies, 1953), *It Came From Outer Space* (Jack Arnold, 1953), *Invasion of the Body Snatchers* (Don Siegel, 1956), *I Married a Monster from Outer Space* (Gene Fowler, Jr., 1958), *The Day Mars Invaded the Earth* (Maury Dexter, 1962), and—if you consider it science fiction—*The Manchurian Candidate* (John Frankenheimer, 1962).

22. Hodgens, "A Brief Tragical History," p. 33.

23. Arthur C. Clarke and Michael Crichton in *Focus on the Science Fiction Film,* ed. William Johnson (New Jersey: Prentice-Hall, 1972), pp. 154; 156.

24. Baxter, *Science Fiction in the Cinema,* pp. 7-8.

25. Richard Matheson in *Focus on the Science Fiction Film,* pp. 164-65.

26. Theodore Sturgeon as quoted by Fritz Lang in *Focus on the Science Fiction Film,* p. 162.

27. Clarens, "An Illustrated History," pp. 118-39; 161-71.

28. Baxter, *Science Fiction in the Cinema,* pp. 39-52.

29. Hodgens, "A Brief Tragical History," p. 30.

30. Ibid.

31. Neil D. Isaacs, "Unstuck in Time: *Clockwork Orange* and *Slaughterhouse Five,*" *Literature/Film Quarterly* 1 (Spring 1973): 123.

32. Michel Laclos, *Le Fantastique au Cinéma* (Paris: J. J. Pauvert, 1958), p. xxviii. Translated freely from the following: ". . . la SF cinématographique . . . assimilé tous les thèmes du fantastique traditonnel. Martiens, Venusiens ou mutants ont pris la relève des vampires, tandis que les robots allient les défaillances des zombis et du Golem. Le Cadre étroit de las maison hantée éclate aux dimensions du satellite peuplé d'invisibles présences extra-terrestres."

33. Denis Gifford, *A Pictorial History of Horror Movies* (London: Hamlyn, 1973), p. 82.

34. Ibid., p. 89.

35. Ibid., p. 82.

36. Ibid., p. 136.

37. Ibid.

38. Susan Sontag, "The Imagination of Disaster," *Commentary* 40 (October 1965): 45.

39. Ibid., p. 47.

40. Chris Steinbrunner and Burt Goldblatt, *Cinema of the Fantastic* (New York: Saturday Review Press, 1972), p. 264.

41. T. J. Ross, "Introduction," *Focus on the Horror Film,* eds. Roy Huss and T. J. Ross (New Jersey: Prentice-Hall, 1972), pp. 2-3.

42. For further discussion—in depth—of the horror film, see Bibliography under Ivan Butler, Carlos Clarens, R. H. W. Dillard, Denis Gifford, Roy Huss and T. J. Ross, and Frank Manchel.

43. Sontag, "The Imagination of Disaster," p. 44.

44. Brian Murphy, "Monster Movies: They Came From Beneath the Fifties," *The Journal of Popular Film* 1 (Winter 1972): 32.

45. Ibid., p. 34.

46. Ibid., p. 35.

47. Ibid., p. 42.

48. Ibid., p. 38.

49. John D. Denne, "Society and the Monster," December 9 (#2/3): 180.

50. Ibid.

51. Joe Kane, "Nuclear Films," *Take One* 2 (July/August 1969): 10.

52. Sontag, "The Imagination of Disaster," p. 48.

53. Murphy, "Monster Movies," p. 38.

54. Baxter, *Science Fiction in the Cinema,* p. 136.

55. Margaret Tarratt, "Monsters from the Id," *Films and Filming* 17 (December 1970): 38.

56. Ibid., p. 40.

57. Hodgens, "A Brief Tragical History," p. 37.

58. Frank Hauser, "Science Fiction Films," *International Film Annual,* ed. William Whitebait (New York: Doubleday, 1958), p. 89.

59. Murphy, "Monster Movies," p. 38.

60. Ibid., p. 39.

61. Denne, "Society and the Monster," p. 180.

62. Ibid.

63. Kane, "Nuclear Films," p. 9.

64. Ibid.

65. Siclier and Labarthe, *Image de la Science-Fiction,* p. 124. Translated from the following: ". . . un'néo-realisme' prophétique, que la realité vient corroborer aprés coup."

66. Robert Brustein, "Film Chronicle: Reflections on Horror Movies," *The Partisan Review* 25 (Spring 1958): 288-89.

67. Arthur C. Clarke in Albert Rosenfeld, "Perhaps the Mysterious Monolithic Slab is Really Moby Dick," *Life* 30 (21 May 1951): 35.

68. Siegfried Mandell and Peter Fingesten, "The Myth of Science Fiction," *Saturday Review* 38 (27 August 1955): 25, 28.

69. Ivan Butler, *Horror in the Cinema* (New York: Paperback Library, 1971), p. 11.

70. Stanley Kubrick in Alexander Walker, *Stanley Kubrick Directs* (New York: Harcourt, Brace, Jovanovich, 1971), p. 15.

71. Bronislaw Malinowski, *Magic Science and Religion and Other Essays* (Glencoe, Ill.: The Free Press, 1948), p. 66.

72. Ibid., p. 70.

73. Ibid., pp. 67-68.

74. Ibid., p. 69.

Chapter 2 Notes

1. Jim Kitses, *Horizons West* (Bloomington, Ind.: Cinema One Series, Indiana University Press, 1969), p. 25.

2. Colin McArthur, *Underworld U.S.A.* (New York: Cinema One Series, The Viking Press, 1972), p. 24.

3. Ibid., p. 25.

4. For further discussion of the theoretical aspects of iconography in genre films, see Edward Buscombe's "The Idea of Genre in the American Cinema," John Cawelti's *The Six-Gun Mystique,* and Tom Ryall's "The Notion of Genre," cited in the Selected Bibliography.

5. Michael Butor, "Science Fiction: The Crisis of its Growth," *SF: The Other Side*

of *Realism,* ed. Thomas D. Clareson (Bowling Green: Bowling Green Popular Press, 1971), p. 157.

6. Ibid.

7. John Baxter, *Science Fiction in the Cinema* (New York: Paperback Library, 1970), p. 150.

8. Jacques Siclier and André S. Labarthe, *Images de la Science-Fiction* (Paris: Les Editions du Cerf, 1958), p. 62.

9. Baxter, *Science Fiction in the Cinema,* p. 151.

10. Ibid., p. 13.

11. Denis Gifford, *Science Fiction Film* (London: Studio Vista/Dutton Pictureback, 1971), p. 118.

12. Renata Adler, Review of *2001: A Space Odyssey* in *A Year in the Dark* (New York: Random House, 1969), p. 103.

13. Penelope Gilliatt, Review of *2001: A Space Odyssey* in *Film 68/69,* eds. Hollis Alpert and Andrew Sarris (New York: Simon and Schuster, 1969), p. 56.

14. Gifford, *Science Fiction Film,* p. 130.

15. Gilliatt, in *Film 68/69,* p. 55.

16. Joseph Morgenstern, Review of *2001: A Space Odyssey* in *Film 68/69.* pp. 61-62.

17. For more information on the design these spaceships, see John Brosnan, *Movie Magic* (New York: St. Martin's Press, 1974).

18. Brosnan, *Movie Magic,* p. 197.

19. Ibid., pp. 191-94.

20. Gifford, *Science Fiction Film,* p. 54.

21. Brosnan, *Movie Magic,* pp. 198-99.

22. Bosley Crowther, Review of *Forbidden Planet* in the *New York Times,* (4 May 1956).

23. Baxter, *Science Fiction in the Cinema,* p. 113.

24. Alexander Walker, *Stanley Kubrick Directs* (New York: Harcourt, Brace, Jovanovich, 1971), p. 255.

25. Ibid., p. 258.

26. Gifford, *Science Fiction Film,* p. 59.

27. Baxter, *Science Fiction in the Cinema,* p. 136.

28. Paul D. Zimmerman, Review of *Silent Running* in *Newsweek* (20 March 1972). p. 113.

29. William Johnson, Review of *Silent Running* in *Film Quarterly* 25 (Summer 1972): 55.

30. Ibid.

31. Called "familiar" and "unfamiliar," these images are briefly discussed in René Prédal, *Le Cinema Fantastique* (Paris: Éditions Seghers, 1970), pp. 9-10.

32. Damon Knight, *In Search of Wonder* (Chicago: Advent Press, 1967), p. 13.

33. For complete information on special effects cinematography, see Raymond Fielding, *The Technique of Special Effects Cinematography* (London: Focal Press, 1965), as well as the less technical but more lively *Movie Magic* by John Brosnan, already cited.

34. Gifford, *Science Fiction Film,* p. 87.

35. "The final impressive shots in *2001,* of the serene, god-like 'star child' approaching Earth, were created with a fibreglass doll, which had originally been shaped in clay by a young sculptress. The eyes, made of glass, were moveable and could be operated by remote control. The doll, which was two and a half feet tall, was superimposed over the glowing bubble which was then matted in the shots of the Earth and surrounding stars." Brosnan, *Movie Magic,* p. 228.

36. Michel Ciment, "The Odyssey of Stanley Kubrick: Part 3: Toward the Infinite— *2001*" in *Focus on the Science Fiction Film,* ed. William Johnson (New Jersey: Prentice-Hall, 1972), p. 135.

37. Raymond Durgnat, *Films and Feelings* (Cambridge, Mass.: The M.I.T. Press,

Paperback Edition, 1971), p. 252.

38. Brosnan, *Movie Magic,* p. 188.

39. Baxter, *Science Fiction in the Cinema,* p. 113.

40. Durgnat, *Films and Feelings,* p. 267.

41. Morgenstern, *Film 68/69,* p. 62.

42. James F. Scott, *Film: The Medium and the Maker* (New York: Holt, Rinehart and Winston, 1975), p. 115.

43. "Rape of the Future," *Esquire* 65 (May 1966): 112.

44. Parker Tyler, *The Shadow of an Airplane Climbs the Empire State Building* (New York: Anchor Press/Doubleday, 1973), p. 128.

45. Baxter, *Science Fiction in the Cinema,* p. 171.

46. Luis Gasca, *Cine y Ciencia-Ficción* (Barcelona: Llibres de Sinera, 1969), p. 92. Translated from the following: ". . . un lugar encantado . . . con sus tornasolados reflejos y fosforescencias emergiendo de una penumbra azulada."

47. Brosnan, *Movie Magic,* pp. 206-7.

48. Ibid., p. 207.

49. Richard Fleisher in *Focus on the Science Fiction Film,* p. 158.

50. George Lucas quoted by Lawrence Sturhahn in "Genesis of *THX-1138:* Notes on a Production," *Kansas Quarterly* 4 (Spring 1972): 53.

51. Brosnan, *Movie Magic,* p. 198.

52. Stanley Kubrick in *Stanley Kubrick Directs,* p. 245.

53. For details on the astronomical effects in *2001,* see Brosnan, *Movie Magic,* p. 226.

54. Siegfried Kracauer, *Theory of Film: The Redemption of Physical Reality* (New York: Oxford University Press, Paperback Edition, 1960), p. 50.

55. Jean Epstein quoted in *Theory of Film,* p. 53.

56. Lotte H. Eisner, *The Haunted Screen* (Berkeley and Los Angeles: University of California Press, First California Paperback Edition, 1973), p. 13.

57. Baxter, *Science Fiction in the Cinema,* pp. 169-70.

58. Philip Strick and Peter Nicholls, "Science Fiction Cinema," *National Film Theatre Bulletin,* (London: May-July 1973), p. 8.

59. Tyler, *The Shadow of an Airplane,* p. 208.

60. This quote from *Tarantula,* unfortunately, is only somewhat approximate. The unpublished script is not available and the lines are quoted from notes taken during my various viewings of the film.

61. T. S. Eliot, "The Love Song of J. Alfred Prufrock," *The Complete Poems and Plays* (New York: Harcourt Brace, 1952), p. 7.

62. Baxter, *Science Fiction in the Cinema,* p. 114.

63. Frank McConnell, "Song of Innocence: *The Creature from the Black Lagoon,*" *The Journal of Popular Film* 2 (Winter 1973): 20.

64. Ibid.

65. Tyler, *The Shadow of an Airplane,* p. 108.

66. Baxter, *Science Fiction in the Cinema,* p. 157.

67. Strick and Nicholls, *National Film Theatre Bulletin,* n.p.

68. Ibid.

69. Tyler, *The Shadow of an Airplane,* p. 108.

70. Susan Sontag, "The Imagination of Disaster," *Commentary* 40 (October 1965): 47.

71. Ernesto G. Laura, *"Invasion of the Body Snatchers," Focus on the Science Fiction Film,* p. 71.

72. Brian Murphy, "Monster Movies: They Came From Beneath The Fifties," *The Journal of Popular Film* 1 (Winter 1972): 42.

73. Charles T. Gregory, "The Pod Society Versus the Rugged Individualists," *The Journal of Popular Film* 1 (Winter 1972): 3-4.

74. Sontag, "The Imagination of Disaster," p. 48.
75. Carlos Clarens, *An Illustrated History of the Horror Film* (New York: Capricorn Books, 1967), p. 134.
76. Don Siegel in *Don Siegel: Director,* Stuart M. Kaminsky (New York: Curtis Books, 1974), p. 104.
77. Ibid., p. 106.
78. Lawrence Alloway, *Violent America: The Movies 1946-1964* (New York: The Museum of Modern Art, 1971), p. 44.
79. Baxter, *Science Fiction in the Cinema,* p. 117.
80. Scott, *Film: The Medium and the Maker,* p. 70.
81. Stanley R. Greenberg, *Soylent Green.* Unpublished Screenplay. M.G.M., pp. 14-14A.
82. Ibid., p. 15.
83. Ibid., p. 24.
84. Martin Rubin, "Film Favorites: *The Incredible Shrinking Man,*" *Film Comment* 10 (July-August 1974): 53.
85. Baxter, *Science Fiction in the Cinema,* p. 125.
86. Rubin, "Film Favorites," p. 52.
87. Ibid.
88. Clarens, *An Illustrated History,* p. 133.
89. Rubin, "Film Favorites," p. 53.
90. William Johnson, in *Film Quarterly* 25, p. 55.
91. It isn't. See Brosnan, *Movie Magic,* p. 170.
92. Ray Harryhausen in Brosnan, *Movie Magic,* p. 167.
93. André Bazin, *What is Cinema?* Trans. Hugh Gray (Berkeley and Los Angeles: University of California Press, 1967), p. 51.
94. Ibid., p. 50.
95. Ray Harryhausen, in Brosnan, *Movie Magic,* p. 167.
96. Bazin, *What is Cinema?,* p. 48.
97. Ibid., p. 51.
98. Sontag, "The Imagination of Disaster," p. 44.
99. Ibid.
100. Fred Chappell, "The Science-Fiction Film Image," *The Film Journal* 2 (Issue 6, Number 3): 10.
101. Rubin, "Film Favorites," p. 53.
102. Frank McConnell, "Rough Beast Slouching," *Focus on the Horror Film,* eds. Roy Huss and T. J. Ross (New Jersey: Prentice-Hall, 1972), p. 32.
103. Sontag, "The Imagination of Disaster," p. 42.

Chapter 3 Notes

1. Pauline Kael, Review of *A Clockwork Orange, Deeper Into Movies* (New York: Bantam Books, 1974), p. 474.
2. Anthony Burgess, "On the Hopelessness of Turning Good Books Into Films," *New York Times,* (20 April 1975), sec. D, p. 15.
3. Ibid., p. 154.
4. Philip Strick, "Kubrick's Horrorshow," *Sight and Sound* 41 (Winter/Spring 1971-1972): 45.
5. *Robinson Crusoe on Mars* (Byron Haskin, 1964), for example, posits an alien "Friday." However, the runaway slave's language sounds emphatically reminiscent of Incan or Aztec, a sound further localized "south of the border" by Friday's hairdo and general appearance. Thus, despite the film's interesting linguistic battle in which a U.S. astronaut attempts to impose English on the alien and finally has to agree to linguistic

reciprocity rather than tyranny, *Robinson Crusoe's* alien looks and sounds like a left-over from *The Captain from Castille.*

6. Penelope Houston, "Glimpses of the Moon," *Sight and Sound* 22 (April-June 1953): 188.

7. Susan Sontag, "The Imagination of Disaster," *Commentary* 40 (October 1965): 42.

8. Brian Murphy, "Monster Movies: They Came From Beneath the Fifties," *The Journal of Popular Film* 1 (Winter 1972): 36-7.

9. Sontag, "The Imagination of Disaster," p. 42.

10. Pauline Kael, Review of *Marooned* in *Deeper Into Movies,* p. 107.

11. Stanley Kubrick in Alexander Walker, *Stanley Kubrick Directs* (New York: Harcourt, Brace, Jovanovich, 1971), p. 185.

12. Neil P. Hurley, *Theology Through Film* (New York: Harper and Row, 1970), p. 164.

13. Ann Marie Cunningham, "Forecast for Science Fiction: We Have Seen the Future and it is Feminine," *Mademoiselle* (February 1973), p. 140.

14. Pauline Kael, in *Deeper Into Movies,* p. 107.

15. Michael Wilson, *Planet of the Apes,* unpublished screenplay based on a novel by Pierre Boule, APJAC Productions, 20th Century Fox, 1967, U.C.L.A. Special Collections, pp. 118-19. N.B. This screenplay does not credit Rod Serling as co-author.

16. Paul Dehn, *Beneath the Planet of the Apes,* unpublished screenplay from a story by Paul Dehn and Mort Abrahams, APJAC Productions, 20th Century Fox, 1969, U.C.L.A. Special Collections, p. 16X.

17. Paul Dehn, *Conquest of the Planet of the Apes,* unpublished screenplay, 20th Century Fox, 1971, U.C.L.A. Special Collections, p. 146.

18. F. Anthony Macklin, "The Comic Sense of *2001," Film Comment* 5 (Winter 1969): 10.

19. A line of dialogue (and subsequent action) in *The Angry Red Planet* (Ib Melchior, 1960).

20. All dialogue from notes taken at a viewing of *Creation of the Humanoids.* I believe they are quite accurate, but as they were not tape-recorded it is always possible that they are not.

21. Parker Tyler, *The Shadow of an Airplane Climbs the Empire State Building* (New York: Anchor Books Edition, 1973), p. 161.

22. See, for example, *Abbott and Costello Meet the Invisible Man* (Charles Lamont, 1951), *Abbott and Costello Go to Mars* (Charles Lamont, 1953), the Three Stooges in *Have Rocket, Will Travel* (David Lowell Rich, 1959), and *The Three Stooges in Orbit* (Edward Bernds, 1962).

23. These credits were taken from a viewing of *Flesh Gordon.* Walt Lee's *Reference Guide to Fantastic Films,* vol. I., p. 142, however, says *Flesh Gordon* was directed by Michael Light. No such name appeared in the directorial credits of the film I saw in theatrical release.

24. John Carpenter quoted in program for *Filmex 1974,* (Los Angeles), p. 27.

25. Richard Combs, Review of *Everything You Always Wanted to Know About Sex* in *Sight and Sound* 42 (Summer 1973): 178.

26. Steven H. Scheuer, ed., *Movies on TV,* (1972-73), edition (New York: Bantam Books, 1971), p. 217.

27. Ibid.

28. Stanley Kauffmann, Review of *Dr. Strangelove, A World on Film* (New York: Delta Books, Dell Publishing Co., 1967), p. 15.

29. Judith Crist, "The Strangelovian Age" in *The Private Eye, the Cowboy and the Very Naked Girl* (New York: Holt, Rinehart and Winston, 1968), p. 45.

30. Walker, *Stanley Kubrick Directs,* pp. 185-88.

31. Ibid., p. 162.

32. Norman Kagan, *The Cinema of Stanley Kubrick* (New York: Holt, Rinehart and Winston, 1972), p. 142.

33. John Baxter, *Science Fiction in the Cinema* (New York: Paperback Library, 1970), p. 176.

34. Joseph Morgenstern, Review of *Wild in the Streets, Film 68/69,* eds. Hollis Alpert and Andrew Sarris (New York: Simon and Schuster, 1969), p. 174.

35. Patrick MacFadden, Review of *Wild in the Streets* in *Film Society Review* (May 1968): 24.

36. Renata Adler, Review of *Wild in the Streets, A Year in the Dark* (New York: Random House, 1969), p. 162.

37. Ibid., p. 163.

38. Clive James, "*2001:* Kubrick vs. Clarke," *Film Society Review* 5 (January 1970): 34.

39. Macklin, "The Comic Sense of *2001*," p. 12.

40. Penelope Gilliatt, Review of *2001: A Space Odyssey* in *Film 68/69,* pp. 54-55.

41. Philip Strick, Review of *THX 1138* in *Sight and Sound* 42 (Summer 1973): 178.

42. Walker, *Stanley Kubrick Directs,* p. 254.

43. Joseph Morgenstern, review of *2001: A Space Odyssey* in *Film 68/69,* p. 62.

44. Michael Sragow, "*2001: A Space Odyssey*," *Film Society Review* 5 (January 1970): 25.

45. Walker, *Stanley Kubrick Directs,* pp. 258-59.

46. Macklin, "The Comic Sense of 2001," p. 12.

47. Kenneth Geist, "Chronicler of Power: an interview with Franklin Schaffner," *Film Comment* 8 (September-October 1972): 33.

48. Ibid.

49. David Zinman, *Saturday Afternoon at the Bijou* (New Jersey: Castle Books, 1973), p. 101.

50. Murphy, "Monster Movies," p. 42.

51. Pierre Kast, "Don't Play with Fire," *Focus on the Science Fiction Film,* ed. William Johnson (New Jersey: Prentice-Hall, 1972), p. 69.

52. Baxter, *Science Fiction in the Cinema,* p. 104.

53. Ibid., p. 175.

54. Gerald Pratley, *The Cinema of John Frankenheimer* (New York: International Film Guide Series, A. S. Barnes & Co., 1969), pp. 107-8.

55. Lawrence Sturhahn, "Genesis of *THX-1138:* Notes on a Production," *Kansas Quarterly* 4 (Spring 1972): 47.

56. Ibid., p. 49.

57. Richard Schickel, Review of *The Groundstar Conspiracy* in *Life,* (11 August 1972), p. 18.

58. Wilson, *Planet of the Apes,* p. 115.

59. Dehn, *Beneath the Planet of the Apes,* p. 53.

60. Ibid., p. 57.

61. Howard Thomson, Review of *The Monitors* in the *New York Times,* (9 October 1969), 55:2. This review gives the name of the character played by Strudwick as Tersh. In my viewing of the film, his character was called Jeterex, frequently enough so as to make me quite sure that Thompson was in error.

62. Ibid.

63. Siegfried Mandell and Peter Fingesten, "The Myth of Science Fiction," *Saturday Review* 38 (27 August 1955): 25.

64. Pauline Kael, Review of *The Andromeda Strain* in *Deeper Into Movies,* pp. 348-49.

65. Philip Strick, "*Zardoz* and John Boorman," *Sight and Sound* 43 (Spring 1974): 73.

66. Marcia Kinder, Review of *Zardoz* in *Film Quarterly* 27 (Summer 1974): 52.

67. Ted Gilling, "The Colour of the Music: An Interview with Bernard Herrmann," *Sight and Sound* 41 (Winter 1971/72): 36.

68. Ibid., pp. 36-7.

69. Bosley Crowther, Review of *Forbidden Planet* in the *New York Times,* (4 May 1956).

70. Baxter, *Science Fiction in the Cinema,* p. 113.

71. Ibid.

72. F. Anthony Macklin, "Sex and *Dr. Strangelove,*" *Film Comment* 3 (Summer 1965) : 55.

73. Ibid.

74. Gilliatt, Review in *Film 68/69,* p. 53.

75. Pauline Kael, *Deeper Into Movies,* p. 474.

76. Kagan, *The Cinema of Stanley Kubrick,* p. 176.

77. Robert Hughes, "The Decor of Tomorrow's Hell," *Time,* (27 December 1971), p. 59.

78. Kagan, *The Cinema of Stanley Kubrick,* p. 185.

79. A. G. L., Review of *Them!* in *Twentieth Century,* (September 1954), p. 197.

80. Baxter, *Science Fiction in the Cinema,* p. 113.

81. Ibid., p. 112.

82. Robert Brustein, "Film Chronicle: Reflections on Horror Movies," *The Partisan Review* 25 (Spring 1958) : 292.

83. National Film Theatre Bulletin, (London: May-July 1973), n.p.

84. Baxter, *Science Fiction in the Cinema,* p. 128.

85. Ivan Butler, *Horror in the Cinema* (New York: International Film Guide Series, Paperback Library by arrangement with A. S. Barnes & Co., 1971), p. 185.

86. Philip Strick, Review of *THX 1138* in *Sight and Sound,* p. 178.

87. Stanley R. Greenberg, *Soylent Green,* unpublished screenplay, MGM, 1972, U.C.L.A. Special Collections, p. 33.

Chapter 4 Notes_____

1. Martin Heidegger, "The Question Concerning Technology," trans. William Lovitt, in *Martin Heidegger: Basic Writings,* ed. David Farrell Krell (New York: Harper & Row, 1977), p. 317.

2. For an elaboration of the sexual "dreamwork" of the traditional SF film, see my "The Virginity of Astronauts: Sex and the Science Fiction Film" in *Shadows of the Magic Lamp,* eds. George Slusser and Eric S. Rabkin (Carbondale: University of Southern Illinois Press, 1985), pp. 41-57.

3. Joan F. Dean, "Between *2001* and *Star Wars,*" *Journal of Popular Film and Television,* 7, No. 1 (1978), pp. 36-37.

4. This recuperation of patriarchy as a response to feminism and the failure of American aggressivity in Southeast Asia is treated not only in relation to the contemporary SF film, but also to the family melodrama/comedy and horror film in my "Child/Alien/Father: Patriarchal Crisis and Generic Transformation" in *camera obscura* #13 (1986). In that text, I also draw attention to E.T.'s physical resemblance to starving Ethiopian children.

5. "Care" here is a philosophical concept that entails a recognition of the meaning of all beings, of meaning as "Being." "Dread" is also a philosophical concept not to be seen as synonymous with "fear"; the latter is specific and connected to a meaningful particular, to something that matters, whereas "dread" is a condition of the denial of particular meaning, a vertigo in which all being and action stand as equivalent and therefore meaningless. The mainstream *Close Encounters,* for example, could stand as a representation of the urge towards a condition of "care" as could *Blade Runner* (Ridley Scott, 1982), whereas the marginal *Liquid Sky* and *Repo Man* manifest the recognition of meaninglessness and equivalency associated with "dread" (albeit in a transformed way yet to be discussed). For a summary of these Heideggerean concepts, see Karsten Harries, "Martin

Heidegger: The Search for Meaning," in *Existential Philosophers: Kierkegaard to Merleau-Ponty*, ed. George Alfred Schrader, Jr. (New York: McGraw Hill, 1967), pp. 183–187.

6. "Futurism" here has a double sense. The term evokes SF's general tendency to project temporally possible (if sometimes improbable) events, technologies, and social relations. But it also is a technical term that describes a "modernist" and "Utopian" art movement of the early twentieth century that celebrated machinery and speed. As Fredric Jameson notes in "Postmodernism, or the Cultural Logic of Late Capitalism," at that time, new technological objects like the machine gun and the motor car "are still visible emblems, sculptural nodes of energy which gave tangibility and figuration to the motive energies of that earlier moment of modernization." (*New Left Review*, No. 146, July–August 1984, p. 78) The "visibility" of such emblems, their existence as some sort of "tangible" evidence and figuration of the dynamism ("the motive energies") that constituted the "modern," are precisely what the new "marginal" SF film both mocks and tries to reformulate. In its recognition that "visibility," "tangibility," and "dynamism" are terms descriptive of a "modern" technology outmoded by an electronic culture to which those terms seem irrelevant, in rejecting the visual celebration and visible display of technology dominating current "mainstream" SF, "marginal" SF films like *Repo Man* or *The Brother from Another Planet* can be seen as consciously embracing what shall be elaborated as a "postmodern" aesthetic.

7. This question can only be briefly addressed here — and as it furthers my discussion of the contemporary SF film. I would direct the interested reader to a most provocative phenomenological exploration of this question: Don Ihde, *Existential Technics* (Albany, NY: State University of New York Press, 1983), and to Section I. "Technology and American Culture" (pp. 11–75) in *The Technological Imagination: Theories and Fictions*, eds. Teresa De Lauretis, Andreas Huyssen, and Kathleen Woodward (Madison, WI: Coda Press, 1980).

8. Interestingly, this phrase is repeated (and makes the same statement of spatial equivalency) in the Australian *Mad Max: Beyond Thunderdome* (George Miller/George Ogilve, 1985).

9. Here, in relation to my use of the term "political unconscious," I would refer the reader back to the new Introduction of this volume, and for further elaboration to Fredric Jameson, *The Political Unconscious: Narrative as a Socially Symbolic Act* (Ithaca, NY: Cornell University Press, 1981). See particularly, pp. 9–102.

10. Jameson, "Postmodernism, or The Cultural Logic of Late Capitalism," *New Left Review*, No. 146 (July–August 1984), p. 87.

11. This "ultimate victory" of cultural totalization is discussed in its form as a technological totalization of nature by Ihde in "Technology and Human Self-Conception," the first chapter in the previously cited *Existential Technics*. See, particularly, pp. 19–23.

12. While the theorization (and idealization) of the "cyborg" is apparent in recent SF, I would direct the reader's attention to the popularity of recent non-SF films that consciously project and display the human body as well-oiled machine, as construction: both *First Blood* (with Sylvester Stallone) and *Conan the Barbarian* (with Arnold Schwarzenegger) in 1982, *Staying Alive* (directed by Stallone and starring his prize "pupil," John Travolta) in 1983, and *Rambo* (with Stallone even more mean and naked this time), *Perfect* (with Travolta and Jamie Lee Curtis), and *Pumping Iron II: The Women* in 1985. While androids and cyborgs have always been part of SF, we have not previously been so self-identified with them, so ready to incorporate them as ourselves, nor have films like *Blade Runner*, *Android* (both 1982), and *The Terminator* (1984) been so cinematically "replicated" in non-SF cinema. For an excellent discussion of this changed cultural perception of the human body and its social implications, see Donna Haraway, "A Manifesto for Cyborgs:

Science, Technology, and Socialist Feminism in the 1980s," *Socialist Review*, No. 80 (1985): 65–107. (Although Haraway is basically hopeful about this new theorization of the body and the possibility for human description it opens up, such a theorization may also be seen as a way for popular culture to respond to the feminist critique of voyeurism with a canny recuperation.)

13. Jameson, "Postmodernism, or The Cultural Logic of Late Capitalism," p. 87. On this issue, see also Jean Baudrillard, *Simulations*, trans. Paul Foss, Paul Patton, and Philip Beichtman (New York: Semiotexte, 1983), and "The Ecstasy of Communication," trans. John Johnston, in *The Anti-Aesthetic: Essays in Postmodern Culture*, ed. Hal Foster (Washington: Bay Press, 1983), pp. 126–134; and Guy Debord, *The Society of the Spectacle* (Detroit: Black and Red Press, 1983).

14. Walter Benjamin, "The Work of Art in the Age of Mechanical Reproduction," in *Illuminations*, ed. Hannah Arendt, trans. Harry Zohn (New York: Harcourt Brace Jovanovich, 1968), pp. 219–226.

15. Jameson, "Postmodernism, or The Logic of Late Capitalism," p. 57.

16. Ibid., p. 77. See also Ernest Mandel, *Late Capitalism*, trans. Joris De Bres (London: Verso Press, 1975).

17. Mandel, p. 191.

18. Jameson, "Postmodernism, or The Cultural Logic of Late Capitalism," p. 78.

19. It is worth noting here that as a capitalist industry and institution, the American cinema has three expansive "moments" equivalent to Mandel's — although, of course, they exist in a more concentrated time frame. In the early 1900s, the first movies are produced, distributed, and exhibited within "market capitalism" (evidenced by all the independent production companies, store-front theaters, pirating of patents and films, general entrepreneurship, etc.). From the 1930s through the 1950s, the motion picture industry becomes a textbook example of successful monopoly capitalism; the major studios have taken over smaller ones or put them out of business, and control both distribution and exhibition. (In Mel Brooks' *Silent Movie*, the rise of monopoly capitalism through the "studio system," which changed the industry's early structure, is humorously, but aptly, figured in the corporate name of "Engulf and Devour.") After the emergence of television in the 1950s (and a good deal of antitrust legislation), the studio system began to fall apart. Seemingly weakened at first, the motion picture industry has nonetheless now expanded its capital in an unprecedented manner — while also consolidating capital into fewer and fewer hands (and centering it in fewer and fewer films). Now films are made as packaged deals and financed as multinational co-productions. (There really is a distribution "company" called National General.) While Hollywood is presently more a state of mind than a place where movies originate, the industry has not so much declined as "decentered" itself. Indeed, it has actually expanded — and through the very electronic media that first challenged its supremacy. Thus, since the 1960s, the motion picture industry has reflected the economic structural logic of late capital.

20. Jameson, "Postmodernism, or The Cultural Logic of Late Capitalism," p. 56.

21. Ibid., p. 57.

22. To distinguish a work as "properly" postmodern would seem to demand that it articulate a consciousness of its own cultural positioning and aesthetic features. In phenomenological terms, we could say that the cultural production influenced by the postmodern but not itself a postmodernist work is one that merely represents "the postmodern experience of consciousness." The cultural production that is properly postmodernist, however, also represents "the consciousness of postmodern experience" and thus reflects upon and recognizes its logic. In regard to the SF film, I have seen what here are described as "mainstream" and "marginal" SF films as, respectively, those unconsciously influenced by postmodern logic and those that consciously embrace that logic (if not its name).

23. Jameson, "Postmodernism, or The Logic of Late Capitalism," p. 53. I might point out here (as Jameson neglects to) that this "inverted millennarianism" with its sense of the "end of this or that" is inherent not only in the previously discussed negativity of a term like "postindustrial," but also in the term "postmodern" — and in my own new chapter title, "postfuturism."

24. Ibid., pp. 54–55.

25. Certainly a form of "inverted millennarianism" has been endemic to the SF film since its beginnings. Nonetheless, there is a difference between the representation and sense of the "end of this or that" in films prior to the last decade. Generic predecessors to *Blade Runner*'s "trashed" futurism tend to be linked to postnuclear holocaust narratives rather than to the expansion of multinational capitalism. The only exception that comes to mind is *Soylent Green* (Richard Fleischer, 1973), which displays the tired and recycled technology of a negatively envisioned "postindustrial" society, but does not visually eroticize postindustrial waste in the manner of *Blade Runner*. Similarly, the generic predecessors to *The Terminator*'s inverted millennarianism locate their time-travel narratives in a "wasted" future rather than a "trashed" present represented as the past. What is striking in an introductory passage of the film is the visual equivalence constituted between a post-nuclear holocaust future and the urban landscape of the present (that future's past): a destructive crushing machine in a "boneyard" battlefield is made to seem identical to a massive garbage truck amid the trash of a contemporary junk yard. These equivalencies are not the stuff of previous time-travel films, which, while evidencing a sense of the "end of this or that," clearly differentiate between past and future and tend to locate themselves not in the former, but in the latter. This differentiation can be seen in *The Planet of the Apes* series, for example, or in *Logan's Run* (Michael Anderson, 1976).

26. Certainly, to a great extent, the cinema as a mass medium and the genre film as its most commercially popular form have never been the province of high culture. Nonetheless, the widespread incorporation of film and popular culture into the academic curriculum (which can be dated back to the 1960s, as can the scholarly interest in popular genres) institutionally articulates this growing "aesthetic populism," which is critically entailed not only with the commodification of aesthetic production, but also with the commodification of education. (Courses in film studies and popular culture, in most instances, have been grudgingly admitted into the academy to boost waning enrollments.)

27. The opening credit sequence of *The Brother from Another Planet* also pays homage to the schlockiness of B-movie special effects; its chintzy spaceship dials and laughable landing announce and celebrate the film's marginal and low-budget status.

28. Andrew Gordon, "*Star Wars: A Myth for Our Time,*" *Literature/Film Quarterly* 6, No. 4 (Fall 1978), p. 319.

29. Jameson, "Postmodernism, or The Cultural Logic of Late Capitalism," p. 54.

30. Ibid., p. 58.

31. Gordon, "*Star Wars: A Myth for Our Time,*" p. 315.

32. Pat Aufderheide, "Sci-fi Discovers New Enemies," *In These Times*, 21 November–4 December 1984, p. 30. Despite the piece's brevity, Aufderheide is well worth reading on the aesthetics and political implications of the new marginal SF.

33. Jameson, "Postmodernism, or The Cultural Logic of Late Capitalism," p. 80.

34. Ibid., p. 81.

35. Jean Baudrillard, "The Ecstasy of Communication," trans. John Johnston, in *The Anti-Aesthetic: Essays on Postmodern Culture*, ed. Hal Foster (Washington: Bay Press, 1983), p. 128.

36. Scott Bukatman, "Terminal Identity: Image and Subjectivity in Postmodern Science Fiction," p. 39. (Unpublished paper). Bukatman here refers to characteristics of postmodern architecture noted by Charles Jencks.

37. Jameson, "Postmodernism, or The Cultural Logic of Late Capitalism," p. 60.

38. A fascinating visual gloss on this equivalence is an IMAX film shot by astronauts, which shows both the earth and the space capsule and extravehicular activity in the same image. What is visually striking is the fuzziness of the earth blurred by its atmosphere and the absolute hard-edged clarity of the capsule and astronauts in a space with no atmosphere. The latter appeared by comparison with the former as electronically generated (rather than cinematographically represented) images.

39. Bukatman, p. 14.

40. Jean Baudrillard, "The Precession of Simulacra," trans. Paul Foss and Paul Patton, in *Simulations* (New York: Semiotexte, 1983), p. 54.

41. Here the reader is reminded that the optics of the cinematic apparatus were developed to replicate the Renaissance representation of space as three-dimensional, and the image as centered in a single viewing subject.

42. Jameson, "Postmodernism, or The Cultural Logic of Late Capitalism," p. 79.

43. Ibid.

44. For discussion of this aspect of the special nature of special effects in SF, see Michael Wood, "Kiss Tomorrow Hello," *American Film* 2, No. 6 (April 1977), pp. 14–17; and Albert J. LaValley, "Thinking about Special Effects," *American Film* 7, No. 8 (June 1982), p. 57.

45. Jameson, "Postmodernism, or The Cultural Logic of Late Capitalism," p. 79.

46. Michael Stern, "Making Culture Into Nature; or, Who Put the 'Special' into 'Special Effects'?" *Science-Fiction Studies*, No. 22 (November 1980), p. 266. This is a particularly insightful article on the ideological implications of special effects and seems to me most persuasive in the context of the weakening of the categories of the "real" and the "natural" in the postmodern culture of the "image" and the "simulacrum."

47. Baudrillard, "The Precession of Simulacra," p. 25. Here it is worth noting that *Tron* — using electronic representation to nearly subsume the cinematic and its traditional representation of the "real" — was produced by Disney Studios.

48. Guy Debord, *The Society of the Spectacle* (Detroit: Black and Red Press, 1983), np., paragraph 1.

49. The term "excess scenography" is borrowed from a particularly fine analysis of *Blade Runner* (also drawing upon Jameson's work on postmodernism) by Guiliana Bruno: "Ramble City: Postmodernism and *Blade Runner*," a paper presented at the 1985 Society for Cinema Studies annual meeting, New York University, and in press for a forthcoming special SF issue of *camera obscura*.

50. Bart Mills, "The Brave New World of Production Design," *American Film* 7, No. 4 (January–February 1982), p. 40.

51. Ibid. Lawrence G. Paull was the "production designer" of *Blade Runner*, Syd Mead its "visual consultant."

52. Ibid., p. 45.

53. Marc Mancini, "The Future Isn't What It Used to Be," *Film Comment* 21, No. 3 (May–June 1985), p. 13.

54. Hal Hinson, "Dreamscapes," *American Film* 10, No. 3 (December 1984), p. 46.

55. Ibid., p. 47.

56. Ibid., p. 48.

57. For an interesting discussion of this issue, see Mancini, *Film Comment* 21, No. 3 (May–June 1985), particularly pp. 13–15.

58. Jameson, "Postmodernism, or The Cultural Logic of Late Capitalism," p. 76.

59. Ibid., p. 77.

60. Ibid., pp. 82–83.

61. This construction of desire from *excess* rather than *lack* is extremely suggestive in

its subversive turn on that Freudian and Lacanian psychoanalytic theory which has so informed film analysis since the 1970s, and poses a transformed model of both desire and identification.

62. This kind of mise-en-scène of dispersal and excessive materiality and activity has heretofore been seen only in the singular works of Jacques Tati and, more recently, Bill Forsyth—neither American and neither working in the SF genre, but both attuned to the spatial relations between humans and things and each other as a field for both comedy and anthropology. The only American herald to this new postmodern mise-en-scène was *Airplane!*, released in 1981. Its popularity and box-office success paved the way for this aesthetic of postmodernist clutter and overabundance.

63. Jameson, "Postmodernism, or The Cultural Logic of Late Capitalism," p. 71. For those not familiar with the linguistic concept of the "syntagmatic," the term refers to the combinatory relations of language in a "signifying chain."

64. Ibid., p. 64.

65. Ibid., pp. 65, 70.

66. In an interview Ridley Scott mentions comic-strip artist Mobius (a not inappropriate name in the context of my present discussion on the postmodern conflation of time) as an inspiration for *Blade Runner*, and points to his creation of "a *tangible* future. . . . one you can see and touch." Harlan Kennedy, "21st Century Nervous Breakdown," Film Comment 18, No. 4 (July–August 1982), p. 66.

67. Jameson, "Postmodernism, or The Cultural Logic of Late Capitalism," p. 72.

68. Ibid., p. 66.

69. Ibid., p. 67.

70. Ibid., p. 71.

71. Conversely, *The Terminator* could not have been other than a melodrama—for its temporal nostalgia is not for a simulacra of the historical past, but for the present-ness of the present. It wants to conserve the direct experience of urban waste, not the indirect experience of televised small-town cleanliness. Thus, while its Moebius strip temporal structure and narrative objective of conserving the present is the same as that of *Back to the Future*, its direction is different, and it well might have been subtitled *Back from the Future*. In this regard, *The Terminator* also differs from *Blade Runner*, which clearly creates its nostalgia for the trashed postmodern present through intertextual reference to the decayed past of 1940s film noir.

72. Jameson, "Postmodernism, or The Cultural Logic of Late Capitalism," p. 71.

73. Ibid., pp. 71–72.

74. Ibid., p. 72. Italics mine.

75. Lisa Jensen, Review of *Repo Man* in *Good Times*, 20 September 1984, p. 47.

76. Michael S. Gant, Review of *Repo Man* in *Santa Cruz Express*, 20 September 1984, p. 39.

77. Ibid.

78. Jameson, "Postmodernism, or The Cultural Logic of Late Capitalism," p. 74.

79. Ibid.

80. Ibid.

81. Ibid., p. 64.

82. Ibid., p. 76.

83. Ibid., p. 73. Jameson, of course, is not writing here of SF special effects. For a more scathing and less dialectical reading of the meaning-effects of SF special effects, see Manfred Nagl, "The Science-Fiction Film in Historical Perspective," trans. David Clayton, *Science-Fiction Studies*, No. 31 (November 1983), pp. 262–277.

84. I recommend the reader to Tony Crawley, *The Steven Spielberg Story* (New York: Quill, 1983), pp. 53–74. Of particular interest here (and throughout the book) is the

rhetoric (both Crawley's and Spielberg's) that continually links special effects with the sublime, the transcendent, the wondrous, and the magical rather than to anything scientific, technological, or "rational." For further commentary on Neary's re-solution as a child and its relation to contemporary patriarchal crisis, see my own "Child/Alien/Father: Patriarchal Crisis and Generic Exchange," in *camera obscura* #13.

85. It is worth noting here that the "new" technology represented in *Brainstorm* hyperbolically thematizes and duplicates the transference of subjective experience by the cinema itself: a mechanism that objectifies the subjective (makes it visible) while still maintaining it as experienced subjectively (actively viewed and made meaningful through the agency of a situated seeing subject). That is, the cinema as a medium represents human consciousness. For further discussion of this major assertion, I would direct the reader to my forthcoming *The Address of the Eye: A Phenomenology of Film Experience* (Princeton, NJ: Princeton University Press).

86. See, for example, Tony Williams, "Close Encounters of the Authoritarian Kind," *Wide Angle* 5, No. 4 (1983), pp. 22–29.

87. I am indebted for this formulation to Zoe Sofoulis, who used it as part of a paper title for a presentation at the Eaton Conference on Science Fiction (University of California, Irvine: April 1986). And lest one example of American corporate capitalism not be familiar to all my readers, let me explain (for its connotations of play, cuteness, and childhood appropriate to this discussion) that Ms. Sofoulis's transformation is not merely from "us" to U.S., but also a reference to a U.S. chain of toy stores, called "Toys R Us."

88. Jameson, "Postmodernism, or The Cultural Logic of Late Capitalism," pp. 76–77.

89. Michel Foucault, *This Is Not a Pipe*, translated and edited by James Harkness (Berkeley: University of California Press, 1982), p. 32.

90. Ibid., p. 44.

91. Ibid., p. 46.

92. Jameson, "Postmodernism, or The Cultural Logic of Late Capitalism," p. 86.

93. Ibid.

94. Ibid., p. 88.

95. Ibid., p. 89.

96. Ibid., p. 92.

97. For a theoretical and critical discussion of *Born in Flames*, see Teresa DeLauretis, "Aesthetics and Feminist Theory: Rethinking Women's Cinema," *New German Critique*, No. 34 (Winter 1985), pp. 154–175.

Selected Bibliography

See Page 329 for Chapter 4 Bibliography

Books

Alloway, Lawrence. *Violent America: The Movies 1946-1964.* New York: Museum of Modern Art, 1971.

Amis, Kingsley. *New Maps of Hell.* New York: Harcourt, Brace & Co., 1960.

Baxter, John. *Science Fiction in the Cinema.* The International Film Guide Series. New York: The Paperback Library by arrangement with A. S. Barnes & Co., 1970.

Bazin, André. *What is Cinema?* Translated by Hugh Gray. Berkeley and Los Angeles: University of California Press, 1967.

Bretnor, Reginald, ed. *Modern Science Fiction: Its Meaning and Its Future.* New York: Coward-McCann, 1953.

Brosnan, John. *Movie Magic.* New York: St. Martin's Press, 1974.

Butler, Ivan. *Horror in the Cinema.* The International Film Guide Series. New York: The Paperback Library by arrangement with A. S. Barnes & Co., 1971.

———. *Religion in the Cinema.* The International Film Guide Series. New York: A. S. Barnes & Co., 1969.

Cameron, Ian. *Adventure in the Movies.* New York: Crescent Books, 1973.

Cawelti, John G. *The Six-Gun Mystique.* Bowling Green, Ohio: Bowling Green Popular Press, 1970.

Clarens, Carlos. *An Illustrated History of the Horror Film.* New York: Capricorn Books, 1967.

Clareson, Thomas. *Science Fiction Criticism: An Annotated Checklist.* Ohio: Kent State University Press, 1972.

———. ed. *SF: The Other Side of Realism.* Bowling Green, Ohio: Bowling Green University Popular Press, 1971.

323

Durgnat, Raymond. *Films and Feelings*. Cambridge, Mass.: The M.I.T. Press, Paper Edition, 1971.

Fielding, Raymond. *The Technique of Special Effects Cinematography*. London: Focal Press, 1965.

Gasca, Luis. *Cine y Ciencia-Ficcion*. Barcelona: Llibres de Sinera, 1969.

Gifford, Denis. *A Pictorial History of Horror Movies*. London: Hamlyn, 1973.

———. *Science Fiction Film*. London: Studio Vista/Dutton Pictureback, 1971.

Hurley, Neil P. *Theology Through Film*. New York.: Harper & Row, 1970.

Huss, Roy, and Ross, T. J., eds. *Focus on the Horror Film*. New Jersey: Prentice-Hall, 1972.

Hutchinson, Tom. *Horror and Fantasy in the Movies*. New York: Crescent Books, 1974.

Johnson, William, ed. *Focus on the Science Fiction Film*. New Jersey: Prentice-Hall, 1972.

Kagan, Norman. *The Cinema of Stanley Kubrick*. New York: Holt, Rinehart & Winston, 1972.

Kaminsky, Stuart M. *American Film Genres*. New York: Pflaum Publishing, 1974.

———. *Don Siegel: Director*. Curtis Film Series. New York: Curtis Books, 1974.

Kitses, Jim. *Horizons West*. Cinema One Series, Bloomington, Ind.: Indiana University Press, 1969.

Knight, Damon. *In Search of Wonder*. Chicago: Advent Press, 1967.

Kracauer, Siegfried. *Theory of Film: The Redemption of Physical Reality*. New York: Oxford University Press, 1960.

Laclos, Michel. *Le Fantastique au Cinéma*. Paris: J. J. Pauvert, 1958.

Lee, Walt., comp. *Reference Guide to Fantastic Films*. Los Angeles: Chelsea-lee Books, Vol. I, 1972; Vol. II, 1973; Vol. III, 1974.

McArthur, Colin. *Underworld U.S.A.* Cinema One Series. New York: The Viking Press, 1972.

McCarthy, Todd, and Flynn, Charles, eds. *Kings of the Bs: Working Within the Hollywood System*. New York: E. P. Dutton & Co., Inc., 1975.

Malinowski, Bronislaw. *Magic, Science and Religion and Other Essays*. Glencoe, Ill.: The Free Press, 1948.

Manchel, Frank. *Terrors of the Screen*. New Jersey: Prentice-Hall, 1970.

Moskowitz, Sam, *Explorers of the Infinite: Shapers of Science Fiction*. New York: World Books, 1957.

Pratley, Gerald. *The Cinema of John Frankenheimer*. The International Film Guide Series. New York: A. S. Barnes & Co., 1969.

Predal, René. *Le Cinema Fantastique*. Cinema Club. Paris: Éditions Seghers, 1970.

Rose, Lois, and Rose, Stephen. *The Shattered Ring: Science fiction and the quest for meaning*. Virginia: John Knox Press, 1970.

Scheuer, Steven H., ed. *Movies on TV*. 1972-73 edition, New York: Bantam Books, 1971.

Scott, James F. *Film: The Medium and the Maker*. New York: Holt, Rinehart and Winston, Inc., 1975.

Siclier, Jacques, and Labarthe, André S. *Images de la Science-Fiction*. Paris: Les Éditions du Cerf, 1958.

Steinbrunner, Chris and Goldblatt, Burt. *Cinema of the Fantastic*. New York: Saturday Review Press, 1972.

Tyler, Parker. *The Shadow of an Airplane Climbs the Empire State Building*. New York: Anchor Books, Edition, 1973.

Walker, Alexander. *Stanley Kubrick Directs*. New York: Harcourt, Brace, Jovanovich, 1971.

Willis, Donald C. *Horror and Science Fiction Films: A Checklist*. New Jersey: Scarecrow Press, 1972.

Zinman, David. *Saturday Afternoon at the Bijou*. New Jersey: Castle Books, 1973.

Articles

Adler, Renata. Review of *Wild in the Streets*. *A Year in the Dark*. New York: Random House, 1969, pp. 162-63.

Amis, Kingsley. "Science Fiction: A Practical Nightmare." *Holiday*, February 1965, p. 8.

Arnold, Francis. "Out of this World." *Sight and Sound* 8 (June 1963): 14-18.

Ascher, Marcia. "Computers in Science Fiction." *Harvard Business Review* 41 (November 1963): 40.

Atwell, Lee. "Two Studies in Space-Time." *Film Quarterly* 26 (Winter 1972): 2-9.

Bernabeau, Ednita P. "Science Fiction: A New Mythos." *Psychoanalytical Quarterly* 26 (October 1957): 527-35.

Blish, James. "On Science Fiction Criticism." *SF: The Other Side of Realism*. Edited by Thomas Clareson. Bowling Green, Ohio: Bowling Green University Popular Press, 1971, pp. 166-70.

Brophy, Liam. "Grave New Worlds." *Catholic World*, April 1954, pp. 40-43.

Brustein, Robert. "Film Chronicles: Reflections on Horror Movies." *The Partisan Review* 25 (Spring 1958): 288-296.

Burgess, Anthony. "On the Hopelessness of Turning Good Books Into Films." *New York Times*, 20 April 1975, Section D, p. 1†.

Buscombe, Edward. "The Idea of Genre in the American Cinema." *Screen* 2 (March-April 1970): 33-45.

Butor, Michael. "Science Fiction: The Crisis of its Growth." *SF: The Other Side of Realism*. Edited by Thomas Clareson. Bowling Green, Ohio: Bowling Green University Popular Press, 1971, pp. 157-65.

Campbell, John Ramsey. "But is it SF?" *Stardock* 1 (August 1968): 4-8.

Chappell, Fred. "The Science-Fiction Film Image." *The Film Journal* 2 (Issue 6): 8-12.

Collins, Richard. "Genre: A Reply to Ed Buscombe." *Screen* 2 (August-September 1970): 66-75.

Combs, Richard. Review of *Everything You Always Wanted to Know About Sex*. *Sight and Sound* 42 (Summer 1973): 178.

Crowther, Bosley. "Outer Space Comes of Age." *Atlantic*, March 1952, pp. 91-92.

Cunningham, Ann Marie. "Forecast for Science Fiction: We Have Seen the Future and it is Feminine." *Mademoiselle,* February 1973, pp. 140-41.

Daniels, Don. *"2001:* A New Myth." *Film Heritage* 3 (Summer 1968) : 1-9.

Denby, David. Review of *The Andromeda Strain. Atlantic,* June 1971, p. 97.

Denne, John D. "Society and the Monster." *December* 9 (#2/3) : 180-83.
de Wohl, Liam. "Religion, Philosophy and Outer Space." *America,* 24 July 1954, pp. 420-21.

Dillard, R. H. W. "Even a Man who is Pure at Heart: Poetry and Danger in the Horror Film." *Man and the Movies.* Edited by W. R. Robinson. Baltimore: Penguin Books, 1969, pp. 60-96.

Dworkin, Martin S. "Atomic Operas." *Contemporary Review* 203 (January 1963) : 27-30.

Evan, Walter. "Monster Movies: A Sexual Theory." *The Journal of Popular Film* 2 (Fall 1973) : 353-65.

Finer, S. E. "A Profile of Science Fiction." *The Sociological Review* 2 (December 1954) : 239-56.

Flatto, Elie. *"2001: A Space Odyssey:* The Eternal Renewal." *Film Comment* 5 (Winter 1969) : 6-9.

Geist, Kenneth. "Chronicler of Power: an interview with Franklin Schaffner." *Film Comment* 8 (September-October 1972) : 29-36.

Gilliatt, Penelope. Review of *The Forbin Project. New Yorker,* 16 May 1970, pp. 114-15.

————. Review of *2001: A Space Odyssey. Film 68/69.* Edited by Hollis Alpert and Andrew Sarris. New York: Simon and Schuster, 1960, pp. 53-57.

Gilling, Ted. "The Colour of the Music." *Sight and Sound* 41 (Winter 1971-1972) : 36-39.

Green, Martin. "Science and Sensibility: Part II. Science Fiction." *Kenyon Review* 25 (Autumn 1965) : 713-28.

Gregory, Charles T. 'The Pod Society Versus the Rugged Individualists." *The Journal of Popular Film* 1 (Winter 1972) : 3-14.

Hauser, Frank. "Science Fiction Films." *International Film Annual.* Edited by William Whitebait. New York: Doubleday, 1958, pp. 87-90.

Herzog, Arthur. "Science Fiction Movies Are Catching on in a Weary America." *New York Times,* 25 August 1974, Section 2, p. 1+.

Hodgens, Richard. "A Brief Tragical History of the Science Fiction Film." *Film Quarterly* 13 (Winter 1959) : 30-39.

Houston, Penelope. "Glimpses of the Moon." *Sight and Sound* 22 (April-June 1953) : 185-88.

Hughes, Robert. "The Decor of Tomorrow's Hell." *Time,* 27 December 1971, p. 59.

Hunter, Tim. *"2001. A Space Odyssey." Film Heritage* 3 (Summer 1968) : 12-20.

Isaacs, Neil D. "Unstruck in Time: *Clockwork Orange* and *Slaughterhouse Five." Literature/Film Quarterly* 1 (Spring 1973) : 122-31.

James, Clive. *"2001:* Kubrick vs. Clarke." *Film Society Review* 5 (January 1970) : 27-34.

Johnson, William. Review of *Silent Running*. *Film Quarterly* 25 (Summer 1972) : 52-56.

Jonas, Gerald. "Onward and Upward with the Arts—SF." *New Yorker,* 29 July 1972, pp. 33-52.

Kael, Pauline. Review of *Marooned. Deeper Into Movies*. New York: Bantam Books, 1974, pp. 107-8.

———. Review of *The Andromeda Strain. Deeper Into Movies.* New York: Bantam Books, 1974, pp. 348-49.

———. Review of *A Clockwork Orange. Deeper Into Movies.* New York: Bantam Books, 1974, pp. 470-75.

Kane, Joe. "Nuclear Films." *Take One* 2 (July-August 1969) : 9-11.

Kass, Robert. Review of *The Magnetic Monster. Catholic World,* April 1953, p. 65.

Kinder, Marcia. Review of *Zardoz. Film Quarterly* 27 (Summer 1974) : 49-57.

Knight, Arthur. Review of *Invasion U.S.A.* and *The Magnetic Monster, Saturday Review,* 21 February 1953, pp. 34-35.

Kolker, Robert Philip. "Oranges, Dogs, and Ultra-Violence." *The Journal of Popular Film* 1 (Summer 1972) : 159-72.

Kosloff, Max. *"2001." Film Culture* #48-49 (Winter-Spring 1970) : 53-56.

Lingeman, Richard R. "There Was Another Fifties." *New York Times Magazine,* 17 June 1973.

McConnell, Frank. "Rough Beasts Slouching: A Note on Horror Movies." *Kenyon Review* 128 (1970) : 109-20.

———. "Song of Innocence: *The Creature from the Black Lagoon." The Journal of Popular Film* 2 (Winter 1973) : 15-28.

McDonnell, T. P. "Cult of Science Fiction." *Catholic World,* October 1953, pp. 15-18.

MacFadden, Patrick. Review of *Dr. Strangelove. Film Society Review,* January 1967, pp. 22-24.

———. Review of *Wild in the Streets. Film Society Review,* May 1968, pp. 22-25.

Macklin, F. Anthony. "The Comic Sense of *2001." Film Comment* 5 (Winter 1969) : 10-15.

———. "Sex and *Dr. Strangelove." Film Comment* 3 (Summer 1965) : 55-57.

Maddison, Michael. "Case Against Tomorrow." *Political Quarterly* (London) 36 (April 1965) : 214-27.

Maddocks, Melvin. "New Note: the Novel as Sci-Non-Fi." *Life,* 30 May 1969, p. 15.

Mandell, Siegfried, and Fingesten, Peter. "The Myth of Science Fiction." *Saturday Review,* 27 August 1955, p. 7.

Merla, Patrick. " 'What is Real? Asked the Rabbit One Day." *Saturday Review: The Arts,* November 1972, pp. 43-50.

Merril, Judith. "What Do You Mean: Science? Fiction?" *SF: The Other Side of Realism.* Edited by Thomas Clareson. Bowling Green, Ohio: Bowling Green University Popular Press, 1971, pp. 53-95.

Morgenstern, Joseph. Review of *2001: A Space Odyssey. Film 68/69.* Edited by

Hollis Alpert and Andrew Sarris. New York: Simon and Schuster, 1969, pp. 60-63.

———. Review of *Wild in the Streets*. *Film 68/69*. Edited by Hollis Alpert and Andrew Sarris. New York: Simon and Schuster, 1969, pp. 173-74.

Murphy, Brian. "Monster Movies: They Came From Beneath the Fifties." *The Journal of Popular Film* 1 (Winter 1972) : 31-44.

Nelson, Joyce. "*Slaughterhouse-Five:* Novel and Film." *Literature/Film Quarterly* 1 (Spring 1973) : 149-53.

Peary, Gerald. Review of *Westworld*. *Take One* 3 (May-June 1972, published 9/26/73) : 31.

"People-Eaters, the New Diet in Hollywood Films." *Life*, 15 September 1972, pp. 74-75.

Pohl, Frederik. "*2001:* a second look." *Film Society Review* 5 (February 1970) : 23-27.

Rayns, Tony. Review of *Sleeper*. *Sight and Sound* 43 (Summer 1974) : 178-79.

Rogers, Ivor. "Extrapolative Cinema." *Arts in Society* 6 (Summer-Fall 1969) : 287-91.

Rosenfeld, Albert. "Perhaps the Mysterious Monolithic Slab is Really Moby Dick." *Life*, 5 April 1968, pp. 34-35.

Ross, T. J. "Introduction." *Focus on the Horror Film*. Edited by Roy Huss and T. J. Ross. New Jersey: Prentice-Hall, 1972, pp. 1-10.

Rubin, Martin. "Film Favorites: *The Incredible Shrinking Man*." *Film Comment* 10 (July-August 1974) : 52-53.

Ryall, Tom. "The Notion of Genre." *Screen* 2 (March-April 1970) : 22-23.

Sargeant, Winthrop. "Through the Interstellar Looking Glass." *Life*, 21 May 1951, pp. 127-42.

Schickel, Richard. Review of *The Groundstar Conspiracy*. *Life*, 11 August 1972, p. 18.

Schwartz, Sheila. "The World of Science Fiction." *The English Record* 21 (February 1971) : 27-40.

Scobie, Steven. "Concerning Horses; Concerning Apes." *Riverside Quarterly* 4 (March 1971) : 258-62.

Shatnoff, Judith. "A Gorilla to Remember." *Film Quarterly* 22 (Autumn 1968) : 30-39.

Sobchack, Vivian. "The Alien Landscapes of the Planet Earth." *The Film Journal* 2 (Issue #6) : 16-21.

Sontag, Susan. "The Imagination of Disaster." *Commentary*, October 1965, pp. 42-48.

Sragow, Michael. "*2001: A Space Odyssey*." *Film Society Review* 5 (January 1970) : 23-26.

Stout, Tim. "The Blurred Borderline between Science Fiction and Horror Fantasy." *Stardock* 1 (August 1968) : 19-22.

Strick, Philip. "Science Fiction at Trieste." *Films and Filming* 18 (November 1971) : 35-38.

———. "Kubrick's Horrorshow." *Sight and Sound* 41 (Winter-Spring 1971-72) : 44-45.

———. Review of *THX 1138*. *Sight and Sound* 43 (Summer 1973) : 177-78.

――――. "*Zardoz* and John Boorman." *Sight and Sound* 43 (Spring 1974) : 73-77.

Strick, Philip, and Houston, Penelope. "Interview with Stanley Kubrick." *Sight and Sound* 41 (Spring 1972) : 62-66.

Sturhahn, Lawrence. "Genesis of *THX-1138:* Notes on a Production." *Kansas Quarterly* 4 (Spring 1972) : 47-57.

Tarratt, Margaret. "Monsters from the Id." *Films and Filming* 17 (December 1970/January 1971) : 38-42, 40-42.

Thompson, Howard. Review of *The Monitors. New York Times,* 19 October 1969, p. 55.

Tudor, Andrew. "Genre: Theory and Malpractice in Film Criticism." *Screen* 2 (November-December 1970) : 33-43.

Zimmerman, Paul D. Review of *Silent Running. Newsweek,* 20 March 1972, p. 113.

Unpublished Materials

Dehn, Paul. *Beneath the Planet of the Apes.* Unpublished screenplay. APJAC Production, 20th Century Fox (UCLA Special Collections).

――――. *Conquest of the Planet of the Apes.* Unpublished screenplay. 20th Century Fox (UCLA Special Collections).

Greenberg, Stanley R. *Soylent Green.* Unpublished screenplay. MGM (UCLA Special Collections).

Menville, Douglas. *A Historical and Critical Survey of the Science-Fiction Film* (M.A. Thesis, U.S.C., 1959).

Wilson, Michael. *Planet of the Apes.* Unpublished screenplay based on a novel by Pierre Boulle. APJAC Productions, 20th Century Fox (UCLA Special Collections).

BIBLIOGRAPHY FOR CHAPTER 4

Books

Amelio, Ralph J., ed. *HAL in the Classroom: Science Fiction Films.* Dayton, OH: Pflaum, 1974.

Annan, David. *Robot: The Mechanical Monster.* New York: Bounty Books, 1976.

Ash, Brian, ed. *The Visual Encyclopedia of Science Fiction.* New York: Harmony Books, 1977.

Atkins, Thomas R., ed. *Science Fiction Films.* New York: Monarch Press/Simon & Schuster, 1976.

Biskind, Peter. *Seeing Is Believing: How Hollywood Taught Us to Stop Worrying and Love the Fifties.* New York: Pantheon Books, 1983.

Bouyxou, J.P. with Roland Lethem. *La Science-Fiction au Cinema.* Paris: Union Générale d'Editions (Collection 10/18), 1971.

Brosnan, John. *Future Tense: The Cinema of Science Fiction.* New York: St. Martin's Press, 1978.

Crawley, Tony. *The Steven Spielberg Story.* New York: Quill, 1983.

DeLauretis, Teresa, Andreas Huyssen and Kathleen Woodward. *The Technological Imagination: Theories and Fictions.* Madison, WI: Coda Press, 1980.

Dowdy, Andrew. *The Films of the Fifties: The American State of Mind.* New York: Morrow, 1975.

Dunn, Thomas P. and Richard D. Erlich, eds. *The Mechanical God: Machines in Science Fiction.* Westport, CT: Greenwood Press, 1982.

Edelson, Edward. *Visions of Tomorrow: Great Science Fiction from the Movies.* New York: Doubleday, 1975.

Erlich, R.D. and T.P. Dunn. *Clockwork Worlds: Mechanized Environments in SF.* Westport, CT: Greenwood Press, 1983.

Frank, Alan. *The Science Fiction and Fantasy Film Handbook.* Totowa, N.J.: Barnes & Noble, 1983.

Glut, Donald F. *Classic Movie Monsters.* Metuchen, N.J.: Scarecrow Press, 1978.

Grant, Barry, ed. *Film Genre: Theory and Criticism.* Metuchen, N.J.: Scarecrow Press, 1977.

Greenberg, Harvey, M.D. *The Movies on Your Mind.* New York: Saturday Review Press/Dutton, 1975.

Hardy, Phil, ed. *Science Fiction.* New York: Morrow, 1984.

Hefley, Robert M. with Howard Zimmerman. *Robots.* New York: Starlog Press, 1979.

Hickman, Gail Morgan. *The Films of George Pal.* New York: A.S. Barnes, 1977.

Kaminsky, Stuart M. *American Film Genres: Approaches to a Critical Theory of Popular Film.* New York: Laurel-Dell, 1977.

Lenne, Gerard. *Le Cinéma "Fantastique" et ses Mythologies.* Paris: Editions du Cerf, 1970.

Menville, Douglas and R. Reginald. *Things to Come: An Illustrated History of the Science Fiction Film.* New York: Times Books, 1977.

Naha, Ed. *Horror from Screen to Scream.* New York: Avon, 1975.

Nicholls, Peter, ed. *The Science Fiction Encyclopedia.* Garden City, N.Y.: Dolphin Books/Doubleday & Co., 1979.

———. *The Science in Science Fiction.* New York: Alfred Knopf, 1983.

Parish, James Robert and Michael R. Pitts, eds. *The Great Science Fiction Pictures.* Metuchen, N.J.: Scarecrow Press, 1977.

Peary, Danny, ed. *Omni's Screen Flights/Screen Fantasies: The Future According to Science Fiction Cinema.* Garden City, NY: Doubleday, 1984.

Pohl, Fredrik and Fredrik Pohl IV. *Science Fiction Studies in Film.* New York: Ace Books, 1981.

Pollock, Dale. *Skywalking: The Life and Films of George Lucas.* New York: Harmony, 1983.

Rose, Mark. *Alien Encounters: The Anatomy of Science Fiction.* Cambridge, Mass.: Harvard University Press, 1981.

Rovin, Jeff. *A Pictorial History of Science Fiction Films.* Secaucus, N.J.: Citadel Press, 1975.

_____ . *From Jules Verne to Star Trek*. New York & London: Drake Publishers, 1977.

Saleh, Dennis. *Science Fiction Gold: Film Classics of the '50's*. New York: McGraw Hill, 1979.

Sayre, Nora. *Running Time: Films of the Cold War*. New York: Dial Press, 1978.

Scholes, Robert and Eric S. Rabkin. *Science Fiction: History, Science, Vision*. New York: Oxford University Press, 1977.

Siegel, Richard, J.-C. Suares and Boylston Tompkins. *Alien Creatures*. Los Angeles: Reed Books, 1978.

Slusser, George and Eric S. Rabkin, eds. *Shadows of the Magic Lamp*. Carbondale, IL: Southern Illinois University Press, 1985.

Solomon, Stanley J. *Beyond Formula: American Film Genres*. New York: Harcourt Brace Jovanovich, 1976.

Strick, Philip. *Science Fiction Movies*. London: Octopus Books, 1976.

Strickland, A.W., and Forrest J. Ackerman. *A Reference Guide to American Science Fiction Films*. Bloomington, Ind.: T.I.S. Publications, 1981.

Suvin, Darko. *Metamorphoses of Science Fiction*. New Haven: Yale University Press, 1979.

Warren, Bill. *Keep Watching the Skies: American Science Fiction Movies of the Fifties, Vol. 1, 1950–1957*. Jefferson, N.C.: McFarland, 1982.

Warrick, Patricia S. *The Cybernetic Imagination in Science Fiction*. Cambridge, Mass.: MIT Press, 1980.

Wolfe, Gary K. *The Known and the Unknown: The Iconography of Science Fiction*. Kent, OH: Kent State University Press, 1979.

Articles

Adair, Gilbert. "*E.T.* cetera." *Sight and Sound* 52, No. 1 (Winter 1982–1983): 63.

Ahrens, John and Fred D. Miller, Jr. "Beyond *The Green Slime*: A Philosophical Prescription for Science Fiction." *Philosophy in Context* 11 (1981): n.p.

Andrews, Nigel and Harlan Kennedy. "Space Gothic." *American Film* 5 (March 1979): 17–22.

Annas, Pamela. "Science Fiction Film Criticism in the US." *Science-Fiction Studies* No. 22 (November 1980): 323–329.

Aufderheide, Pat. "Sci-fi Discovers New Enemies." *In These Times* 21 November –4 December, 1984, p. 30.

Auty, Chris. "The Complete Spielberg." *Sight and Sound* 51, No. 4 (Autumn, 1982): 275–279.

Bates, William. "Body-Snatching Pods Are Back, Courtesy of Philip Kaufman." *The New York Times*, 7 January 1977, p. D1.

Bell-Metereau, Rebecca. "*Altered States* and the Popular Myth of Self-Discovery." *Journal of Popular Film and Television* 9, No. 4 (Winter 1982): 171–179.

Biskind, Peter. "War of the Worlds." *American Film* 9, No. 3 (December 1983): 37–42.

Blair, Karin. "Sex and *Star Trek.*" *Science-Fiction Studies*, No. 31 (November 1983): 292-297.

Boyd, David. "Mode and Meaning in 2001." *Journal of Popular Film and Television* 6, No. 3 (1978): 202-215.

Carroll, Noel. "Nightmare and the Horror Film: The Symbolic Biology of Fantastic Beings." *Film Quarterly* 34, No. 3 (Spring 1981): 16-25.

Chase, Donald. "War of the Wizards." *American Film* 7, No. 8 (June 1982): 52-59.

Chevrier, Yves. "*Blade Runner*; or, The Sociology of Anticipation." Trans. Will Straw. *Science-Fiction Studies*, No. 32 (March 1984): 50-60.

Chion, Michel. "Les Visages et les Noms: DUNE de David Lynch." *Cahiers du Cinéma* 368 (February 1985): 50-51.

Cinefantastique (periodical, bi-monthly).

Clarens, Carlos. "SciFi Hits the Big Time." *Film Comment* 14, No. 2 (March-April 1978): 49-53.

Davis-Genelli, Tom and Lyn. "*Alien*: A Myth of Survival." *Film/Psychology Review* 4, No. 2 (Summer-Fall 1980): 235-240.

Dean, Joan F. "Between *2001* and *Star Wars.*" *Journal of Popular Film and Television* 7, No. 1 (1978): 32-41.

Dempsey, Michael. "Q: What's H.G. Wells Doing in San Francisco? A: Chasing Jack the Ripper." *American Film* 4, No. 6 (April 1979): 60-65.

_____ . Review of *Blade Runner*. *Film Quarterly* 36, No. 2 (Winter 1982-1983): 33-38.

Dervin, Daniel. "Primal Conditions and Conventions: The Genres of Comedy and Science Fiction." *Film/Psychology Review* 4, No. 1 (Winter-Spring 1980): 115-147

Donnelly, Jerome. "Humanizing Technology in *The Empire Strikes Back*: Theme and Values in Lucas and Tolkien." *Philosophy in Context* 11 (1981): n.p.

Eisenberg, Adam. "*Jedi*'s Extra Special Effects." *American Film* 8, No. 8 (June 1983): 36-39.

Elitzik, Paul. "*Blade Runner.*" *Cineaste* 12, No. 3 (1983): 46-47.

Elkins, Charles, ed. "Symposium on *Alien.*" *Science-Fiction Studies*, No. 22 (November 1980): 278-304.

Entman, R. and F. Seymour. "Close Encounters with the Third Reich." *Jump Cut*, No. 18 (1978): 3-6.

Fairchild, Jr. B.H. "An Event Sociologique." *Journal of Popular Film and Television* 6, No. 4 (1978): 342-349.

Farber, Stephen. "Hollywood Maverick." *Film Comment* 15, No. 1 (January-February 1979): 26-31.

_____ . "Brainstorming." *Film Comment* 19, No. 5 (September-October 1983): 77-82.

Franklin, H. Bruce. "Don't Look Where We're Going: Visions of the Future in Science Fiction Films, 1970-82." *Science-Fiction Studies*, No. 29 (March 1983): 70-80.

_____ . "Future Imperfect." *American Film* 8, No. 5 (March 1983): 47-49, 75-76.

Freund, Charles. "Pods Over San Francisco." *Film Comment* 15, No. 1 (January-February 1979): 22-25.

Geduld, Harry M. "Return to Melies: Reflections on the Science Fiction Film." *The Humanist* 27, No. 6 (November–December 1968): 23–24, 28.

Glass, Fred. "Sign of the Times: The Computer as Character in *Tron, War Games,* and *Superman III.*" *Film Quarterly* 38, No. 2 (Winter 1984-85): 16–27.

Gordon, Andrew. "*Star Wars*: A Myth for Our Time." *Literature/Film Quarterly* 7, No. 4 (Fall 1978): 314–326.

_____ . "*The Empire Strikes Back*: Monsters from the Id." *Science-Fiction Studies* 7, No. 3 (November 1980): 313–318.

_____ . "*Return of the Jedi*: The End of the Myth." *Film Criticism* 8, No. 2 (Winter 1984): 45–54.

_____ . "*Close Encounters*: The Gospel According to Steven Spielberg." *Literature/Film Quarterly* 8, No. 3 (1980): 156–164.

_____ . Review of *Flash Gordon. Film Criticism* 5, No. 3 (Spring 1981): 53–55.

_____ . "*E. T.* as Fairy Tale." *Science-Fiction Studies* 10 (1983): 298–305.

_____ . "The Power of the Force: Sex in the *Star Wars* Trilogy." In *Eros in the Mind's Eye: Sexuality and the Fantastic in Film*, ed. Donald Palumbo. Westport, CT: Greenwood Press (forthcoming 1986).

Gourlie, John M. Review of *Liquid Sky. Film Quarterly* 38, No. 2 (Winter 1984-85): 55–58.

Gow, Gordon. "The Non Humans." *Films and Filming* 20, No. 12 (September 1974): 59–62.

Grant, Barry K. "From Film Genre to Film Experience." *Paunch*, Nos. 42–43 (December 1975), pp. 123–137.

Greenberg, Harvey R. "In Search of Spock: A Psychoanalytic Inquiry." *Journal of Popular Film and Television* 12, No. 2 (Spring 1984): 52–65.

Haraway, Donna. "A Manifesto for Cyborgs." *Socialist Review* 80 (1985): 65–107.

Harmetz, Aljean. "George Lucas — Burden of Dreams." *American Film* 8, No. 8 (June 1983): 30–36.

_____ . "Today's Hottest Movie Stars." In *Rolling Breaks and Other Movie Business*. New York: Alfred A. Knopf, 1983, pp. 230–237.

_____ . "The Great and Powerful Wizard of Lucasfilm." In *Rolling Breaks and Other Movie Business*. New York: Alfred A. Knopf, 1983, pp. 244–263.

Heung, Marina. "Why E.T. Must Go Home: The New Family in American Cinema." *Journal of Popular Film and Television* 11, No. 2 (Summer 1983): 79–85.

Hinson, Hal. "Dreamscapes." *American Film* 10, No. 3 (December 1984): 44–50.

Hoberman, J. "1975–1985: Ten Years that Shook the World." *American Film* 10, No. 8 (June 1985): 34–59.

Ihde, Don. "Technology and Human Self-Conception." *The Southwestern Journal of Philosophy* 10, No. 1 (Spring 1979): 23–34.

Jacobson, Harlan. "Thunder on the Right." *Film Comment* 19, No. 4 (July-August 1983): 9–11, 74.

Jameson, Fredric. "SF Novels/SF Film." *Science-Fiction Studies*, No. 22 (November 1980): 319–322.

_____ . "Towards a New Awareness of Genre." *Science-Fiction Studies*, No. 28 (November 1982): 322–324.

_____ . "Postmodernism, or The Cultural Logic of Late Capitalism." *New Left*

Review, No. 146 (July–August 1984): 53–94.

Jameson, Richard T. *"E. T."* *Film Comment* 19, No. 1 (January–February 1983): 11–14.

Jurkiewicz, Kenneth. "Technology in the Void: Politics and Science in Four Contemporary Space Movies." *New Orleans Review* 9, No. 1 (1982): 16–20.

Kael, Pauline. "Fun Machines." *The New Yorker*, 30 May 1983, pp. 88–90.

Kellner, Douglas, Flo Leibowitz, and Michael Ryan. *"Blade Runner:* A Diagnostic Critique." *Jump Cut*, No. 29 (February 1984): 6–8.

Kellner, Douglas and Michael Ryan. "Chapter Nine: Fantasy, Technology, Dystopia." In *Politics and Ideology in Contemporary American Film* (Forthcoming).

Kennedy, Harlan. "21st Century Nervous Breakdown." *Film Comment* 18, No. 4 (July–August 1982): 64–68.

Kirkeby, Marc, "Computer Graphics: Is There Life After *Tron?" American Film* 8, No. 4 (January–February 1983): 42–45.

Kottack, Conrad. "Social-Science Fiction." *Psychology Today* (February 1978): 12–18.

Lancashire, Anne. "Complex Design in '*The Empire Strikes Back*'." *Film Criticism* 5, No. 3 (Spring 1981): 38–52.

_____ . *"Return of the Jedi:* Once More with Feeling." *Film Criticism* 8, No. 2 (Winter 1984): 55–66.

Landrum, Larry. "A Checklist of Materials about Science Fiction Films of the 1950's: A Bibliography." *Journal of Popular Film* 1, No. 1 (Winter 1972): 61–63.

_____ . "Science Fiction Film Criticism in the Seventies: A Selected Bibliography." *Journal of Popular Film and Television* 6, No. 3 (1978).

Lauren, Byron. "Time after Wells." *Ampersand* (January–February 1979): 12–13.

LaValley, Albert J. "Thinking about Special Effects." *American Film* 7, No. 8 (June 1982): 57.

Lehman, Peter and Don Daso. "Special Effects in *Star Wars*." *Wide Angle* 1, No. 1 (1979): 72–77.

Lewis, Jon. *"Return of the Jedi:* A Situationist Perspective." *Jump Cut*, No. 30 (1985): 3–6.

Mancini, Marc. "Thunder & Lightning." *Film Comment* 19, No. 4 (July–August 1983): 52–55.

_____ . "The Future Isn't What It Used To Be." *Film Comment* 21, No. 3 (May–June 1985): 11–15.

Markey, Constance. "Birth and Rebirth in Current Fantasy Films." *Film Criticism* 6, No. 1 (Fall 1982): 14–25.

Martin, James M. "The Best of All Impossible Worlds." *American Film* 1, No. 5 (March 1976): 29–49.

McCarthy, Todd. "Sand Castles." *Film Comment* 18, No. 3 (May–June 1982): 53–59.

Miller, Martin and Robert Sprich. "The Appeal of *Star Wars*: An Archetypal-Psychoanalytic View." *American Imago* IMAGO 38, No. 2 (Summer 1981): 203–220.

Mills, Bart. "The Brave New Worlds of Production Design." *American Film* 7, No. 4 (January–February 1982): 40–46.

Nagl, Manfred. "The Science-Fiction Film in Historical Perspective." Trans. David Clayton. *Science-Fiction Studies*, No. 31 (November 1983): 262–277.

Panisnick, David. "Who Among Us . . ." *Hawaii International Film Festival Program*, December 1984, pp. 24–26.

Pielke, Robert G. "*Star Wars* vs. *2001*: A Question of Identity." *Extrapolation* 24, No. 2 (Summer 1983): 143–155.

Pye, Michael and Lynda Miles. "The Man Who Made *Star Wars*." *The Atlantic Monthly* (March 1979): 54.

Pym, John. "The Middle American Sky." In *Sight and Sound: A Fiftieth Anniversary Selection*. Ed. David Wilson. London: Faber and Faber/BFI, 1982, pp. 286–291.

Roth, Lane. "Bergsonian Comedy and the Human Machines in 'Star Wars'." *Film Criticism* 4, No. 2 (1980): 1–8.

––––––– . "The Rejection of Rationalism in Recent Science Fiction Films." *Philosophy in Context* 11 (1981): n.p.

Samuels, S. "The Age of Conspiracy and Conformity." In *American History/American Film*, eds. J.E. O'Connor and M. Jackson. New York: Ungar, 1979, pp. 203–217.

Scanlon, Paul. "The Force Behind George Lucas." *Rolling Stone*, 25 August 1977, pp. 40–48, 50–51.

Scigaj, Leonard M. "Bettelheim, Castenada and Zen: The Powers Behind the Force in *Star Wars*." *Extrapolation* 22, No. 3 (Fall 1981): 213–230.

Sobchack, Vivian. "Child/Alien/Father: Patriarchal Crisis and Generic Exchange." *camera obscura*, #13, 1986.

Sofia, Zoe. "Exterminating Fetuses: Abortion, Disarmament, and the Sexo-Semiotics of Extraterrestrialism." *Diacritics* 14, No. 2 (Summer 1984): 47–59.

Steffen-Fluhr, Nancy. "Women and the Inner Game of Don Siegel's *Invasion of the Body Snatchers*." *Science-Fiction Studies*, No. 23 (July 1984): 139–153.

Stern, Michael. "Making Culture Into Nature; or, Who Put the 'Special' into 'Special Effects'?" *Science-Fiction Studies*, No. 22 (November 1980): 262–269.

Stewart, Garrett. "Close Encounters of the Fourth Kind." *Sight and Sound* 47, No. 3 (Summer 1978).

Strick, Philip. "The Age of the Replicant." *Sight and Sound* 51, No. 3 (Summer 1982): 168–172.

––––––– . "'That has such people in't . . .'." *Sight and Sound* 52, No. 3 (Summer 1983): 214.

Studlar, Gaylyn, ed. "Trumbull on Technology." *The USC Spectator* 3, No. 1 (Fall 1983): 7.

Telotte, J.P. "The Doubles of Fantasy and the Space of Desire." *Film Criticism* 6, No. 1 (Fall 1982): 56–68.

––––––– . "Human Artifice and the Science Fiction Film." *Film Quarterly* 36, No. 3 (Spring 1983): 44–51.

––––––– . "'The Dark Side of the Force': *Star Wars* and the Science Fiction Tradition." *Extrapolation* 24, No. 3 (Fall 1983): 216–226.

Tesson, Charles. "Y a-t-il 'E.T.' dans la Salle?" *Cahiers du Cinéma* 370 (April 1985): 58–59.

Tuchman, Mitch. "Close Encounters with Steven Spielberg." *Film Comment* 14, No. 1 (January–February 1978): 49–55.

Williams, Tony. "Close Encounters of the Authoritarian Kind." *Wide Angle* 5, No. 4 (1983): 22–29.

Wood, Denis. "Growing Up Among the Stars." *Literature/Film Quarterly* 7, No. 4 (Fall 1978): 327–341.

————. "The Stars in Our Hearts—A Critical Commentary on George Lucas's *Star Wars*." *Journal of Popular Film and Television* 6, No. 3 (1978): 262–279.

————. "The Empire's New Clothes." *Film Quarterly* 34, No. 3 (1981): 10–16.

Wood, Michael. "Kiss Tomorrow Hello." *American Film* 2, No. 6 (April 1977): 14–17.

Zito, Stephen. "George Lucas Goes Far Out." *American Film* 2, No. 6 (April 1977): 8–13.

Unpublished Materials

Bruno, Giuliana. "Ramble City: Postmodernism and *Blade Runner*." Paper presented at the Society for Cinema Studies Annual Meeting, New York, 1985.

Bukatman, Scott. "Terminal Identity: Image and Subjectivity in Postmodern Science Fiction." New York University, Dept. of Cinema Studies, 1985.

Index

See Page 342 for Chapter 4 Index

337

Index for Chapter 4

345